The Reminiscences

of

CAPTAIN EARL K. RHODES

U. S. Coast Guard (Retired)

U. S. Naval Institute
Annapolis, Maryland
1971

This manuscript is the result of a series of tape recorded interviews with Captain Earl K. Rhodes, USCG (retired) at his home in Takoma Park, Maryland, during the year 1970. These interviews were conducted by Mr. Peter Spectre for the Oral History Office in the U. S. Naval Institute.

Only minor emendations and corrections have been made by Captain Rhodes. The reader is asked, therefore, to bear in mind that he is reading a transcript of the spoken word rather than the written one.

DECLARATION OF TRUST

The undersigned does hereby appoint and designate as his (her) Trustee herein, the Secretary-Treasurer and Publisher of the United States Naval Institute to perform and discharge the following duties, powers, and privileges in connection with the possession and use of a certain taped interview between the undersigned and the Oral History Department of the United States Naval Institute.

1. Classification of Transcript.

   ( )a. If classified OPEN, the transcript(s) may be read or the recording(s) audited by the qualified personnel upon presentation of proper credentials, as determined by the Secretary-Treasurer of the U. S. Naval Institute.

   (X)b. If classified PERMISSION REQUIRED TO CITE OR QUOTE, the user will be required to obtain permission in writing from the interviewee prior to quoting or citing from either the transcript(s) or the recording(s).

   ( )c. If classified PERMISSION REQUIRED, permission must be obtained in writing from the interviewee before the transcribed interview(s) can be examined or the tape recording(s) audited.

   ( )d. If classified CLOSED, the transcribed interview(s) and the tape recording(s) will be sealed until a time specified by the interviewee. This may be until the death of the interviewee or for any specified number of years.

2. It is expressly understood that in giving this authorization, I am in no way precluded from placing such restrictions as I may desire upon use of the interview at any time during my lifetime, nor does this authorization in any way affect my rights to the copyright of my literary expressions that may be contained in the interview.

Witness my hand and seal this _FIRST_ day of _FEBRUARY_ 19_71_.

Earl A. Rhodes
Capt USCG Ret.

I hereby accept and consent to the foregoing Declaration of Trust and the powers therein conferred upon me as Trustee:

R. E. Bowker Jr.

Public Information Division
U. S. Coast Guard Headquarters
Washington, D. C.

Biographical Data

CAPTAIN EARL K. RHODES, USCG
(RETIRED)

Earl King Rhodes was born on September 4, 1906, at Lake Ann, Mich. After graduating from Manistee (Mich.) High School in May 1925, he entered the U. S. Coast Guard Academy, New London, Conn., with an appointment as cadet.

Graduating from the Academy with a commission as Ensign on May 15, 1928, he served his first assignment on board the Destroyer PORTER out of New York on anti-smuggling patrol and other missions.

Reassigned in 1929 to the Cutter MOJAVE at Boston, Mass., he served the 1930 and 1931 seasons on International Ice Patrol. During 1931 and 1932, he served on board the Destroyer WAINWRIGHT out of Boston. He then was ordered to Hampton Roads, Va., for flight training which he continued at the Naval Air Station, Pensacola, Fla. He returned to sea duty in 1933 to serve in the Cutter PERSEUS at New York and later at San Diego, Cal.

From 1935 to 1937, CAPT Rhodes served as navigator on board the Cutter NORTHLAND in Alaskan waters, and later in 1937 was ordered to the Chicago Division to serve as Communications Officer and as Personnel Officer.

In 1940 he was transferred to Washington, D. C., where he first was assigned to the U. S. Army Signal Corps School until 1942, at the outset of World War II, and then served in the Communications Division at Coast Guard Headquarters until 1944. During the remainder of the war he served as Executive Officer of the Coast Guard-manned troop transport USS GEN. M. C. MEIGS (AP-116), transporting Brazilian troops from Rio de Janeiro to Naples, Italy. In the early part of 1945, he also served as Ice Pilot for a Naval Expedition to Point Barrow, Alaska. In June of 1945, he assumed command of the Coast Guard-manned attack cargo vessel USS THEENIM (AKA-63), assisting in the occupation of Japan.

After the war, he returned to Coast Guard Headquarters to serve as Assistant Chief, Communications Division from 1946 to April 1949. He then commanded the Icebreaker NORTHWIND on Bering Sea Patrol until October 1950, at which time he returned again to Headquarters to serve as Chief, Communications Division. During that tour of duty he also served as liaison for the Treasury Department to the President's Communications Policy Board. During 1951 he was lauded by the State Dept. for helping solve a telecommunications problem between the U. S. and Canada through his technical abilities and cooperation. He also served as a member of the U. S. Delegation to the Extraordinary Administrative Radio Conference convened at Geneva, Switzerland, in August 1951.

(more)

Biog. - CAPT E. K. Rhodes, USCG (Ret)

In April 1954, CAPT Rhodes became Chief of Operations for the 14th Coast Guard District, Honolulu, his last tour of duty until he retired on November 1, 1955.

CAPT Rhodes' World War II campaign service medals and ribbons include the following: American Defense; American Area; European-African-Middle Eastern Area; Asiatic-Pacific Area; World War II Victory; Navy Occupation Service with Asia Clasp; Brazilian Expeditionary Force medals.

Following is a resume of his appointments in rank: Ensign, May 15, 1928; Lieutenant (jg), May 15, 1930; Lieutenant, May 15, 1932; Lieut. Commander, May 23, 1941; Commander, September 15, 1942; and Captain, March 25, 1945. Retired November 1, 1955.

CAPT Rhodes and his wife, the former Christena Hunter of Somerville, Mass., had one daughter, Shirlee H. Mrs. Rhodes died on December 28, 1964. The Captain still maintains the home they lived in at 7412 Holly Ave., Tacoma Park, Md., 20012.

Rev.
Nov. 1969 - cas

Interview #1 with Captain Earl K. Rhodes, USCG (ret.)

At his home - Takoma Park, Maryland   23 May 1970

Subject: Biography   by Peter Spectre

Mr. Spectre: Captain, could you tell me a little bit about your early life, where you were born, the date you were born, and so forth?

Captain Rhodes: I was born in what we used to call a shanty on a farm outside of Lake Anne, Michigan, on September 4, 1906. My father's family came through Pennsylvania, Ohio - I remember he went out in Indiana and Missouri. He was three years in the Spanish-American War, where he was a sergeant in the light artillery fighting in China and in the Philippines. Later he came back and married my mother, whose name was Fanny King. My father's name was Howard Rhodes. My mother also lived on a farm up in northern Michigan. My father purchased a farm up near Lake Anne, and to make ends meet, he also became a rural mail carrier, so that he was able to pay off the indebtedness on the farm and at the same time build up the land and the stock and equipment for the farm.

Q: Where is Lake Anne near?

Rhodes: Lake Anne is about fifteen miles from Traverse City, Michigan. It's also practically between Empire, which is on Lake Michigan, and Traverse City, which is on Grand Traverse Bay.

Q: What type of farming did your father do?

Rhodes: Very general farming, mostly stock farming - cattle, pigs, horses, we bred horses. Actually my father was a great horseman. Being in the light artillery, they had teams of six horses drawing the artillery pieces, and he was in charge of all of the horses. He could do all kinds of tricks with the horses —somewhat of a trick rider. He enjoyed breeding horses and raising them, but generally you had all kinds of stock. We had saddle horses, pigs, geese, ducks, chickens, turkeys.

Q: Was it a large farm?

Rhodes: The first farm we had was a hundred and sixty acres. He kept on getting more property, and at the time I went to high school we had three farms of about a hundred and sixty acres each. The lakes were very thick up in Michigan, creeks and so forth, and we had at least one lake on each farm and generally the same farm would border at least two lakes. The house had a dammed up creek in front where we had a saw mill and a grist mill by water power.

Q: So this wasn't just a subsistance farm, it was a fairly large business?

Rhodes: It was quite a large business, although transportation was such up there, it was very difficult to get your produce to market. So the main thing was that you raised enough produce to feed your family, sell locally, and then certain things such as cattle and so forth could be sold at market, milk, cream, butter, things of that sort, also poultry and pork.

Q: I take it that you worked on the farm?

Rhodes: Yes, I did. That was one reason why I wanted to bring this up because I definitely learned to work very young. We always had many chores to do, and by the time I was ten years old, I was doing a man's work. I handled the mules and the horses and many jobs that an ordinary farm hand could not do because I was very mechanically inclined even at that time.

Q: Did you have any brothers or sisters?

Rhodes: I had four sisters --two sisters older than myself, Miriam, the oldest, and then Norma, and two sisters younger than myself, Doris and Lida. No brothers.

Q: So you were the only son and you worked like a dog.

Rhodes: That's very true. Anytime that a boy's work was needed, I was called on. However, my sisters were often called on to do quite a few chores that normally a boy would do. My mother also worked. She always had a garden and most of that was her responsibility. Of course, the children helped raise the garden. We had about an acre of garden crops, and we had to can, and so forth, getting ready for the winter. It was quite primitive in those days compared with what it is now.

Q: When did you start school? Did you start at the normal age?

Rhodes: I started school, I believe when I was seven years old. I was always curious, and my two older sisters taught me a lot even before I went to school. School was just a natural to me. The difficulty out there was that we generally had a long ways to go to school, except that my father would often move into town during the winter months because carrying the mail was very difficult in northern Michigan, to get around with a horse and cutter. Often when you couldn't get through on the roads, he would go on horseback, and when the horses couldn't get through, he would go on foot. While we were small children and he was on the mail route, generally we lived in town during the winter months.

Q: What town was this?

Rhodes: Lake Anne. As soon as he got settled and was doing well in farming, he resigned from his position on the rural mail route and put all of his time in farming.

Q: What was the school like that you went to?

Rhodes: We never went to anything but a one room school house that had all eight grades and one teacher. All grades were generally represented, and you had generally quite a promotion at the end of school. In those days, the teacher maintained discipline. There were plenty of bushes outside, and if the boys started cutting up too much, we had to go out and cut our own switches and then they were used on us. My father always told all of us that if we got a spanking in school, we'd get another one when we got home. That was a policy in those days. They didn't raise cain, because they figured if a teacher spanked a child, he needed it.

Q: Did you go through all eight grades in this school?

Rhodes: Yes, I went through all eight grades. Michigan had a particular system where-by you took an examination for the eigth grade, and the highest boy, the one who received the highest marks from each county was sent, all expenses free, to the Michigan State Fair, outside of Detroit.

Q: I notice you have something next --you were there?

Rhodes: That is correct. I believe that that had a great influence in my life. Receiving the highest mark in the county on the eigth grade examination gave me confidence that I should go on farther. That led, then, to my going to high school. But there was no high school closer than fifteen miles from Lake Anne, so I had to find a place where I could attend high school, and we were able to make arrangements where I could work for my room and board with a family in Manistee, Michigan. Their name was R.G. Peters. Actually, the G. stood for Gould and he took great pride in the fact that he was a cousin of the famous J. Gould. They had a very large house in the middle of a block down there, so there was plenty of work for me especially shoveling sidewalks, keeping the furnace going. I had to act as chauffeur for the family car. Mr. Peters was over ninety years old at the time but very, very active, so I enjoyed working with him. Actually the last time that I ever stayed home for any length of time was when I left for high school. I made my way from then on.

Q: How did your parents feel about your going away, and how did they feel about you going to high school?

Rhodes: My parents were very sad that I went away but they did everything they could to help me in my education. On the other hand, they always expected that I would come back as soon as I received my high school education. They had me start in a commercial course. We didn't know much about high school in those days. After the first semester I changed to college preparatory on my own because the type of subjects that I was studying in the commercial course were not the type I was interested in. I was interested in math, science, and learning more about the world around us, rather than learning to become an accountant, or something of that type. On my own, I decided to go into the scientific and mathematical --

Q: When did you decide that you didn't want to be a farmer?

Rhodes #1 - 6 -

Rhodes: I decided that long before I went to high school because I was very sensitive, and having to help out in butchering pigs and killing chickens -- one of my main jobs when I was a young kid was killing the chickens and rabbits, and so forth. I enjoyed hunting, but I didn't enjoy going and picking up the animal and preparing him for food. Also one of the toughest things that ever happened to me was having to kill veal, a six week old calf. Those were the things that made me decide that I could not be a successful farmer because there were many things that you just had to do. I would rather do almost anything else than indulge in that --very sensitive.

Q: When you went away to high school, your parents thought you were going to come back as a farmer, and you decided to go on?

Rhodes: That is true although they felt that since I had done an outstanding job and was able to use machinery and all the rest, they thought that I would go into that type of thing. But I really wanted to do more complicated things than just work on farm machinery.

Q: What was your strongest subject when you were in high school?

Rhodes: I would say the sciences such as chemistry, physics; mathematics such as algebra, geometry, trigonometry; also the natural sciences such as physiography which has to do with the weather and our surroundings of various types.

Q: What was your weakest subject?

Rhodes: My weakest subject was probably English, grammar. I especially liked history in high school. Actually I was not weak in any courses, as such, because they had a rule in my high school that as juniors and seniors, if you received all A's, you were excused from the afternoon classes. You could arrange all your classes in the morning and have the afternoon off. So by doing that, it enabled me to go out for basketball and football, and although I wasn't very successful in either because many times I couldn't appear at practice, still I could not have appeared at all if I had not been able to get my afternoons off so that I could do most of my chores around home where I was working. Then I could go out for practice and come back and do the rest of them with a little studying on the side.

Q: You went four years to high school?

Rhodes: Four years to high school and in those days they didn't have such things as junior high school out in Michigan. It was four years of high school in Manistee, Michigan.

Q: Did you go back to the farm in the summertime?

Rhodes: No, I worked, generally speaking, with the Peters. I worked two summers there, and then one time I worked down at Lansing, Michigan. My father got me this job and he worked along with me. We were laying water mains down in Lansing. In that short summer, I learned how to do all phases of it. I could run the trencher, cut the pipe where it was supposed to be cut, lead the joints. The gentleman who owned the company who was putting in that, told me that as soon as I finished high school I could come with him and he would give me my own crew. That was just a short period. I was sixteen years old at the time --around 1922. Our salary was six dollars a day for a ten hour day, and six days a week. There wasn't much time to do anything but it was a tremendous salary for a sixteen year old boy to make, six dollars a day in those days.

Q: What happened after high school?

Rhodes: By the way, we might enter the fact that there was a Coast Guard life-saving station at Manistee, and I got quite familiar with that while I was there.

Q: What lake was this on?

Rhodes: This was on Lake Michigan.

Q: How did you first come in contact with the Coast Guard?

Rhodes: All that I knew about the Coast Guard was life saving stations. I didn't know that they had larger vessels even all the time I was going to high school. However they had some literature sent out and the captain of the life boat station delivered literature to the school, and told them about the examinations that were being given for the Coast Guard Academy. The nearest place to take the examinations was at Detroit, Michigan, which is three hundred miles away. There were a few people in the class ahead of me which had graduated the previous year, and also some people in my class who were interested in taking the examinations, so we had the principal write to the Coast Guard in Washington and find out if the examinations could be given at Manistee rather than have these people go all the way to Detroit. The Coast Guard said that if they could obtain ten applicants for the Academy, they would arrange to give the exams in Manistee. So I was approached as a possible applicant, to see if I could help build up the number to ten. I thought it would be fun to get out of school for a couple of days to take the examinations, so I agreed to take the examinations, having no idea that I would ever go to the Coast Guard. The brochure

Rhodes #1 - 9 -

that they sent to us said that the highest rank you could get in the Coast Guard was a captain. We had a captain in charge of life boat stations down there and I had no intention of spending all my life and the highest I could get was captain of a life boat station. So I took the exam and I was the only one that passed out of ten, and also the only one in the state of Michigan. The local high school and the local newspaper made a big thing about it. My father didn't even know I was taking the exams, but when I told him about it he drove right down. I hadn't yet had my physical exam. It took a weekend to drive to ~~Traverse City~~ Detroit to the hospital down there where I was directed to take the exam. I passed that. My father, of course, knew what a commissioned officer was, I didn't at that time. He insisted that I go regardless of anything. My father gave me a lot of backing even though he wanted me to come back to the farm and live with them.

Q: Was your mother in favor of it?

Rhodes: Oh yes. But she didn't know very much about what it meant other than what my father was able to tell her. He being a sergeant in the Army many years ago, he knew very well that going to the Academy and becoming a commissioned officer was a very fine thing to do.

Q: What did you have in mind before you took the examinations?

Rhodes: I planned to go to Michigan State College where I was going to take up preferably electric engineering. That seemed to me the most interesting thing I would be able to take up, and while I was in Lansing working on the water main, my main interest was going out to visit Michigan State and seeing all the facilities they had out there. They had a very good reputation for engineering and agriculture both. It used to be called Michigan Agricultural College.

Rhodes #1 - 10 -

Q: Had you applied to Michigan State?

Rhodes: No, I had not, but I planned on it. Actually, I would have had to stay out of school for one year in order to earn enough money to start going to Michigan State. I knew that I would have to earn my own way because I could expect to receive very little help from my family. They would help some, but very little.

Q: What did you think about going to the Coast Guard Academy?

Rhodes: I thought it was very interesting. It was the first trip I ever made to the East. At New London with the lay of the land there, the ocean right next door, right from the beginning, I loved the atmosphere. Even then I had no intention of staying in the service all of my life. However I think the challenge of the fact that when we first got there we saw some upper classmen having to leave because they had failed in certain subjects, and the word got around that it was a very tough school to get through. I think perhaps my stubborness and determination was such that I decided that I would not be kicked out, if I wanted to resign, that was one thing but certainly I was going to watch myself and see to it that I didn't fail any subjects and was able to make the grade. As I went along I gained a great deal of respect --I learned a lot about the Coast Guard and what they had done in past years --what the history of the Coast Guard was. It wasn't long before I decided that I wanted to stay in the service and be grouped with men that had performed such exploits in past years. Our summer cruises, and so forth, also gave it a feeling --

Q: Before you went to the Coast Guard, did you ever consider the Naval Academy, or West Point?

Rhodes: I had considered them but when I realized that it would require an appointment from a representative in Congress or a senator, I didn't feel that I had a great deal of hope. If I had known how to obtain an appointment, I probably would have tried to obtain the appointment. But I was pretty much on my own in those days and I didn't know too much about either West Point or Annapolis. I had heard about them. I knew other people who had gone and I would have been very proud to have gone to either West Point or Annapolis. When I found out that the Coast Guard Academy compared with West Point and Annapolis as far as an education and preparation of an officer in the service was concerned, the fact that I had always respected, very much, those who had gone to West Point and Annapolis, helped me decide that I wanted to stay with the Coast Guard.

Q: Did you have any nautical experience before you got there?

Rhodes: I had no nautical experience except in small boats. Being so many lakes up in Michigan, Lake Michigan and so forth, we loved the water. We were on the water all the time, either fishing, swimming, canoeing, rowing a boat, sailing a boat. We enjoyed water very much. I think once you've been around the water, you're very lonely once you get away from it.

Q: What was the Coast Guard Academy like when you first arrived there?

Rhodes: It was very small --we had, I would say around forty enter our class; however when the class graduated, only ten of us graduated, so you had quite a little loss as you went along in the curriculum.

Q: Was it a three year course?

Rhodes: I went to the Academy in 1925 and right at that time they were starting to get more officers because of the anti-smuggling program that the Coast Guard had gone into at that time because of the smuggling of alcoholic beverages into the United States. They were trying to build up the size of the Coast Guard at that time. They were taking in larger classes but the courses were very difficult and they were squeezing a four year course into three years. A great many of my classmates had had experience in college --they had gone one, two, or three years to college before they went to the Academy. We had to compete against those for marks and regardless of what one may say, there is an influence on a professor when you have several people in the class who have already had the subject and know it very well, and you have others who haven't had the course; they have a great deal of difficulty in keeping up with the top men of the class. It's nip and tuck to just get a passing mark to graduate.

Q: What was the geographical distribution of the cadets that were in your class?

Rhodes: We had, of course, a preponderance from the East coast. However, two of my classmates were from the Finger Lake District in New York, a few from the Middle West. I do not recall any from the West Coast. The Middle West and the East supplied most of the cadets who went to the Coast Guard Academy.

Q: What about the other cadets there? Do you know why they came to the Academy?

Rhodes: There were various reasons why they came. Many had prepped for either West Point or Annapolis and perhaps were not the prime appointee and perhaps took the Coast Guard examination as well as being a secondary or later appointment to Annapolis or West Point. That was quite prevalent. On the other hand many perhaps had started through college and finding financial difficulties, they took the examination and this way they could get a fine education at government expense. I did find though, that generally speaking, if the person went to the Academy for reasons such as that, after they were there awhile, they became very loyal to the Coast Guard. When they saw what was required --we were out in boats a great deal, summer cruises, and so forth, and learning various exploits of the Coast Guard in past years, the history of the Coast Guard, it usually got in their veins. I think making it as tough as it was, it really encouraged determination among those to make the grade. If it had been too easy, I have a feeling that the ones who graduated wouldn't have been quite as sold on the service as they would have been having it tough. They figured if they could get through, it had to be tough.

Q: You said that in your class forty entered and ten graduated. What happened to the other thirty?

Rhodes: Some resigned voluntarily. They decided that they didn't like that type of life. However a great majority resigned because of failure of subjects. They just couldn't get through. That was the big reason for the attrition.

Q: In order to be asked to resign, to be kicked out or whatever you want to call it, what was the minimum that you had to fail?

Rhodes: If you failed two minor courses, you might still stay in the Academy. If you failed a major course, such as mathematics, or engineering, or navigation, or something of that type, that might be sufficient if your conduct was on the down side. In other words, we had a system of demerits there, and if you got caught with a fifty demerit offense, you were right on the border line of being kicked out. If you got, say, a hundred and fifty demerits in a whole year, you might be kicked out for no other reason. Actually, the Coast Guard Academy, when you took your first examination, one of your major marks was a mark in adaptability. I don't know any other academy that allows a mark in adaptability before you can enter the academy. That is determined from your scholastic record --whether you were good in athletics, a leader in the community and school, church affairs, things of that type. Also the recommendations that you may have received from the local people who knew you. That particular mark wasn't too important when you first entered the Academy, but it was counted in your competitive mark for entrance. Then each year you were also marked in adaptability. It was possible to be kicked out with passing all your subjects very high and getting a low mark in adaptability. Some people just are not suitable. They have two left hands, all their fingers are thumbs. They've got to be able to actually do things, and do things well, as well as just learning subjects out of a book.

Q: What was the physical aspect of the Academy, like buildings, equipment, facilities?

Rhodes: Actually, facilities were very, very poor. They had it at the location of old Fort Trumbull, which is a stone fort overlooking the Thames River and Long Island Sound. Old wooden barracks buildings had been constructed there --they were just temporary buildings and yet that was converted to the barracks and studyhall and classroom. It was actually quite adequate except that it was not very imposing. You hated to bring your friends there and say, "This is the grand Academy that I'm attending." And they were getting dilapitated. Each year they were getting worse because they had not been built for permanency.

Q: They were permanent temporaries.

Rhodes: They were permanent temporaries like the Munitions Building and the

Navy Building here in Washington.

Q: When you were there the course was divided into engineering and deck?

Rhodes: Yes. When I first went to the Academy, I entered as a Cadet engineer. After I had been there a year, they combined both engineering and line at the Academy, and from then on we all had to take the same subjects, and some of us had to take additional subjects. For example, the engineers would have to study navigation and the line cadet would have to catch up in engineering so that we could all be lumped together in one class.

Q: How did they determine you were going to be an engineer?

Rhodes: I liked engineering right from the beginning in high school. On the application you had a chance to decide whether you wanted to go for line or whether you wanted to go in for engineering. I was planning to go to college as an engineer, and the idea of engineering appealed to me so I put down engineering. I didn't know what a line cadet would mean anyway. However, I was very happy when they did change it to both line and engineer combined as one course. I think in a small service it is better to have everyone competing with each other instead of having one group be the navigators and the other the engineers because it's far better when you get in command if you understand both navigation and engineering. I think a commanding officer can do a far better job and when you get into administration I think it's far better that you know a great deal about all the problems that enter into the engineering and also the operation and navigation of a ship.

Q: How many engineers were there in the beginning of your class?

Rhodes: I've forgotten but it seems to me that about twelve were engineers and the rest of them were line deck, but that is only a recollection. It might be a few one way or the other.

Q: Awhile back you mentioned major and minor courses. In general which were the major courses and which were the minor courses?

Rhodes: The major courses were generally courses in science such as physics, chemistry; courses in mathematics were trigonometry, geometry, calculus, mechanics. There were many major mathematical and scientific courses that we had. Then you might fail a course in literature if you spent too much time on that. You might fail a course in French and still get a passing grade. We had a course in logic which many of us figured was the most important course we had. That would be a minor. You might fail history and that would be a minor. The real major courses were the basic mathematical and engineering subjects. When I say engineering, I include navigation in that because that was scientific as well as very much akin to engineering.

Q: You later became a communications man. Was there communications?

Rhodes: Yes. We had to take communications. We all had to take Morse code and pass in that. Also visual signals such as flag signals and semaphores. Then we had blinking light signals. Aboard ship you use a lot of blinking lights at night So we all had to become proficient in actually sending and receiving the signals as such. We also had a course in radio communications at the Academy. That was the technical phase of it --the beginning of electronics, you might say, at that time. So you had the understanding of radio communications when you got aboard ship. Communications in those days were very primitive. They were just getting into radio you might say, and the vacuum tube had been discovered just a short time before that. Most of the transmitters on the ship at that time were the old spark transmitters, no vacuum tubes at all. A very primitive method of communicating. However, you've got to remember in those days we thought it was marvelous.

Q: I'm sure the things we have now will probably be primitive to somebody in later years. This is sort of a very general question, but in light of the fact that later on you did become more-or-less a specialist in communications, did anything that happened to you at the Coast Guard Academy, or before, play a part in pushing you in that direction?

Rhodes: No, nothing at that time or before had any relationship to me later becoming interested in communications. However, the operations of a group of ships getting messages where they needed to be and as rapidly as possible, that is always a problem. I don't care what service you're in, and in the Coast Guard that is perhaps the most important thing. I became interested because in operations, I could see how important it was to be able to communicate from one place to another. Your operations could be no better than your communications, because if they didn't know what was desired and you didn't know where they were or who was closest to help out in an emergency, you could have the whole fleet out there but if you couldn't get word to them, they were worthless. So I got to thinking and through various examples I got extremely interested, and therefore I studied up on it on my own and when the time came when I was assigned communications, I was probably better able to handle it. It was my top interest and I had studied a great deal about it and figured that it actually was the most important thing in the Coast Guard because rapid communications are very, very important when you are dealing in emergencies, whether you're dealing in stopping smugglers, quite often if you knew what they were going to do and you could get the word out to the ships in the field, you could make a successful seizure. If you were unaware of what they were going to do, and even if you were aware but you still couldn't get it into the hands of the people who could do something about it, your whole system was worthless for that particular occasion. Also if someone is in distress, if you can't get someone there in a hurry, chances are they'll be dead by the time you get there. So speed and accuracy seem awfully important to me. The more cases you see where a little bit more speed, alittle bit more accuracy could have done a better job, you tried to make it better next time. The Coast Guard was actually doing a far better job that anyone realized could be done in communications and I admired what they were doing, and I wanted to be a part of it. It's very many things. It's not that I was not satisfied with what was being done; I thought they were very forward looking in doing what they were doing, but naturally, knowing it was so important, I wanted to make it better. That gave me a real interest in it.

Q: Getting back to the Academy, how did you feel about the staff at the Academy?

Rhodes: Some were excellent; some were just natural instructors. Generally speaking, they were not trained as instructors, they were trained in operations, and so forth. I found that at least the amount a person knows, his brilliance, and so forth, does not always make the best instructor. Quite often a person who is interested in something and works very hard to get it, even though he might not be brilliant, he understands these young people who are trying to get it and understands how to put it over much better than a brilliant man. One thing that I did note, that if you got a regular, average person in there, they were much better able to put over their subject, than someone who was really a brain who knew his subject, but he would skip a few steps and you couldn't get it at all because he left out some of the steps that you'd have to know. He was thinking so fast that he wouldn't realize that you were not getting it. On the whole we had an excellent staff, but there were a few misfits in there and you just could not get their subject --they just couldn't put it across.

Q: Were there any professors in the real sense there?

Rhodes: Yes, we had one real professor, Chester Dimock. He was the mathematics professor. We all loved him. He was a fine gentleman and very capable. He inspired most of us, at least, because he could put over his subject very well. He was very patient. He would go over it over and over again. You might say that generally we were the pick of a group having come in through competitive examinations, still we all felt ourselves very dumb when it came to getting all these very difficult subjects rapidly; but we had to get them rapidly because we had so many subjects, and trying to take the whole curriculum in three years was very difficult. Professor Dimock was by far better than most professors I believe.

Q: Were there any instructors there who had an influence on you?

Rhodes: I think that the executive officer of the Academy --when I first went there, he was there my first two years. His name was Derby. He was a very, very fine gentleman. His logic was very good; he could see when you were trying to put something over on him --just sense it. He also taught the subject of logic, and most of my classmates who took the subject of logic under Derby thought that was the best subject they had ever taken anywhere. He was a very fine gentleman operationally as well as academically. He later, of course, became superintendant of the Academy. He was greatly admired, and I did feel that his influence was very great. Then, of course, the Commandant of cadets, first McElligott, and then O'Neill; they I believe influenced us greatly because they set the type of example which you would be happy to follow. They were straightforward and just fine gentleman, and you had to respect them. They were also instructors and I think that type of person at the Academy can influence young boys greatly.

Q: What about the military end? Would you characterize the Coast Guard Academy at that time as a militarily oriented school?

Rhodes: It definitely was, however there were limits to what you would call military oriented. Certainly we had to be qualified. For example, on one of the cruises they took us down to Parris Island and turned us over to the Marines, and told them to treat us just like Marine recruits, and put us through the rifle and pistol ranges. I look back at that as one of the finest experiences I've ever had, because we had excellent training there. We certainly learned how to shoot and that's what we were sent there for, and do it properly. In the military, we had military drill practically every day, and all of our activities at the Academy were military. The upperclassmen had to *drill* the lower classmen --you might call it hazing now but definitely that was part of the military training at that time. They'd call you out in the hall now and then, and make you stand at attention, and you had to keep your control even though they would maybe insult you, but you could not lose your control --lose your cool so to speak. That is one of the most important things, I think, in military training is to keep your temper under all conditions. You can't control others unless you can keep your control of yourself.

Q: Did you find it difficult combining the two-studies and the military training at the same time?

Rhodes: Yes. On the other hand, without the military training, I don't believe any of us would have been able to keep up with our courses, because they not only had military training but they had study hours, and you had to be studying during those study hours. That was set aside for study and everything had to be quiet -- no one could come in and interfere with you, and they kept inspecting to make sure that everyone was quiet and engaged in study. If an ordinary school someone can come in and start shooting the breeze with you, he interrupts you, interrupts your train of thought. It is very difficult to study under those conditions. We had to really concentrate on our studying and I don't think we could have done it to that extent without military discipline.

Q: Did you have enough time to study?

Rhodes: No. You never had enough time even if you put all the time allotted on it, so, therefore, you had to budget your time. You couldn't go ahead and get one subject very well at the expense of another, because you had to have all your subjects and not just one. You had to put so much time on one and even if you didn't get it you had to go on to the next one. You learned to budget your time and you realized that it wouldn't do you any good if you passed half your subjects and didn't pass the others. If you got a hundred percent on one, it wasn't going to do you any good if you flunked the other one. So you had to budget your time and I think that was one thing we learned to do there. You couldn't possibly study hard enough to have all your subjects in real good shape.

Q: If you were having trouble with a course, did you get help from instructors to bring you up to the standard that was expected?

Rhodes: So far as I know of, it was almost unheard of to get help from an instructor. Sometimes we would get help from other men in your class. As I say, some were very good. They'd had these courses in college before they came to the Academy so they could get that course very well --it didn't take them very long. Then those who were having trouble would have little sessions, maybe with four or five of them, and explain some difficult thing that they hadn't been able to see. We did work very well as classmates. We stuck together as classmates. I think that that is probably one of the things that I remember most. It just seemed like everyone was against you except your own classmates. Later on, of course, that loyalty was transferred to the Coast Guard as a whole and we realized that all of this was necessary in the particular type of school that we were going to. Definitely you were very loyal to your own class and you help each other out. Seldom would the instructor have time to help the students.

Q: In later years, did you and your classmates help each other out in the service

Rhodes: Not nearly to the extent that you might, say, in a larger service because the Coast Guard was such a small service at that time that we became loyal to the service. You would never be serving with your classmates, and you would be just as loyal to your shipmates as you had been to your classmates. On the whole, that loyalty was transferred to the Coast Guard, as a whole, because you were all working for the same thing, and that's really what you were loyal to your classmates for --you were all working for the same thing. The Coast Guard being so small, you get a great many other friends after you get out in the service-you have your shipmates. You make a six months cruise with a group of shipmates and you get pretty loyal to them, too. Then you're transferred and you get other shipmates, and pretty soon you just feel that there's a devil of a lot of good men in this outfit, and you become loyal to the outfit as a whole. It developes that way.

Q: Captain, we talked a lot about your theoretical training at the Coast Guard Academy, what about the practical?

Rhodes #1 - 23 -

Rhodes: The practical training was extremely important. We had sail boats that we could go out in. Generally every morning we had to get up early and row across the river and back for exercise. We had a sail loft where they taught us practical seamanship --this was to practice the seamanship which we had learned out of the book. In operating boats, the junior class men would be the ones that did the work and the senior class men would be the ones who operated the boat. Through the years we became adept at doing various phases of the work. Then our summer cruises were extremely important --making cruises on the sailing vessel, the old ALEXANDER HAMILTON. We had to fire the boilers and then go up on deck and work on the sails whenever necessary, because generally we used the engine and sail both, or your engine for stand-by while you had a good breeze, favorable breeze. If you wanted to go against it, you'd use your engines but you'd still have to go up and furl your sails. So there was making sail, furling sail, tacking the ship, and so forth. We all got used to that.

Q: What type of engine did the HAMILTON have?

Rhodes: She had the old triple expansion up and down steam engine. It was not very powerful --it only had the one engine and that was strictly when the sails wouldn't work. When she was built the people didn't believe in engines, they had to have sail as an auxiliary anyhow. The sail was the main thing on the ALEXANDER HAMILTON, but when there wasn't any wind, or the wind was unfavorable, you'd use your engine. And it was coal burning, also, so we had to coal ship every now and then. Dressing up in white uniform and coaling ship is a very miserable job.

Q: Was there a regular crew on the ship?

Rhodes: Just a nucleus of a crew. They would only have maybe one engine for each watch, but the cadets would do all the work, he would supervise it and tell them what to do. Generally, the cadets, themselves, would do all the work. The same on the sail --you'd have one boatswain in there, and perhaps the chief boatswain's mate, but the cadets would actually do all the work. They were there to tell them what to do. Of course, you had your upperclassmen who had already done the work, they would be leading it, and the lower classmen would be doing the work on the sail, and so forth. I know on the last cruise on the way to Europe on the ALEXANDER HAMILTON, I was on the bridge as junior officer of the deck, and the senior officer of the deck was an engineer officer who had never worked on sails. He had no idea about sailing. In that condition, I was somewhat in charge, and at two o'clock in the morning we lost our propeller. We sent down and notified the captain that we had lost the propeller, and he said, "Set sail, and head back for New London." I asked for permission to call all hands, and he said, "No, set sail with the watch on deck." Here I was, a former engineer cadet; I was then a senior classman, however, and with the watch on deck, I had to turn around, set sail and head for New London. Actually it developed, a very odd thing, because here it was two o'clock in the morning, everyone dressed in white, of course, out at sea in the summertime, and I saw this man in white --the cadets were straining on the rope- I saw another one just standing there, doing nothing. So I said, "Here you! Grab this rope. What are you doing there?" He did grab the rope, and in going by closer, I saw it was Captain Hinckley, the skipper of the Academy, in his white pajamas. I got out of there in a hurry and I noticed that he went back down to the cabin --he figured everything was in good hands.

But we got headed back, and we got about half way back and they sent a destroyer to come down and tow us in the rest of the way. We weren't making very good headway --the winds were not proper. We then transferred to the MOJAVE, and made the rest of the cruise with the MOJAVE. Since she had more speed, we were able to make the whole cruise but we did not get all the experience in sail work that we would have had otherwise.

Q: What did the ALEXANDER HAMILTON do in the winter time?

Rhodes: She was just stripped down, all the sails were removed --that was one of the things we had to do. Then in the spring run up all the sails again, and refurbish her, and get her painted, and so forth, and ready for the next cruise. One of the jobs the cadets had to do was to get her ready for the next cruise.

Q: That must have kept you really hopping.

Rhodes: It certainly did. That was extra duty, you might say, but looking forward to the cruise, all of them were willing to do double duty.

Q: You mentioned before that there were students at the Academy who had had advanced education and had been to college and studied some of the subjects, were there cadets at the Academy that had more experience at sea than others?

Rhodes: Yes, there were. For example, Captain Capron, a cadet classmate of mine, had been at sea on a yacht for a year or so. He had a lot of experience at sea. He came from Newport, which was a seafaring town. Another classmate of mine was a warrant officer in the Coast Guard before he came to the Academy. Others had been in the service in various grades. I think two or three classmates had a year or so at Annapolis before they came to the Coast Guard Academy. They had a jump on the rest of us, and of course, we looked to them for advice and guidance, but frequently we might think that we were more capable than they after we had a little bit more experience.

Q: Did you have trouble keeping up with them at first?

Rhodes: Yes. We had a great deal of difficulty keeping up with them because they did know a great deal more about going to sea and sea-going terms than we did. We were strictly landlubbers, but generally, it didn't take us long to catch up because with the type of experience that we had, it was always different than the type of experience that they had had, and many of the things that they had learned they would have to un-learn, and get the phraseology used at the Coast Guard Academy. Also we were operating with different type ships, and they had to un-learn some of the things they had been taught and their experience had showed them. So, I think, in the end, we had it just as good as they did, however they could lord it over us in the beginning because they knew a lot of things that we did not know, and that was to their advantage in the beginning. They were very good at showing us how to do it, and many times the cadets helped each other. It wasn't the competition, you might say, at the Academy, because we learned that we had to stick together pretty well because it just seemed like all the forces were going to bring our downfall if we didn't stick together.

Q: It was us against them.

Rhodes: That's right. I think when you come right down to it, the feeling of a person at that age is that the establishment is against them and you've got to stick together and do your best. It seems that no matter what age it is, a group of youngsters of college age, have a particular feeling that they've got to prepare themselves to take over because everyone else is making such a mess of it. They're inclined to stick together because they don't think that the older people understand them. That's been so in all history, I believe.

Q: The Coast Guard, during the time that you were at the Academy, was getting involved in anti-smuggling activities. Did you have special attention Paid toward anti-smuggling and that type of activity being taught to you?

Rhodes: Yes. We did. They gave courses in law enforcement. The Coast Guard is very much involved in law enforcement, not only in anti-smuggling. This goes back to the old revenue cutter days. The old Revenue Cutter Service was established to prevent smuggling, at least to cut it down. Since then the Coast Guard has been charged with enforcing customs laws. When they started smuggling alcoholic beverages, that was just a continuation of the Coast Guard's duties as customs officers at sea. There was a great deal of publicity about it, and people thought that the Coast Guard was just out there to prevent smuggling of alcoholic beverages. But we did have a very good course on powers of the Coast Guard, customs laws, and so forth, what we could do, what we couldn't do, and the various techniques involved. That was not strictly because of the smuggling of alcohol, it was smuggling of all types. It just happened that our big job at that time was the prevention of the smuggling of alcohol. A great deal of our effort went into that, but it actually was a continuation of effort over many years, and continuing to this day. You seldom read about it now, but at that time it was in all the papers --headlines on the front pages. However, we were well prepared in the enforcement of the law. The Coast Guard is charged with the enforcement of all Federal laws at sea, so we needed to get a good course in law enforcement, and also we had a good course in international law which also involved whenever you were up against foreign vessels, or in foreign ports, and so forth. You should know the basis of international law, and we had a good course in that.

Q: Did they teach you not only the letter of the law, but did they teach you how to conduct yourself as officers?

Rhodes: Yes. That probably is more important than just the enforcement of the law, because that is one thing that we learned in military discipline, to control yourself and to control your manners. I think that we are certainly learning now in this age that it is very important when you are enforcing law that your men not get out of hand. You've got to control them at all times, and you've got to treat the people as honorable human beings, and not treat them as criminals, especially until the court has convicted them as criminals. You have to make sure that they have their rights in all cases. You can't just assume that they are criminals even though they are caught in the act until it's actually proven. I think that our military establishment in the Coast Guard helped a great deal where we got involved in very, very sticky cases. We were pretty well able to maintain discipline and come out with a good record. We didn't take advantage of people because at that time many people held the Coast Guard in low esteem because we were enforcing what they thought was a very --certainly an unpopular law. We were only enforcing that phase of it that had to do with smuggling.

Q: What did you and your fellow cadets feel about the law itself? Prohibition.

Rhodes: We were in general, the cadets as a whole, were not in favor of Prohibition, but none of us felt that enforcing the customs law had anything whatsoever to do with the law of Prohibition. It was strictly the law of the land. We were charged with enforcing it --whether it was enforcing it against dope, enforcing it against aliens, enforcing it against contraband of any kind. I think there was great loyalty that we had to maintain the law. That's what we were there for and the people expected us to do it. Perhaps some were overzealous in enforcing it -- that's very true, but on the other hand, in those days, we were being shot at and in some cases the Coast Guard was shooting back. The trouble is when you start shooting you never know what's going to come of it.

Q: Was it uncomfortable knowing that you were doing you duty, when you were at the Academy you were studying to do your duty, and knowing that a good proportion of the country was not happy with what you were doing?

Rhodes: Yes, it was to some extent. You run into that all the time because the ordinary public is not informed of what you are actually doing. We always felt that those who knew what we were doing generally supported us.
They certainly would not have had any respect for us at all if they knew that we were out there to do this job and we just looked the other way. We felt that if the honorable peole were in our place they would be doing the same thing we were. They had the power to change the law --they had our vote to change the law if they wanted to put it up for change. I think it was almost unanimous when it was put up that we would vote against Prohibition. But while the law was on the book, the only way you could get it off the book was to enforce it. If you enforced it and the people didn't like the law, then we would do something about it. We've had laws on the books for hundreds of years that haven't been enforced and they're still on the books. Just as soon as you start enforcing them, they take them off the book. I think generally, the best way to get an unpopular law off the book is to enforce it.

Q: That's fairly true. It happens with the Blue Laws a lot.

Rhodes: But we had an awful lot of kidding from our friends about what we were doing, there's no doubt about that. It's hard to take at the time, but on the other hand, you just realized that if they understand the whole circumstances they'd be doing the same thing you were.

Rhodes #1 - 30 -

Q: You studied law enforcement in class and international law, did you have any practical training for customs duty?

Rhodes: Not strictly. However, every now and then they would have us go out on these smaller patrol boats, seventy-five footer, having us get used to running without lights at night, sneaking up on vessels, identify them, and every now and then you would get into interesting situations. It gave us the background of what we might expect to go into later on because we had a lot of the small patrol vessels that we could get authority to go out on, say the weekend, while we were still at the Academy, and quite a few of us took that opportunity.

Q: Can you tell me something about the cruises that you went on, and where you went?

Rhodes: Having come in as a cadet engineer, I did not make the first cruise as soon as I went to the Academy. We went there in May and the engineers stayed at the Academy doing engineer work, taking engineer courses, and so forth, while the line cadets took the cruise. Then the next year we made a coastwise cruise. One stop was Parris Island, which I mentioned before where we got target practice. Then we went over to Bermuda and up to the city of Port Halifax, then down through Maine -- we went to Rockland, Portland, and places like that. We got experience at our coastwise harbors. The next cruise, I mentioned, we started out on the ALEXANDER HAMILTON, lost our power and had to come back in and take the MOJAVE on a cruise -- that was a European cruise. That was very interesting. We stopped at Le Havre and we got a trip to Paris. We stopped at La Coruna, Spain and went sailing around there. They arranged a very nice cross country trip, and also the local people gave a big party for us -- a dinner party and dancing. Then at Casablanca and Rabat the officials gave us a real native high level party where you eat with your hands and so forth, and taught you all the customs --you had to take off your shoes before you came in. It was very, very interesting. By making these cruises, we were often entertained by the local people, high level people, who would give a party using their own native customs, and we were able to learn a lot more than we could have as ordinary tourists. The local people were showing us what the native customs were. Those were the only two cruises I made as a cadet.

Q: Did you get a chance to visit any of the Coast Guard stations, or go on board any of the ships for short periods of time?

Rhodes: Yes. We would do a lot of that on our own. On the other hand, they frequently had us take tours also. Right there in New London, one of the biggest operations we had against smuggling was right in New London. We had several destroyers and several patrol boats operating. We often would go over there and visit, and they encouraged that. Then the officers from the destroyers would come to the dances and get acquainted with us. They invited us out for a short cruise, and it was encouraged that we should accept voluntary invitations and we could get off for a few days for that reason. The ships officers also were encouraged to take cadets around and show them the ropes, so to speak.

Q: Did you have any special training in search and rescue?

Rhodes: Not at that time. We had a lot of training in handling ships. That was one of the main things but in search and rescue if you could handle a ship, every search and rescue case was a case in itself. In those days we didn't have aircraft, communications were not too good, and generally it was left to the commanding officer to become proficient, and to train his crew so that under any conditions of weather, he would be able to handle his crew, his boats, and his ship in such a way to effect a rescue regardless of what the circumstances were. It was mostly seamanship. Also they trained us to become familiar with all the coastline and all the harbors that we might be involved with in our cruising area. In the old days, they had winter cruises and the cutters just had to stay out cruising up and down, going into different harbors and becoming completely familiar, and being out there when something might happen, but that generally, was also before radio. It was found that if you maintained your position in a strategic spot, when radio became almost universal, you could get a message and get out there and do your job perhaps better than just cruising back and forth. You never know exactly where something's going to happen, anyhow. But in the days of the old sailing ship, many years ago, the only way you could find out if someone was in difficulty was accidentally run across them out at sea. There was no communications otherwise.

Q: I had a very interesting discussion once with somebody about the nature of the Coast Guard after 1915. In 1915 the Life Saving Service and the Revenue Cutter Service amalgamated and became the Coast Guard, and from that point on the Coast Guard remained more or less oriented around the Revenue Cutter Service --they were ship oriented and less shore base life saving oriented. Would you say that was true?

Rhodes: I would say it was true to a great extent. On the other hand, there was a great deal of coordination between life saving service and the larger ships in this anti-smuggling organization. We did work together. On the other hand, I would say that the top echelon in the Coast Guard probably had a tendency to pay more attention to the larger ships and patrol vessels than they did to the lowly life boat stations along the coast. They maintained them and got new equipment and so forth, but for quite some years, I believe they pretty well maintained the status quo as far as the life boat stations were concerned. Then later on they did start giving

Rhodes #1 - 33 -

them more modern equipment. There's no doubt about it, for some time, especially during the terrific anti-smuggling effort that was made in the 20's, the life boat stations just went along about as they were in years before.

Q: What about your training at the Academy? Were you trained in how to operate a life boat station, the activities that would go on there, and that sort of thing?

Rhodes: We were trained a little bit in the equipment of life boat stations, but not with the idea that we would ever operate them, but with the idea that we would often be operating with them, in coordination with them, and we had to know what their problems were, how they operated, and what their capabilities were. By operating the breeches buoy, we could pretty well determine what they would be able to do if we had to call on them for help. If a ship was aground and we were there, and we were going to help them, but the life boat station was there also, they had their life boat and breeches buoy, we should know pretty well what their capabilities were. It was more to coordinate efforts than it was to actually look at it from our personally operating life boat station itself. If you had qualified people on that end, it was just coordinating your effort. We had to become familiar and actually use these boats and breeches buoy in order to know exactly what their problems were.

Q: So that really when you get right down to it, the actual fact, even though the service was combined, The Life Saving Service and the Revenue Cutter Service, what remained of them in the Coast Guard was still more or less separated.

Rhodes: Yes. They remained separated until about 1938 or '39. I was greatly involved at that time in inducting the life boat station people and the light house people into the regular Coast Guard on the assumption then that officers and men would be transferred back and forth between the cutter operation and between the life boat and *light* station operation, so that they would understand each other's problem and work together. Since that time, I think there has been great improvement all along, because everyone knows a lot more about the life boat station and the *light* station, their purpose, their problems, and also the new electronic equipment that has come into being that has helped greatly in our operations. Some of them have been able to convert strictly to unmanned operations, and they are probably some ways more reliable. We have better equipment, and it's all operated automatically, rather than keep these men out there in an isolated place and no one know what the problems were, and no one seemed to care very much. After this happened, the Coast Guard did care a lot more about what was happening to the boys out there in isolated places. I think it was better for them, better for the whole Coast Guard when that happened.

Q: What was life like at the Coast Guard Academy when you were there, generally?

Rhodes: In many ways it was awfully tough. You were so busy all the time doing things, and as I said before, you just could not do everything you should do. You had very little time to indulge in social affairs, for example. However, we always had a formal dance every month, and as the old saying goes, all cadets are invited and will attend. We had to go to church every Sunday --that was required; it didn't make any difference what church you went to, you had to go to church. Many times we would be on the conduct *list* for having too many demerits. That meant you couldn't go ashore at all except to church. That helped us, though, catch up with our studies. Without being restricted to the Academy we might not be able to get through at the end. So it was considered, generally, an ordeal, and yet we stuck with our classmates and figured that every one else was against us. We had a lot of good times because there's nothing like having good comrades to tell your troubles too. But we didn't have very much time to even discuss our troubles because we were so busy doing the things and trying our best to get through the Academy.

Q: Did you get any leave?

Rhodes: Yes, we got about a little over two weeks leave in September after the summer cruise, and we'd get about ten days leave at Christmas time. Generally I spent my Christmas leaves in New York. I knew people down there and that was a really interesting place to go especially as long as you're acquainted. Generally on my September leave, I'd go home to Michigan.

Interview # 2 with Captain Earl K. Rhodes, USCG (ret.)

At his home, Takoma Park, Maryland   May 31, 1970

Subject: Biography   by Peter Spectre

Mr. Spectre: Captain, on your last cadet cruise, there was a casualty on the cruise. Can you tell me a little bit about it?

Captain   Rhodes: Yes. The under classman, Jones, lost his life when he went overboard during a terrific roll of the ship. Actually, it was morning and the cadet officer of the day, Samuel Gray, classmate of mine, had held the morning formation and while he went up to the bridge to report to the officer of the deck, he left me in charge of the formation on the after deck. This was the Coast Guard cutter, MOJAVE. We had a following sea at the time and the MOJAVE had quite an overhanging fantail, and she had a reputation of riding smoothly with a following sea, but suddenly taking a very sudden and deep lurch as the sea would catch under the fantail and push her over in a deep roll. This happened while we were still in formation on the after deck and it knocked all cadets in the formation off their feet. The deck was awash with several feet of water. Many of the cadets, including myself, were washed through the rail, however, as we went through we were able to catch onto a piece of the pipe railing or the gutter of the ship.

Q: This was the outside rail?

Rhodes: Yes, the outside rail. We were actually over the side. When we finally got to our feet, we noticed cadet Jones was treading water astern of us and waving his arms. Immediately I sent word to the officer of the deck on the bridge "man overboard", and we threw all the available life preservers in that vicinity overboard hoping that he would be able to reach one of them. The ship was turned around to return to the area and by the time we got back we could find no sign of Jones in the water. Apparently he had not been able to reach the life preserver. We searched all day in that vicinity, and of course, the spot was marked by the many life preservers we had thrown overboard, but no trace was ever found of cadet Jones.

Q: How did that effect you and your fellow cadets at the Academy?

Rhodes: That actually was a very, very sad occurrence because Jones was well liked by his class and my class also. He was an outstanding cadet and we all knew him personally. It saddened the rest of the cruise and I believe that it was an experience which matured all of us considerably. We realized that going to sea was an experience that was exhilarating and fun, and yet there were those hazards that we must face. I didn't see any sign of it really breaking up anyone. It saddened us and we were all resolved that anything we could do to avoid such an occurrence again, we certainly would try to foresee any contingency to avoid such a thing happening again.

Q: Was there any specific thing that you did in later years to try to prevent an occurrence of that?

Rhodes: We always tried to string a netting in the rails, if possible, to keep anyone from going overboard. However on a Coast Guard cutter we generally had to be ready to tow, and often would be towing, with men having to work back there on the hawser, and so forth. So regardless of every safety device that we tried to install, nevertheless, there were bound to be hazards from a vessel where you had men working on deck trying to save people from other vessels, and so forth, and that worked with boats, worked with towing hawsers out there in the very worst kind of weather. So there were always hazards, yet we resolved that we would never take any unnecessary chances. Nevertheless there were necessary chances that we had to take. However, men were trained and cautioned against the possibility of occurences such as that, and during the rest of my career, although many times there have been close calls, I have never actually lost a man overboard that was not recovered.

Q: How did you feel about the duties of the Coast Guard which you would perform when you were in the Academy and later on when you were performing them, when a good part of the time Coast Guard duties were hazardous duties, especially the search and rescue activities? Did you feel as if you were in constant danger?

Rhodes: I think to the contrary because when you are so concentrating on helping someone else, if you are busy and using all your energy and the energy of the other men around you on doing a job and helping someone else, the dangers of the assignment seldom occur at that time. After you have completed the task, sometimes you break out in a cold sweat when you realize how close you've come --how close some of the men have come to losing their lives or having a bad accident. But during the time you are so concentrating on doing the job at hand, and the more dangerous it is, the more hazardous it is, the less likely you are to worry about the consequences. You think about that and try to avoid any loss, however you aren't inclined to worry about that until it's over.

Q: What about beforehand? Say you're on stand-by and you know you could be called out for a rescue case at any time, you know what the consequences could be and it's something that's always there for Coast Guardsmen. How did that effect you, not particularly during the incident itself?

Rhodes: We spent a great deal of time in the Coast Guard studying contingencies that might arise. We do a lot of drilling under practical conditions --even rough water conditions. We perhaps take chances in holding the drills during rough water, but unless you hold the drill during the bad condition, rough water and bad weather conditions, the men just will not be able to handle them when they must handle them in actual conditions. So we did take all the precautions we possibly could, such as life preservers, life lines, and so forth, and drill the men under good weather so they were able to handle themselves well, and gradually build up a crew who felt they could handle the situation under any conditions. It's the drilling and practicing, and trying to foresee all contingencies that give you the confidence that you will be able to handle a bad situation. When the situation does come, everyone is so concentrating on doing a good job, it's worth doing, it's worth taking the risk, but nevertheless, we do have confidence that we will be able to accomplish it. And although, as I said, sometimes something will happen that was not foreseen, you really feel quite fortunate that you were able to overcome that difficulty, nevertheless, the fact that the men had been drilled under all kinds of conditions, they as well as you, can slightly change your operations in order to overcome that difficulty that suddenly arose. It could be likened perhaps to that last moon shot when a dangerous contingency arose, they had drilled and figured out just what they would do if something like that occurred --sure enough they were able to take care of it and come back safely. The planning and figuring out just what might happen and then drilling to take care of all those contingencies allow your men to do things that the ordinary person would not believe possible to accomplish under the conditions.

Q: You mentioned that you thought the risk was worth taking. Did any time arise that you didn't think the risk worth taking?

Rhodes: I don't recall any actual time that we were actually working on a case that risk was not worth taking. We worked on many cases that quite often you did not know how bad the case was, and not knowing you had to assume that it was very hazardous. So even though we found later on that the ship we were assisting would not have sunk, nevertheless there was no way of knowing it at that time. So therefore if the hazard is there even though you think the hazard is worth it, and it actually is, you feel that your effort is worthwhile. Many times in drilling under adverse conditions, having something unusual happen that perhaps almost causes a loss of life or injury, it makes you feel that that particular drill may not have been worthwhile. You feel that at the time, but looking back on it, you and the crew learned a great deal when that hazardous condition arose. Perhaps it's things of that type that allow you to figure out methods of avoiding a similar case, and therefore you are able to actually take care of a real true to life case. But in drilling you are bound to feel that when you're taking chances with the men's lives it's hardly worth while but you're awfully glad that you have held the drill when you really have a tough case to handle.

Q: What about a case where you actually decided to take the risk, and you did the job, and when you were done did you ever have any reservations afterwards about having an actual job?

Rhodes: That is difficult to say because many times those cases that you handle are touch and go. I remember one time I had to take a man off a trawler in the very roughest kind of weather on the Grand Banks of Newfoundland because the man had appendicitis. We were on a hundred and sixty-five foot patrol boat at the time. We lowered the boat and towed the boat over toward the trawler on the sea painter. The only man who put his oar in the water at all was the coxswain with a steering oar. We sent up the stretcher and strapped the sick man to the stretcher, tossed him over the side into the boat, then we recovered the boat with a sea painter, the men still not putting out their oars. When the boat got tossed up on a wave even with the gunwale, the men tossed the stretcher aboard. In recovering the boat, we completely broke the boat into kindling wood, it was so rough, we could not hoist the boat under that kind of weather. Yet we recovered the patient and all of the men in the boat were recovered safely --no injury. I remember at the time that it didn't seem possible that we could have put a little nineteen foot boat into the water in that kind of weather, the north Atlantic, and recover a sick man from another ship, and recover our own crew again. It was remarkable, by the drills we had had, we were able to do it. However, in hoisting a boat you can't hoist it fast --the deck was all full of ice. The men had to hoist the boat by hand, they didn't have any footing on the deck and considering the fact that the deck was so icy, and it was so rough, and the ship was rolling so badly, we were surprised that we were even able to recover the sick man and the crew of the boat. That cruise was so rough and the water coming back toward Boston was so rough washing over the decks that we lost all of our other boats on the way back. The waves coming over just splintered them into kindling wood. When you can operate like that, and lower a boat at sea, and recover a sick man, and still get him and the boat crew back aboard, that is almost accomplishing the impossible. And that was on a small patrol boat that we did that.

Q: Do you remember when that was?

Rhodes: That was about 1933, I believe. That was the PERSEUS, a one hundred sixty-five foot patrol boat. I was the executive officer of the ship at that time.

Q: Assuming that you were married at the time or prior to this particular incident, what did your family think about the type of work that you were doing and the hazards that you were confronted with.

Rhodes: I was married at that time and so far as my wife was concerned she would worry but she would never know when I was actually in danger. Most of the time, she wouldn't know what I was actually doing. She knew that I was out at sea but outside of that, that was all. Therefore a person is not likely to get keyed up about it until after the deed is over and then they might draw a deep breath. Our whole crowd, my family and all the other families, really knew what it was all about. I think they had a feeling that it was well worth while also. They were bound to know that we were going to take chances out there every now and then, but they wouldn't know ahead of time when we were going to take them, and therefore they weren't too much inclined to worry about us.

Q: What about after you would come back from a few patrols such as you just described and you told your wife and family what had happened, after telling a few tales like that, what did they think?

Rhodes: I think they had a great deal of difficulty visualizing just what happened and knowing that we often told tall stories, I think they felt that we were embellishing it a great deal. They couldn't tell when we were telling a true story or with a few trimmings, or else telling a dull story with a great deal of exaggeration. So I don't think they placed too much confidence in our stories. We were naturally inclined at that stage when we would come home and talk about this, to do a lot of kidding, and therefore it's very difficult for the wives to know what the real story is.

Q: Were you ever out on a mission or on a case and had a chance to stop and think and say, "My gosh, what am I doing here? As soon as this is over, I'm getting out. I've made a mistake."?

Rhodes: I personally never have felt that way. It's true that sometimes I've had disagreeable assignments, that I get pretty well fed up with that kind of life, but they never lasted very long. I found that as long as I felt that these jobs were worthwhile, I was very, very fortunate to be in a position to be of some help. The tougher things got, as long as people were really in trouble and needing assistance, the happier I was that I had something worthwhile to do. I've known of other people that have somewhat humdrum existence and I would much prefer a little excitement along the way even though it was quite hazardous at times and naturally you're always thinking of the hazards that your men are running rather than the hazards to yourself personally. That is the thing that really worries you and gets you keyed up because when you watch your men operating, true they are doing it in a professional way, yet they are inclined to be overconfident and take chances that they really shouldn't take. That's when you really start to worry. Nevertheless you aren't going to run away, you're going to stay right there and try to see to it that they do take the proper precautions and take care of them. There is nothing about it that would make you feel that you wanted to do something else. You want to stick with it. That is my personal feeling and always has been.

Q: Why don't we get back to the last days of the Academy, how you got your assignment --did you have a choice in your assignment?

Rhodes: Yes, we were all given a chance to request assignments. All my Christmas leaves had been taken in New York --I knew people down there and had gotten quite well acquainted and therefore I requested assignment in New York City. It happened that I got that to the destroyer PORTER. However, just before graduation, the monument to the Coast Guard World War dead had been placed in Arlington Cemetery, and they took us all as cadets down there to dedicate this monument in Washington, D.C., in Arlington Cemetery. That was a trip that we all took just before graduation. I remember that as a very fine and pleasant trip as the last days at the Academy. Then we all got leave before we reported to our assignments, and while I was home on leave I received a telegram from my new commanding officer to report back early so I would be there when the ship sailed. So my first leave was cut short and many leaves after that were cut short in order to be back in time to catch a ship before it went to sea.

Q: When was this --what month and what year?

Rhodes: We went on leave in May. This would be around the first of June, 1923.

Q: Did you think, before you reported aboard, between the time you got your orders and the time you went aboard, what went through your mind about whether you were prepared for the assignment, what you might expect?

Rhodes: I think a youngster who graduates from the Academy has a terrific amount of over confidence. It's not just confidence, but over confidence. We felt that we could do anything that we were called upon perhaps better than anyone else who ever tried it. We soon found out that that was definitely over confidence, however, when you reach the apex, which is a first classman and a graduating first classman and a commission which you have looked forward to for so long, you're inclined to have a very good opinion of yourself. That's somewhat the same as graduating from high school. We thought we were very fine men but they soon took that idea out of our heads when we reached the Academy. Then when we graduated from the Academy, we thought we were world beaters but after we got aboard ship that idea was soon lost, and rightfully so. I found over many years of experience that a youngster just getting out of the Academy is likely to be somewhat dangerous unless he's watched carefully because he does have that terrific amount of confidence. He knows a lot

Rhodes # 2 -- 45

but he doesn't know all the contingencies that might happen, and therefore you've got to have someone supervising him until he settles down and has had some experience on board ship.

Q: Would you say this was true of the cadets you came in contact with after you came out of the Academy that reported aboard a ship that you might have served on?

Rhodes: Yes. This is only natural. This thing has been formed over the years that when a cadet goes through the Academy and rises up class by class and then to the apex and receives his commission, he feels that he is a finished product. It's very necessary to watch this over confidence that I think all college graduates, and especially academy graduates, are inclined to feel when they first get out that they pretty well know all the answers. It's a gradual process of their finding out that there's still a lot to learn. You've got to generally set them down fairly hard when they first report aboard ship because they must realize that this is the real thing now. You're somewhat practicing while you are at the Academy --now you're going to have real experiences and you've got to be prepared for them. From then on you learn mostly by experience and drilling under actual hazardous conditions. Gradually the young officer becomes a finished product through experience. He's had a lot of experience before he gets there, but nevertheless he's just been going to sea during the summertime when the weather is good. When you get out in the north Atlantic in the winter time, the decks are all iced down, and you're called on to do some hazardous operation, it's a lot different than it is going on a summer cruise.

Q: We've talked a lot about officers and cadets and this is a general question that you could apply to the end of the 20's and through the 1930's before the war.

What was the state of the enlisted men in the Coast Guard? What type of men did you have and how good were they?

Rhodes: When we got out of the Academy in 1928, the Coast Guard had gone through a very rapid expansion due to the rum war, that's what it was called in those days, it was the anti-smuggling activities which we had to take care of which required that the Coast Guard be expanded to take care of expanded operation of the smuggler. We had to recruit a great deal of men. We took in many men from the Navy and many of those men had been discharged at one rate and the Coast Guard would offer them a higher rate if they would enlist in the Coast Guard because we took over twenty-five destroyers at one time from the Navy, World War I destroyers that we had to recondition and put in operation, and needed men experienced on that type of ship, which the Coast Guard had not had. So the Navy men that we got were very valuable in operating these destroyers, say machinist mates and so forth that had to keep those destroyers going --the machinery going. They were much more complicated and high powered than the Coast Guard was used to. We also took in some officers which we temporary commissioned officers. Some had been Naval Academy graduates who had resigned and decided they liked the service life and took these temporary commissions from the Coast Guard. Many of those officers stayed in and got permanent commissions because of the expansion of the Coast Guard. So the Coast Guard at that time, you might say was somewhat conglomerous. Also our ships had to be run short-handed. We just did not have enough men, officer or enlisted, to operate these ships. So most of the time we were standing watch and watch. Sometimes we'd have to stand watch six hours on, six hours off, and we got in port, we never were able to stand anything but watch and watch --you'd have one day off and one day on. When you figured that, you didn't get ashore very often. In the meantime you had an awful lot of work to do even on your day off. You just had to stay aboard during the working hours to supervise your men and sometimes you wouldn't even be able to go ashore on your day off or your night off. You had to keep your department up. So it was very, very, tough, slim times in those days and we had a great deal of work to do in port, as well as at sea. They tried to keep those ships at sea as much as possible to accomplish the work which we had out there. We had to cover a large area with comparatively few ships. So the object was to keep the ships at sea and even when we came in port, we certainly had plenty of work and we seldom got ashore in those days.

Q: Were the men up to par? Were they what you would expect for Coast Guardsmen?

Rhodes: No. Not up to par especially to what we were in the '30's in depression times. We had the finest outfit, of course, during the depression, because of the fact that you could get almost anyone you wanted and there was practically no promotion in the '30's, whereas during the '20's these were the roaring '20's, and people didn't want to go to sea and work like the Coast Guard had to work. You had to take who you could get in those days and we did remarkably well. Don't get me wrong --there were some fine people and perhaps we didn't deserve to have such fine people, enlisted as well as the officers. Our standards had to be, somewhat necessarily lowered in order to entice men to get out of civilian life and come into the Coast Guard in those days because it was pretty rugged and they could always get a good job in those days in the outside civilian life where they did not have to go to sea. Under those conditions it's very difficult to keep morale real high.

Q: Were you any worse off, or any better off than the other services?

Rhodes: I would say we were probably worse off because we had to expand during the '20's. If we had just had to maintain our status quo we perhaps could have made it but we were fortunate at that time --I don't say the country was fortunate, I say the Coast Guard was fortunate-- in that the disarmament conference did away with some battleships the Navy was building and reduced the amount of ships the Navy would keep at sea, and as a result the Coast Guard was able to entice some of these fine Navy men, who had taken their discharge thinking there wasn't much chance for advancement --we would offer them an advancement over the rank that they had held in the Navy just to enlist in the Coast Guard. So I think the timing was such that we were able to get some fine former Navy men that we would not have been able to get otherwise.

Q: Did this disarmament conference effect the Coast Guard anyway materially?

Rhodes: No, it did not effect the Coast Guard in any way whatsoever because the Coast Guard ships were not the type that would be covered in the naval disarmament conference. The Navy could have all kinds of patrol type ships that they wanted. They were not limited. I don't believe that had anything to do with the Coast Guard. The fact that we were expanding while the Navy was cutting back gave us quite an advantage in getting qualified personnel.

Q: What was the PORTER like? Your first ship.

Rhodes: The PORTER was a --her nickname was "The Showboat." We had a very public relations minded skipper, name of Steve Yardell. He wore a red goatee and mustache; he had a tiger as mascot on the ship; he was very socially minded. The ship was kept up very well --we were very proud of her, but shortly after I reported aboard after a couple of patrols we had a casualty to one of the turbines and that required that she be layed up in the Brooklyn Navy Yard for over three months for repairs. I just mentioned that the Coast Guard was short handed, the ships always were short handed so every time the other ships went to sea, I always had to go to sea on one of them to fill out their compliment. So although the PORTER was layed up for three months, I never missed a cruise. Sometimes I had to make two cruises instead of one to take care of the short-handedness of the other ships.

Q: So you weren't laid up at all.

Rhodes: No, I was kept very busy. I found, however, that that probably was one of the best things that ever happened to me because life on the PORTER was entirely different than life on the other ships. Your skipper can make a great deal of difference in the feeling of the officers and men on the ship and each ship that I'd go on with a different skipper would have a different attitude, so, very young, I was able to see the differences of the ships, the different way they were run and so forth, and I think that having it occur so early in my career helped me a great deal in later life because I could see the difference the skipper made and I could also see the good and the bad features in the way they were running their ships.

Q: What were the names of some of the other ships that you served on during this time?

Rhodes: I remember one was the ABEL, one was the PAULDING, I believe one was the McCORMICK, I think one was the NOMA --that's all that I can remember right at this time.

Q: These were all former Navy destroyers?

Rhodes: These were former Navy destroyers. Some of them were smaller destroyers than the PORTER. The PORTER was a thousand tonner and then they had even older ones which were called seven forty tonners. They were smaller and generally had three stacks, and the thousand tonners had four stacks. The seven forties had less power but they could go almost as fast because they were lighter than the thousand tonners but they rode entirely differently. Nevertheless the World War I destroyers were very rough riding. I could see what the boys had to go through in those days of World War I and we put a lot of winter cruising on them up in the north Atlantic out of New York.

Q: Were they all the same type? The flush deck destroyers --the broken deck destroyers.

Rhodes: No, these were before the flush deck destroyers. These were so-called broken deck destroyers which had a high forecastle and the officers had their quarters up in the fore part of the ship on the raised forecastle part. That was the roughest part of the ship, by the way, so the officers weren't able to get out of any of the rough riding --they had it just as bad as the men. It may be of interest to know in those days you only had cold water piped to your wash basin without any drain. We had a slop jar underneath that the drain washed into. When you wanted to wash up and shave in the morning you had to ring for the boy and he could bring some warm water in a pitcher and you could use that to clean up and shave with. Showering -- you had to shower in cold water. And that isn't so long ago when you stop to figure it. Those were World War I destroyers, fairly new ships back in the '20's, and yet that is the type of construction that they had even for the commanding officer. He didn't have any warm water in his state room.

Q: Captain could you tell me about the type of duty, the type of work that you did during those days on the POMPE and the other destroyers?

Rhodes: Mostly the duties in those days were locating the foreign supply vessels carrying alcoholic beverages and then trailing them, keeping right next to them until they would run out of fuel and have to return to their foreign port to get fuel and supplies. That was the objective because the large vessels such as the destroyers, for example, it was so bad in the early days that they would even use sailing vessels as supplying as supply boats. They could, of course, stay out there a long time. They would just anchor out there but it required that you keep a ship right there to keep speedboats, which would come out and load up and then go into port, from contacting them. So our main duty was to keep track of the larger vessels who would come in from Canadian, French, and English ports. We couldn't touch them as long as they were outside of the territorial limits, so, of course, the main supply vessels never came into American waters. They would just stay outside and be contacted by the American speedboats which would load up and then at high speed, run into harbor and unload there. So our main duty was to keep track of those vessels. Then, of course, in case of emergency, if some other vessel got into trouble, we could be called off that duty that we were on to help rescue anyone in trouble. But mostly the real reason for being on the destroyer was to trail and keep track of these larger foreign vessels to keep them from contacting any American vessels which were running between the shore and the larger supply vessels.

Q: How big were these supply ships?

Rhodes: Some of the supply ships would be quite large. I would say nearly as large as the destroyer herself. Of course, more of a cargo type than a destroyer but most of them I would say would be a little over a hundred feet long, which is of the small type, built low to the water so that they were not too visible. It's very easy for a vessel like that to go unseen in the foggy, misty type weather that you have off the East coast.

Q: In other words, there were supply ships that were specially built for the --

Rhodes: Yes, that's very true. Of course, they could use a fishing trawler type also as a supply vessel. He could look exactly like a fishing vessel then, and outside of the fact that he was hovering off our coast and maybe he was from the British West Indies, you'd know from his home port that he had no business up there off our coast. He wasn't there for fishing. As a result of that we had pretty good intelligence as to who the supply vessels were. We had a whole list of their names and, of course, they might paint another name on them but you could still pretty well tell whether they were the rum running type or rum supply vessels, or whether they had ligitimate business.

Q: How did your intelligence work? Were you familiar with that?

Rhodes: Yes. Actually that is one of the things that got me involved in communications because on the POWER, Ensign L. L. Jones was one of the foremost successfull officers who had come up from the enlisted and warrant grades. He had boarded and seized a large supply steamer right in New York Harbor. It was standing in and he took her.

Q: This was when he was an enlisted man?

Rhodes: That was when he was a warrant officer just before he made commission. That was one reason he got his commission, because of that. So as a hobby we got to breaking codes of these foreign vessels, and it's surprising how crude some of them were in those days. There were other activities, also, along that line, and that's where I first became intensely interested in communication, because you could have intelligence forces by using communications and by using the enemy communications as well as your own you were able to operate much more efficiently. So the two of us together as hobbies, we used to work in communications in trying to figure out how we could break down their information which they were transmitting to each other. Now we didn't have too much to go on because we weren't able to intercept their messages. We just had to get them as we could. But later on the Coast Guard as a whole had a very efficient intelligence operation. Most of our information was excellent.

Q: Could you use agents?

Rhodes: We used them but that was a very small amount. Actually, if you were able to read all of their communications which they were sending in code, you could get an awful lot of information and you wouldn't need a lot of agents. That was a lot cheaper and easier to get that type of information. Also as they would transmit you could take radio bearings and find out their locations and so forth. With that type of information it was far better than agents, generally, because we would have all the information that the agent would have.

Q: What about the other law enforcing agencies in the federal and state governments? Did they support you in any way? Like the FBI, the --

Rhodes: Yes, suprising how little support we got. We were supposed to get quite a little support from the customs agencies but in that day and age you probably know from reading that prohibition was very unpopular. It would not have been so successfull except for the fact that local law enforcement let them operate freely, you might say. As a result of that, where ever we operated we were generally very unpopular on shore because we were preventing the running of the alcohlic beverages in great quantities, and you might say what we were accomplishing was raising the price and also making them rely greatly on this very dangerous product called bathtub gin, or whatever else they were using to make bootleg type liquor. So if we had just laid off the smuggling part of it, they would have been getting good foreign liquor at a fairly good price. So many of the people on shore were very much against the Coast Guard in those days. We ran into a great deal of opposition, say when our men would go ashore and so forth. The newspapers would be inclined to run the Coast Guard down because we were making it so tough for the smugglers. The smugglers were the popular boys in those days.

Q: Even though you wore white hats you were still --

Rhodes: That's right.

Q: You mentioned before that you and Ensign Jones became involved in breaking codes. How did you do this? How did you learn, how did you begin?

Rhodes: Actually, we were both interested in it to begin with and we had somewhat similar hobbies. You know there were plenty of books you could get on that, and then if you could get ahold of a regular message from, say, a smuggling outfit, and treat that or different codes in an ordinary way you can determine what kind of an encipherment it is and perhaps in very short order you might derive plain text from it. That's where you have the crude type code that children learn to use. It's surprising how many people not familiar with code and ciphers will resort to a very simple type --either substitution or transposition type code --it's a cipher rather than a code.

Q: What do you mean by simple? Can you give me an example?

Rhodes: For example, if you have substitution you can just call one letter another. In other words you say "a" will be "t", and "b" will be "f", and "c" will be "l", and things of that type. Once you arrange that you can determine quickly by a count of the letters whether that is substitution. E is the most frequently used letter and maybe you can determine right away that they are using an "m" for an "e". Pretty soon in trial and error substitution and probability, you can have that plain texted in maybe a half an hour. That's a simple type and yet a lot of people who don't realize that that can be solved so easily will use that, thinking they are perfectly safe. Then ther is the transposition type which you write a message down horizontally and then take out vertical columns. The simple type, you can solve that in maybe an hour or two. So it's just a matter of testing these things to see what type of encipherment they use. Anyone can do that after they've studied up on the subject. It's surprising how crude a method people will use in an operation of that type.

Q: Did they know that you were onto them?

Rhodes: They didn't know at that time, but I have a hunch that they did later because we always happened to be right where the action was. They'd have to be very dull if they couldn't put two and two together. Of course, I think that a lot of the time they figured that someone in their own outfit was telling us what was happening.

Q: As you got better, did they get better with their codes?

Rhodes: Yes, they did. They improved. That's what makes me think they suspected that we were reading their codes and ciphers. Yes, they got much better later on.

Q: Were you and Jones the only ones?

Rhodes: No, there were others also. I think Meals was one of the ring leaders in that and he was in charge of it later on. We were only doing it on our own. We never got into the real activities. We were too junior at that time. But we could see how easy it could be done and reported what we could do in our spare time. It certainly gave us a great impetus in our interest in that kind of work.

Q: Did some of the people at headquarters or the people in your squadron know that you were doing this?

Rhodes: Oh yes, they knew that we were doing this and they were very much interested and of course, the fact that we were able to get some information of that type, that was very encouraging. I think that might have had something to do with expanding that activity. That's the cheapest way you can get your information, as long as you can get it that way.

Q: Did you teach other people?

Rhodes: No. Not at that time. Actually, a few months later I was transferred to the MOJAVE so it was only a short period of time that I was on the POMPEY. I was on the POMPEY from June, 1928 until March, 1929. It wasn't a full year.

Q: You must have learned very quickly.

Rhodes: That's why I say that we had already had the hobby and it was odd that the two of us on the same ship had a hobby of that type. Working together it was a good thing to do on these long patrols and long duty hours on board ship.

Q: Sort of a crossword puzzle.

Rhodes: That's right. Better than crossword puzzles. It's really a puzzle but it gives you great satisfaction to work on them.

Q: How far away could you receive messages from.

Rhodes: It depends on the frequency, of course, but at the frequency they were using I would say around fifty to a hundred miles.

Q: How did you know what frequency they were going to transmit on?

Rhodes: We had radios and you could always hear them, and we had that information that different ones would transmit on different frequencies. That way you could have the radio room listening in on those frequencies, and if they picked up a message on those frequencies, they would pass it on to us.

Q: If some of the supply ships were so big, couldn't they outlast the destroyers that were trailing them?

Rhodes: Yes, they could. But we would be on patrol for a certain time, and we would have to stay on patrol along with that ship until the next group of ships came out and one of them was assigned to take over the trailing of this supply ship. She might be there for two or three months so you had to keep a ship there all the time that she was there.

Q: So while they only had one ship they could use, you had many ships.

Rhodes: That's right true and they had a long ways to go, and as long as they were right off our coast we didn't have very far to go.

Q: Did any of them use what we call now, underway replenishment?

Rhodes: No, not the large ships. If one was short of meat and the other was short of potatoes, they might go alongside of each other and trade but generally they didn't have any mother ship, so called. I believe in certain locations, though that they did try that out, that the mother ship would be there to supply fuel and provisions. I wasn't personally involved in that type of supply, but I did hear that they were using it in some locations.

Q: How did the supply ships try to evade you?

Rhodes: Just by staying out of range of our waters. On the other hand, these large vessels loaded with contraband would use fog mostly to evade us. Of course, they never used lights at night. That was contrary to international law and yet they never ran with lights, unless you were coming up on them and they saw you, then they would put their lights on so you didn't dare hit them. But generally they would be waiting until you were going in one direction in a fog --see you always had to circle them to keep close to them-- you would be headed in the opposite direction in a fog, and they would get under way and go off through the fog and try to lose you in the fog. But that is dangerous because while you're running at high speed and trying to find them, you could cut them in two.

Q: Did that ever happen?

Rhodes: It happened to quite a few of them, but they were out there without lights and they were run into by Coast Guard vessels and sunk on the spot. I think in almost every case they were able to recover the crews of those vessels, but it was that type of attrition --it would cost them maybe a million dollars each time one of those vessels was sunk, and that type of attrition really hurt a great deal.

Q: It brings up an interesting point. Say a Coast Guard cutter ran down a rum runner during a fog, did the rum runners ever claim protection under international law saying that they were deliberately run down?

Rhodes: So far as I know, they didn't. They may have as far as newspaper copy was concerned, but I never heard of them bringing a case in court, claiming that it was deliberate because in every case they were running without lights and it was well known that that was their habit of running without lights. Therefore with a Coast Guard cutter cruising around, of course he would be without lights too, but he was not violating United States law when he was running without lights any more than Navy ships were violating law when they ran without lights during war time. That's a common thing, and it was common for Coast Guard vessels to run without lights. If we ran into a vessel that had its lights on, we would definitely be at fault when we were running without lights. So we had that hazard to contend with but if you ran into a vessel that had no lights on it, you were not at fault --he was at fault. There's nothing which allows him to be out there without lights whereas you have the law in back of you when you were running without lights.

Q: When you were out there did you ever have the thought at the time that this thing is out here and it's really bothering us and we could run it down and claim that it was running without lights, and so forth, and do it deliberately?

Rhodes: It never occurred to me, especially on a destroyer, because probably the destroyer would get the worst of it because they have very thin skins, but certainly you could see the logic of a thing like that. You could have an honest collision and that would probably solve a great deal of problems. But, so far as I know, there was no discussion of that type except in, you might say, very light vein. There was no serious thought of it whatsoever, as far as I personally ever heard about. I know that the rummies who suffered from it tried to get a lot of propaganda going to that effect --that in those cases where it had happened that it might have been deliberate. That is the only thing that I have ever heard is where they were trying to convince the press that that might have been what happened.

Q: What about harassment of rum runners?

Rhodes: Every now and then they would see that because they would be taking us farther and farther away from our home port, when it was time for us to be relieved. Every now and then when we were up close they would throw objects at the ship and the crew in turn would maybe throw potatoes at them. But that was always good fun. I don't think anyone ever was hurt over it. Or you might, if they were making it miserable for you, you might accidentally as you were running to windward of them, blow tubes and let a lot of soot come over, but that type of thing is all in fun. We had no difficulty of that type. There was one very interesting incident while I was on the PORTER. I was only on it for a short time, and my skipper, Steve Yardel was very publicity minded, so he took a photographer from the <u>Daily Mirror</u>, I believe it was --this was in New York while we went out on patrol. Then, me being junior officer, he set me up for boarding. We boarded a lot of vessels as well as followed the big ones. We could board American vessels anywhere on the high seas. Quite often these fishing vessels would take a few cases off these foreign rum runners and try to get ashore, so we did a lot of boarding in that way. This trip that we had was quite rough water out there off New York and the eastern coast, so the skipper wanted the newspaper photographer to get some good pictures, but it was too rough to lower a boat for boarding purposes, so he'd run close to these vessels that he wanted me to board, and just as the vessel would rise right toward the gunwale of the ship I had to jump from the destroyer over onto the vessel to be boarded. After I made the inspection, they would toss me a line and it was up to me to watch just the right time when a little fishing vessel would rise on the crest of a wave, I would have to jump and by the use of the line swing myself over to the deck of the destroyer. The pictures turned out much better than I thought of it, and actually both the front and the back pages of the Mirror when we got in port were covered with pictures of me making these flying leaps from the ship to the small boat in this rough weather. It actually looked far more daring than it was, because the photographer must have been good.

Q: I imagine it probably was a little bit risky.

Rhodes: The next cruise, the captain took a photographer out and he made a cruise on Long Island Sound, and he personally took a boarding boat and boarded the vessel. But it was nice smooth water, very calm, and lots of pictures taken, but when we came in port, none of the pictures had appeared in the paper. That was quite a talking point --we all had a lot of fun out of that. Well, he had quite a bit of publicity having a leopard on board as a pet, and things like that. He just loved publicity.

Q: Was he an Academy graduate?

Q: Yes, he was. But he had been in command of the Coast Guard cutter APACHE, which was based at Washington, D.C., and he had become quite well acquainted with the people around Washington, and he actually, also had been an aide to the Commandant of the Coast Guard so he was more of the public relations person than a sea-going person. A great deal of his time had been spent in public relations work --that was his hobby.

Q: What became of him?

Rhodes: He retired many years ago. I never heard just exactly what became of him later on.

Q: Did he serve during the war?

Rhodes: I don't believe so. I think he retired before the war started.

Q: Speaking of public relations, how were your public relations?

Rhodes: At that time they were very poor. In other words, anything good about the Coast Guard was not published and anything bad got the front pages.

Q: Were there people, aside from your skipper, who were actively trying to promote a good image? Or was it left up to chance?

Rhodes: No. We had different people who were, but in those days the Coast Guard had no funds for that purpose. It was only many years later that we ever had what you'd call a public relations department. We never had any public relations except just each command trying to maintain good relations and good contact with the press. Of course, in your life saving activities, and so forth, we always did have fairly good contact with the press. Also we always had the contacts with the press because of the activities we were in --they would come and contact us and ask us questions.

It was just a question of whether we could turn a bad story that they intended to write into a story that perhaps showed a little bit of the good side of it, too. Most of the time, the press in those days were in favor of public opinion which was that the Prohibition Act should be abandoned. We got caught in the middle because of our major concern with smuggling. We were against smuggling --that's all we were against. We were sworn to enforce the anti-smuggling laws.

Q: When you were on the PORTER did you ever intercept speedboats that came out from shore to pick up supplies from a supply ship?

Rhodes: No, we never did. We saw them a few times but they always operated from fairly near shore, and they had high speed. You couldn't follow them in shallow water. As a result a large ship like the PORTER was not able to follow them into the shallow water. They would never try to contact the ship that you were tailing and generally they operated at night. You needed a small vessel of that type and generally that's what we used. The Coast Guard could not afford to build vessels of that type because they were very expensive and we didn't have money to build real fast large speedboats. That problem was solved by seizing certain speedboats from the rummies with the goods, having them FORFEITED because of illegal use and then the Coast Guard would turn them into Coast Guard vessels and use their own boats against them. That is the way we captured many more speedboats is after we got a goodly supply of boats which they had had to forfeit. Then we could man them and without a load, we could catch them when they had a load. So that's how we were able to get many more.

Q: In the line of communications, if you saw a speedboat that you couldn't follow were you able to communicate with a shore station that had a speedboat or directly with a Coast Guard patrol boat that could come out and --

Rhodes: You always could do that but at that particular time our communications themselves were not good enough and rapid enough to get results. We were talking last time, our life boat stations were not closely geared in those days to our ships. If we could have communicated directly with our life boat stations along the coast, we could have done a much better job, but we would have to communicate on shore and then they would have to send a land-line telephone call or telegraph to the local stations and by the time all this was done it would be too late for them to act. In later years we equipped all our ships and stations with radio so they could talk directly with ships along the way, and also yachts and so forth, who might be in trouble. Radio changed the picture entirely but this was all after the prohibition amendment was repealed.

Q: What value do you think that your experience on these destroyers had for you and had for the service in general?

Rhodes: I would say that one big thing it kept us at sea a great deal more than we might have been otherwise. We got to be real sea-faring men rather than people who just went out now and then when the weather was good, or when there was a special call for us. Another was that we got a lot of practice in maneuvering larger ships on short notice and we not only had to keep close to these vessels but we had to be careful that we didn't hit them. We had to keep them in sight in very rough weather and often very foggy weather, and still with them maneuvering you were both without lights and you had to be very, very, careful that you didn't hit them because you couldn't say you didn't know they were there. Therefore it gave our younger officers a great deal of seaman experience in handling a larger vessel at sea under various adverse weather conditions, and he had to use his own judgement. Even the junior officer who would be on watch couldn't always wait for the captain to get up there. He had to maneuver the vessel himself. Generally speaking, on a regular cruise you can't change course except in an emergency without calling the captain, but while you were trailing these vessels you had to handle your ship with split-second accuracy in order to maneuver properly. So I think a lot of our junior officers had a great deal of good experience from that.

Q: A question of semantics. Coast Guard ships are called Coast Guard cutters. All Coast Guard ships, at least now are called Coast Guard cutters. Were the destroyers called cutters?

Rhodes: No, we generally called them destroyers. Where the name originated was the Revenue Cutter Service, they called it the Revenue Cutter Service, and the first law passed appropriated money to build, I believe, ten cutters. That's what the type of the ship was called. So that's come down over the years and generally we call a ship that's painted white --we call that a cutter, and the others painted gray such as a destroyer --we call that a destroyer; you call the others patrol boats even the hundred and sixty-five foot long patrol boat that I was on. In the old days perhaps if that was painted white, we'd call it a cutter, but painted gray we called it a patrol boat.

Q: Why were some painted white and some painted gray? Now they're all painted white.

Rhodes: All of the Coast Guard cutters were painted white. Some of the smaller boats are painted white but we might call them if their size is such, if they were not able to go to sea and make long cruises at sea, you'd call them patrol boats.

Q: What I mean though, say a destroyer is painted gray, why wasn't it painted white?

Rhodes: The big reason is that during the rum war, you couldn't see a vessel nearly as well when it's painted gray as you can when it's painted white, especially in a fog. So all of our patrol boats and destroyers, and so forth, used in the rum war were painted gray. Also that was the paint color of the vessel and it was a lot cheaper to keep it that color than it would be to try to change the color to white. In that day we were trying to conserve funds as much as possible. For example during World War II even our white ships were painted gray.

Q: What was your next assignment after the PORTER?

Rhodes: The Coast Guard cutter MOJAVE was my next assignment. I joined the ship in Washington D.C. about the first of March, 1929 just in time for me to take over command of a company of bluejackets to parade in the inaugural parade of President Hoover. That was, I believe, the last parade on the fourth of March when the President was inaugurated at that time. That was a very, very, wet day as I remember it. Instead of wearing rain coats, they had us wearing overcoats. Our overcoats not only were heavy when they were dry but they were really heavy when they were wet. So during the whole parade we were sloshing along through this cold rain, we were soaking wet all the way to our skin, the soles of my shoes completely wore through and by the time I got back, there was nothing but the uppers of my shoes left. Most of the men parading were about in the same situation. That is a recollection that I have of an inauguration parade. I wished many times that they had waited a week before assigning me to the MOJAVE. That was a very difficult day as I remember it.

Q: Why were you re-assigned?

Rhodes: Generally officers are re-assigned fairly frequently when they are young.

It happened that they needed an officer on the MOJAVE and there were plenty of applicants for jobs in New York. For some reason, I haven't the least idea why I received the assignment --perhaps my own skipper might have had something to do with it because he was public relations minded and he might have wanted to get someone else on there after I made the splash on the <u>Mirror</u>. I always had a hunch that might have been rankling. Also I was quite well acquainted in New York and it might well have been that he thought I was too well acquainted and didn't spend enough time on board ship, although as I said before, there were very seldom times when you could get ashore under any conditions.

Q: Was Washington the home port of the MOJAVE?

Rhodes: No, Boston was the home port of the MOJAVE but she had been brought down here to enter men in the Inauguration parade. So that was her main reason for being here, and I, being junior officer, had to lead a company of men in the parade.

Q: Then you went back to Boston?

Rhodes: As soon as the inauguration ceremonies were over we went right back to Boston.

Q: What kind of work did the MOJAVE do?

Rhodes: The MOJAVE made regular ice patrols off of Boston, and during those patrols, they would start probably in May and last at least four months. We would be based at Halifax in Nova Scotia, and then we would patrol off the Grand Banks of Newfoundland for icebergs. We would locate the icebergs and then keep steamships advised through regular broadcasts of the location of the iceberg that was nearing the steamer lanes. The Coast Guard had the authority that if too many bergs started getting down toward the steamer lanes, they could change the steamer lanes farther south, because the ships going east toward Europe, their lane would be about sixty miles south of the lane of the ships coming from Europe toward the United States. There was so much fog around those localities that they had to have the ship lanes divided a great distance to avoid collisions with ships going the opposite direction. Also you had to keep the ship well south of the location of the icebergs as they drifted down from Greenland—they would drift down toward the steamer lanes and toward the Gulfstream. The Gulfstream actually comes right by the Grand Banks in that location. Sometimes you will find water about sixty degrees on one side and on the other side down near freezing, maybe just a hundred feet apart. That's what causes a lot of the fog up through there —warm water on one side and cold water on the other side. Of course, right around an iceberg itself you often have cloudy conditions that you would not have if it wasn't for the presence of the iceberg. Once the iceberg gets into the Gulfstream it only lasts a few days and disappears rapidly. But as long as it's in this cold water it will last a very long time. They're tremendous big hulks out of the water but that's only one/seventh of the iceberg —six/sevenths of it is under water. Often there's large shelves under water that a ship could run onto and tear its bottom right out of it. Our job was to keep the transatlantic ships away from the icebergs, locate the icebergs and keep the ships advised of their location.

Q: This was part of the International Ice Patrol?

Rhodes: Yes, this was the International Ice Patrol and the Coast Guard operated it. Since those days we have been able to do a far better job, with modern methods. In those days we didn't have radar, we didn't have planes that could cover the area.

Now we have scouting planes that can pick up the icebergs, keep them plotted. We have very excellent navigational facilities in the way of Loran, radar. We can locate the icebergs now even in fog with radar, so we can keep them very well plotted and we know we're not missing anything. In those days with so many days of fog, you couldn't be sure that you weren't missing icebergs now and then. It so happened that as soon as the International Ice Patrol was established, back, I believe in 1914, there's been no ship lost as a result of collision with an iceberg such as the TITANIC --which was the reason for establishing the International Ice Patrol in the first place.

Q: Were there other ships involved in this?

Rhodes: Yes. We alternated with another ship, either the TAMPA or the MODOC. The MODOC was based at New Bern, North Carolina, and she would come up to help out with the International Ice Patrol. Then the TAMPA, based in Boston, was also a sister ship, would be a stand-by vessel so if anything happened to the MOJAVE or the MODOC the TAMPA would come out and take their place. Generally the time of each patrol, you would have fifteen days on station and the other vessel would have fifteen days on station, but you actually had to relieve on station where the Ice Patrol observer would transfer from ship to ship, he would have his other scientist also transfer along with him so that you had an observer group that stayed at sea for a whole month out there making the observations. They were the, you might say, the scientific group that remained out on station all the time. So going to and from the station meant that you spent about twenty-one days at sea and nine or ten days in port. Most of your time was spent at sea under those conditions.

Q: What was the function of the Ice Patrol observer and his staff?

Rhodes: We took scientific soundings continually out there. We would take samples of the ocean water at various depths. You would lower them down so far with bottles hooked on at intervals and then when you got your wire out so far with these bottles on it, you would trigger all these bottles which would fill with water at that particular level. You'd bring them up and you could then sample the contents of the water, get the temperature of the water at the various depths, and from all those observations they're fairly well able to chart the ocean current in that locality. For many many years we've been taking those samples every year, and we call it an oceanographic cruise as well as an Iceberg Patrol because you're taking scientific observations continually while you're on patrol. As you cruise along, you're taking them in different locations. So you can chart the underwater current, temperatures, contents of water, salinity, many other things that they get. So the scientific observation party on board was not only getting the location of the icebergs themselves, but they were charting the ocean currents, and so forth, to predict the flow of the icebergs so in case of fog, and you knew where the icebergs were, you could figure out where they would be in two days, or three days, or a week from now just knowing the current. It's a similar study that they make of the weather so they know which direction or how strong the wind is going to blow. There you have your atmospheric observations and this is an underwater observation to chart the contents of the ocean water and the temperature, so you could predict the ocean currents.

Q: Were there ships there from other countries?

Rhodes: No. We also had another cutter which was called the GENERAL GREENE, at that time, which was strictly an oceanographic cutter. She would go right up the Greenland waters where the icebergs were breaking off from the Greenland ice cap, and make underwater soundings all the way through that whole territory. She would go up several months ahead of the regular patrol. She was strictly a scientific vessel; she wasn't interested in the icebergs down near the lanes where we were watching. She would chart the waters up near the source of the iceberg and help count the icebergs as they were coming down.

Q: Is that the same GENERAL GREENE that I know --the hundred and twenty-five footer?

Rhodes: That's right. The hundred and twenty-five footer that was converted to an oceanographic vessel way back in the early '30's.

Q: Why such a small ship? That must have been hazardous duty.

Rhodes: It was but there again money had a lot to do with anything like that and in the first place, we had the ship; second place the rum war was pretty well dwindling out and she was especially built for that. Those hundred and twenty-five footers are one of the best sea-boats that we ever had --far better than the hundred and sixty-five footers, so it made a good stable base. Also the hull is much stronger. She's a slow vessel but the hull plates are very strong so if she should hit ice, it wouldn't hurt her very much. We actually used her for ice breaking in our ports down here. She was probably almost as good a vessel as one could be that had been designed for the purpose. She was small, carried a very small crew, had long cruising ranges because of her diesel engine and she was a very staunch, very seaworthy type of vessel.

Q: What about the MOJAVE? Was that reenforced for ice?

Rhodes: No, the MOJAVE was not reenforced for ice. Actually she had what you might call a thin skin type. Her main reputation came from the fact that it was one of the first turbine electric vessels built. The steam drove the turbine and the turbine drove the generator which in turn powered the electric motors. That was an experiment in the Coast Guard and it proved quite satisfactory --more maneuverable generally than a geared turbine type vessel. That's one thing you've got to have on a Coast Guard cutter, rapid maneuverability. You've got to back and fill in tight quarters whether you're out at sea or in port.

Q: What makes it maneuverable?

Rhodes: The big thing is your generator and turbine are turning in the same direction and all you have to do is reverse the leads on your motor, so your motor will stop and turn in the opposite direction. A steam turbine, you often have to close the valves while your turbine is going ahead, and then when you get those valves, of the ahead turbine closed, you've got to open the valves of the reverse turbine to change the direction of motion. You can't very well put a clutch on an engine of that power. It would tear up almost any clutch that they could think of. What happens is, your electric motor serves as your clutch. You can stop that motor in a hurry by reversing the leads and then start it turning in the opposite direction without stopping your turbines or your generator.

Q: How did you physically track these icebergs? Once you discovered them, did you follow them?

Rhodes: You can keep track of an iceberg when you're several miles from it because it's so high out of the water, generally. Knowing an iceberg was there, you would have several icebergs to keep track of, and you would be cruising where you expected them to be after you had plotted the ocean current. Say it had been foggy for three or four days, then you had to relocate those icebergs, and you would figure out where they should be and generally, they would be in that position, within five miles of it. You could also then determine whether they had melted very much or whether they were still good and solid. You would cruise around those southern icebergs, the ones nearest the steamer lanes and if the weather held out after locating them, and broadcasting their positions, you would then cruise north to see how many more were on the way down. Then you start plotting them. But your main, urgent job was to locate and plot the southern most icebergs so you could warn the ships, then you would see what you could in the time allotted, depending on clear weather, you would locate all those you possibly could farther to the north.

Q: Say you discovered an iceberg and left it, searching for more icebergs, then you started tracing the route that you followed coming back, how would you know that you were looking at the same iceberg you were looking at before, or that it might not be the same one --it might be a new one?

Rhodes: All of our scientific work in plotting the ocean current in that area was a great help because we could predict within a very reasonable space where that iceberg would be a day from now, two days, ten days, and invariably you would come very close to your predictions. So once the weather cleared, you would go and relocate it, and the chances are that your prediction was very close. Icebergs do not travel very rapidly because they can only travel with the ocean current. Six/sevenths of them are under water and the wind has very little effect on their drift. If you know the direction and speed of your ocean current, you can predict very closely where your iceberg is going to be ten days from now. You also know your location of your Gulfstream. That is one of the easiest things to locate. Your main difficulty in the old days was navigation because you would have a week or ten days that you couldn't see the sun. With all your ocean currents, and so forth, you had to go on dead reckoning. Unless you knew your ocean currents real well, you could be way off where you figured you would be. That, again, was another reason for knowing your ocean currents as accurately as possible. If you could predict what the current was doing to even in the fog, you'd find that you were within a very reasonable distance of where you thought you should be.

Q: Did you ever experiment in marking icebergs?

Rhodes: Yes. We experimented with it. We experimented with shooting our heaviest guns against them. We experimented with putting mines against them trying to blow them apart. It's no more effect than using a little ice-pick on a great big cube of ice. You could peck away at it, but you hardly make any dent in it at all. They have made experiments in putting lamp black on the icebergs, trying to get them to melt faster, but even that has practically no effect because there's very little sun up there, and the sun has got to shine in order for it to absorb the heat. Also what little area is exposed above the water is so small compared to the total area of the berg, you could melt that top area very rapidly and still have hardly any effect on the part underneath the water. It would be just a very gradual pattern.

Q: You'd be worse off because you couldn't locate the iceberg.

Rhodes: When that iceberg gets into warm water it doesn't last long, and that's the real enemy of the iceberg --warm water-- because that's where the main part of the iceberg is, under water.

Q: What about your actual operations in the ice? Were you ever in danger with your ship?

Rhodes: We have come very close to icebergs in fog. That is probably the worst danger of all. One time when we were standing right close to an iceberg and had broadcast it's position, all of a sudden out of the fog a great big steamer loomed. We flashed the lights, what ship? and instead of answering by flashing light, she flashed a great big sign on the superstructure, BREMEN. I don't know why they ever came that close to the iceberg but they must have had confidence that they knew where we were and we'd broadcast the position of the iceberg very carefully. Also we were sending out a radio signal that they could take bearings on, that we located a southern iceberg in the lane. She came cruising at high speed right past us and past the iceberg. It wasn't a dense fog but it was very misty --you couldn't see very far.

Q: They call it the International Ice Patrol but from the way you describe it, only the United States was involved in it. Where did the international aspect come in?

Rhodes: All of the maritime nations who have signed the International Ice Patrol agreement participate in the cost of the Ice Patrol. At the end of the season the Coast Guard figures how much it costs them to maintain the Ice Patrol and then the cost is figured out on a pro-rata share of north Atlantic nations which have a great amount of commerce across the north Atlantic. It's figured out on who has the most ships, and so forth. It's a formula which has been worked out and signed into the treaty. The cost of the International Ice Patrol is payed for by several different nations who are interested in maintaining an International Ice Patrol.

Q: While you were involved in the International Ice Patrol, what was going on

Rhodes #2 - 76 -

in improving the methods of detecting icebergs? Where there people who were pushing, for instance, for aircraft support?

Rhodes: No not at that time because, if you will remember, long airplane flights were mostly in the experimental stage at that time. It hadn't been many years before that that Lindberg had flown the Atlantic in a single engine plane. There were no planes that could fly over water with any degree of accuracy. You'll remember when Roosevelt came to office he had the Air Force take over the air mail and there were a tremendous number of crashes even among the Air Force and they were fairly well equipped at that time. You just shouldn't fly even on land when the weather wasn't just right. You go off and fly over the ocean in a place where fog is very prevalent and your methods of navigation are very poor, you're going to lose an awful lot of planes in that day and age.

Q. Did anyone consider using sea-planes that could be launched by the Coast Guard cutter?

Rhodes: We talked a great deal about that, but there again, there is so much fog up there that even when it's clear fog may set in at any moment. It's rough water up there, too. The airplane that we had available couldn't land in that rough sea. You'd have to have a harbor for it to land in. Newfoundland, at that time, was not any place to try to land a plane. They had to build air facilities up there during the second World War. They had no real air facilities in that locality -- no special navigation devices for airplanes or ships, so it was just considered too hazardous for the equipment at hand and the state of the Arctic? at that time. It was quite hazardous for ships to be up around the icebergs because we had no radar, no means of adequate navigation other than the old fashioned sun, star sights, which is not pin-point navigation by any means. It wasn't until World War II when they started developing long range aircraft that there was any thought at all of using aircraft up in those areas. It really takes a great deal of accurate navigation and methods of bringing a plane down under poor weather conditions to go up in that area because the weather is a main feature of the whole operation.

Interview # 3 with Capt. Earl Rhodes, USCG (ret.)
At his home, Takoma Park, Maryland   June 7, 1970
Subject: Coast Guard   by Peter Spectre

Mr. Spectre: Captain, the last time we talked, we talked about the International Ice Patrol and your experiences on the Coast Guard cutter, MOJAVE. What did you do on the MOJAVE when you weren't on ice patrol?

Capt. Rhodes: We engaged in regular patrols off the New England coast, and during the summer time we would patrol yacht regattas and general law enforcement, and be available for assistance work as required. During winter cruising, we generally had considerable assistance work, mostly the fishing vessels and so forth, that might get in trouble off the New England coast, and fishermen that might become ill out at sea, we would bring them in. Any vessel that broke down, we would be towing it in, and things of that nature.

Q: Your home port was Boston. If you had a sick fisherman --nowadays it's a fairly simple operation for the fishing boat to contact the Coast Guard by radio-- how was it done during this period of time we're talking about now?

Rhodes: Generally it was done by radio in those days, also. However radio was not nearly as sure and efficient as it is today. Sometimes another fisherman with radio would be informed by the fisherman in trouble by either signals or sighting, and then the vessel with the radio would send the message in. Of course, this was in the early '30s and radio was pretty well in use by the larger fishing vessels as well as the Coast Guard, and many commercial vessels in those days. Although it was not as wide spread and efficient as it is now, it still was far and above the standard that it was in the early '20s.

Q: Do you have any idea what percentage of the fishing boats carried radios?

Rhodes: Practically all the larger trawlers carried it and many of the small deep sea fishing boats carried it. Those who stayed close to the shore would seldom have any radio at all, but those who stayed several days at sea and cruised considerable distances off the coast would have radio, almost invariably.

Q: How did the communications net work?

Rhodes: In those days the Coast Guard had radio stations which was in direct communication with the district office, and Coast Guard vessels would then communicate through their district office directly. The Coast Guard vessels also maintained watch on the international distress frequency of 500 kcs, and also on the voice calling frequency of 2670 kcs. In that way the fisherman could call the Coast Guard vessel or Coast Guard station because we continually maintained watches while at sea on our calling frequencies and international distress frequencies.

Q: How about the Life Saving stations. How did they communicate?

Rhodes: Life Saving stations in those days had better communications than they had previously because of --this was the last days of the rum war and we had generally installed radios in some of the most important stations, and they had telephone communications between themselves up and down the coast. The communications had been improved a great deal during the later 1920s at the stations.

Q: Was there any one person who was responsible for this change? I think you mentioned that the Life Saving stations didn't have radio in the early days.

Rhodes: That's right. I would say that Commodore Webster --actually at that time he was Cdr. Webster, a retired officer placed on active duty, retired after the first World War and went on duty after some experience in commercial communications. He went back on active duty with the Coast Guard and he was chief of communications for the Coast Guard. He was greatly responsible for building up Coast Guard communications. In those days I would say that generally, the Coast Guard had better and more modern communications than commercial services or either of the military services, due to the fact that communications were so important to the Coast Guard in anti-smuggling work, in search and rescue work, and so forth. He was able to show that good communication was far more important than almost any other thing you could do to do a good servicable job in the type of work we were supposed to accomplish.

Q: If Webster retired right after World War I, then he originally started off in one of the original services, at the Coast Guard.

Rhodes #3 -81-

Rhodes: Yes, he was started with the Coast Guard and served with the Coast Guard during the first World War, and then he retired for physical disability after the war was over.

Q: Was he in the Revenue Cutter Service before the war?

Rhodes: That's right.

Q: Could you explain to me the type of equipment the Coast Guard was using during this period of the first years of the '30s? The original equipment that was brought in.

Rhodes: The original equipment was the regular CW spark-gap type equipment. We had no voice equipment in the beginning. It was only during the late 20's that we started getting reliable voice equipment so that we could equip our smaller patrol boats with reliable radio. That was greatly the result of Cdr. Webster developing this type of equipment. Of course, he had commercial companies working on it, but he was able to get the money and had the foresightedness to see the need for it. As a result, we were getting voice radio, which you can use on smaller units, as well as larger units. Where you have the Morse code, CW type radio, you must have radiomen on every unit to use that type of equipment. But on the voice equipment, you can use it directly on the bridge, with the captain of the ship being able to talk with that. And also life boat stations could use it for ship to shore. So the Coast Guard vessels were able to talk directly with the life boat station with this voice equipment. So it got the message to a point that it should go directly rather than have to pass through several channels.

Q: What would you say was the main driving force that pushed the Coast Guard along in developing better communications at that time?

Rhodes: I would say the reason we were able to get the radio equipment that we did, we were expanding at the time because of, you might say, the rum war. There was no reason to spend a lot of money on personnel and ships unless they are effective. They only way they could be effective was through good reliable communications. I think it was a very excellent selling job through the Congress to the higher ups in the Coast Guard, and to everyone concerned, it just made sense that without good communications we were just almost throwing our money away. With good communications, we could do a far better job with the men and vessels available to us. The selling job was done, we got the good communications and we were able to do a far better job than we could have done without good communications.

Q: How about the training of radiomen during that period? What type of training did they receive?

Rhodes: They set up special radio schools for training radiomen. We also sent them to commercial schools. I know various types of commercial schools were established at that time, and our outstanding radiomen were sent to those schools to learn radio maintainence, radio theory, etc..

Q: By commercial schools, do you mean schools like RCA?

Rhodes: Yes. We used RCA and CREI, that's Capital Radio Institute right here in Washington, D.C. Many of our students went there. Actually when Arthur Godfrey was a radioman in the Coast Guard, he was sent to CREI, and he often mentioned it on his program. So we not only got good radio equipment, but we trained our men to maintain it and operate it properly. With all that training, the different men with experience would come in and recommend certain changes that would be more effective. On the whole, the communications department was very forward looking at that time. They wanted to improve communications as much as possible. Once you get started in that direction, you snowball, and everyone starts getting interested in it.

Q: What about your relationship with the Navy in communications? Were you developing your procedures along the same lines as the Navy?

Rhodes: Yes, to some extent, except that our uses of radio were so much different than the Navy's that they were completely incompatible as far as operations were concerned. The Navy would want to maintain radio silence at sea, for example, and broadcast a message and assume the vessel for which it was intended picked it up. With our use of radio, every vessel, every mobile unit would be using their radio to talk to each other, and to talk to land stations, and also talk to commercial vessels, fishing vessels, yachts, etc, that may be in trouble or have some information from someone who was in trouble. So we wanted direct contact with a great many units by each one of our floating units to obtain information and to act on it immediately because time was very important out there working directly with all types of different vessels, and also shore stations. By coordination between each other you'd be able to do a much better job. Also in rum running, we had to communicate directly with each other when we were coordinating a search. So this was a much different type operation than the Navy would be conducting.

Q: The Coast Guard by law, becomes a part of the Navy during war time. Was there any coordination developed to make sure that the Coast Guard knew Navy procedures if war should develop, and of course, it did.

Rhodes: Yes, that's true. The Coast Guard did study Navy procedures and we transmitted and received, especially in our larger cutters. We would strictly adhere to Navy procedures. All of our more powerful transmitters would adhere to naval procedure. Our instruction books were according to the Navy, so that our radiomen and communications officers had to operate along Navy regulations and procedure as far as communications were concerned. But there again, generally Navy procedures were somewhat different than the procedures that we actually used on our small vessels. Seldom would the Navy operate the way that our small vessels operated between shore stations and patrol vessels, and along with yachts and fishing vessels, etc., where you get down to the lower operator. He's a seaman rather than a radioman, but still radio was giving him a tool with which he could do his job.

Q: Going back to the MOJAVE, did you engage in anti-smuggling patrols in the MOJAVE?

Rhodes: Yes, we did to a lesser extent than we did on the destroyer force. MOJAVE, of course, was a ~~smaller~~ *slower* vessel, she was painted white and they could see her a long ways off, and she was far more useful as a rescue vessel and towing vessel, helping other vessels in distress. Therefore, if there was any distress case the MOJAVE would be called upon and the destroyers left to take care of the anti-smuggling operation. So when she was doing nothing else, she was out there patrolling for possible smuggling operations, but often when she was working on a search mission, or something, she'd be called upon to take care of a distress case.

Q: Do any distress cases come to mind during this period?

Rhodes: Right now I can't think of any outstanding cases on MOJAVE. I remember that we had a great many, actually, but I can't remember the name of the vessels involved, and they were not too important at that time. The MOJAVE had done some real important cases before I went on her, and of course, during her whole career she had quite a career of taking care of distress cases, and every year she had a great many. Since you have a great many, unless something is outstanding, it doesn't really stick in your mind too well.

Q: What type of regattas did you patrol?

Rhodes: We would patrol yacht regattas off Gloucester, say the fishing vessel regatta. When I was on the MOJAVE we patrolled the International America's Cup Regatta down at Newport. I believe that was the last SHAMROCK that Lipton brought over here. Of course, the America's entrant won. My recollection is that it was the ENTERPRISE but that's a long time ago and it had so many names that I'm not sure whether that was the correct name or not for that particular race.

Q: What did your duties consist of in this type of patrol?

Rhodes: The cutters formed a line on both sides of the course and patrolled right alongside at some distance off, a couple hundred yards off, the racing vessels. Then we had patrol boats to keep other vessels away from the racing vessels themselves. They were supposed to stay outside of the line of cutters on each side of the racing vessels. This way it allowed the racing vessels to maneuver without interference. Whenever they changed course, the cutters had to change course so that they would keep a so-called alley way cleared for the racing vessels to maneuver.

Q: About how many Coast Guard cutters would be involved?

Rhodes: I believe there were about ten cutters involved at that time and there were several smaller patrol vessels.

Q: It must have been pretty complicated if you had to change course with the racing boats and they didn't know when they were going to change course.

Rhodes: That's very true, and they weren't telling you when they

Rhodes # 3 - 87 -

were going to change course either, otherwise they'd be tipping their hand to the other vessels. But since there was two yachts racing at the time, it did help make it simpler, and, of course, we did have patrol vessels up ahead trying to keep the course clear as well as on each side of it. But there were several hundred yachts, and the larger yachts also were there so you had to be very, very careful not to allow little vessels or even larger yachts to foul up the course. If one of the contestants could call foul because someone got in his way, the whole days racing would be called off, and since it was an international race and highly publicized, it was figured that everything possible should be done to keep the course clear, allow the spectators to see what was going on and still not be close enough to allow a foul to be called.

Q: You see even now, pictures of the America's Cup races, and it's like thousands of spectator boats. Did you ever participate in a regatta where bad weather ever came up during the regatta with all these boats and yachts and racing craft, and all of a sudden it turns into pandemonium? Has that happened, or could it happen?

Rhodes: Yes, it has happened. One time in Chicago we had twenty yachts capsize all together. This was some time after the period that I'm talking about. Generally speaking the vessels that were participating up there at Newport, and places of that nature, they were able to stand the type of weather you might encounter up there. Off Newport the wind gets pretty strong and the water gets pretty choppy and they really shouldn't go out there unless they can stand fairly rough weather.

Actually, during those races, we had no difficulty. Sometimes off Gloucester these fishing vessels racing, these Gloucester schooners, they could take pretty heavy weather and they liked heavy weather. If some smaller vessels went out, they might get in trouble. However, that was one big reason why so many Coast Guard vessels were assigned to a big race of this type. We often would have to tow in the smaller vessels that got into trouble, but generally the major portion of the vessels could handle themselves quite well under the type of weather that was encountered.

Q: What did happen in Chicago?

Rhodes: When these twenty sailing vessels capsized, we had to rescue the people from them first, of course. Then we went out and righted the sailing vessels themselves, which was a considerable slow operation. My recollection there is that some of the owners were quite upset because we hadn't rescued their vessels before we did because of the fact that there was some damage done to some of them, they capsized in water in heavy seas, whereas they felt that if we had been able to right them immediately so much damage might not have been done. However, we had to rescue the people first and we finally did rescue all the sailing vessels without severe damage being done to any of them.

Q: How many Coast Guard cutters were involved?

Rhodes: We had five Coast Guard life boat stations involved and I believe it was four of the smaller type Coast Guard patrol boats that were involved in that particular case.

Q: Do you remember the date of the event?

Rhodes: This would be around 1938, which is sometime after the period we were talking about. I remember it so vividly now because I was in charge of the whole operation of bringing these life boat stations and Coast Guard vessels together to do the job. What a complicated job it was because one of those sudden squalls --it was a beautiful day and then a sudden squall came up and capsized these vessels. We were very fearful that we were going to lose quite a few people. It happened that no one was drowned and all vessels were eventually saved but it was touch and go there for awhile, so naturally a thing like that does pop up in my memory.

Q: It must have been a nightmare for you.

Rhodes: It certainly was.

Q: When the Coast Guard goes out on a rescue mission, the thing that comes first is rescuing the people, saving lives, and then after all lives are saved, then property is concerned. I can imagine some of the difficulties that must arise in things like that, like what you just mention now. Did it cause a lot of trouble with the owners of these ships?

Rhodes: Some of them felt that when we rescued the people from the boats we should immediately right the boat instead of our boat going off with the people and maybe rescuing some people from another boat, that we should have righted the boat on the spot. However, after reviewing the whole thing with them, they all believed that we had done the proper thing to first see to it that all the people were saved before we tried to right any of the boats. That is a long drawn out job sometimes when you try to pull a boat upright from a capsized position in a very rough sea. It takes time. Whereas you could snatch people out of the water in a hurry, and that was the important part as far as we saw it. Even though you might have been able to right a boat in a hurry, it would be somewhat accidental and being in charge of the whole affair, you had to issue orders to save the people first before trying to right other boats.

Q: Say you are on a Coast Guard cutter and you receive a distress call from a ship that's sinking or disabled. You go out and begin your rescues, take the people on, and at the same time you receive another call from another ship that's having the same type of problem, it's an emergency, so you can't tow in this disabled ship or craft. You have to go over and rescue these other people. Did you ever have a situation similar to that and what did the owners of the first ship have to say to you? Did they ever try to sue you?

Rhodes: That is a very excellent question. Of course, you're somewhat covered under your instructions and international law in that you are required to go to the assitance of a vessel whether you are a Coast Guard vessel or a commercial vessel, if you are in the near vicinity, and you shall not leave it until you have made sure that the people on board are safe and no longer need assistance. Therefore, if you are engaged in a rescue mission, no matter how important some other mission might be some distance away from you, you must stay on the scene as long

Rhodes #3 - 91 -

as there is some assistance that you can render, as long as there is still danger to the people that you are trying to assist. That has always been our basic TENET that if a vessel was already on the scene assisting, she could not go to another assistance case until she had taken care of that particular one. You'd try to get another vessel on the way to the other case, but release this one as soon as possible so that no further assistance was necessary. Then she could go on to the next one. But she could not leave it until the people, at least, were out of danger. That doesn't mean that you have to rescue the ship itself. If a ship can stay afloat, while you go and rescue the people off another vessel, you'll go and rescue the people off another vessel and then come back and try and save the ship, if you're pretty sure she's going to stay afloat. But if it's going to take you a long time to try to save the other vessel, and you're not sure at all you can do it, under the circumstances, you definitely would have to go over and rescue the other people before you stayed there on a hopeless case of trying to rescue a vessel that was probably doomed anyhow.

Q: What about questions of negligence? You've performed a rescue and someone got injured during the process of it. Has this ever happened to you or a ship that you were on?

Rhodes: Yes, it has happened quite frequently, and each case deserves an investigation. I remember one case, I believe I was on the MOJAVE at this time, and we and a destroyer were trying to tow a large vessel that had gone aground, I think it was off New Bedford somewhere in the sound down there, and the hawser on the destroyer broke and it snapped and hit one of their boatswain's mates and it mangled his arm. We rushed him to the hospital. This is where one of our own men was hurt, but here again, in each case a very high level investigation was held whenever any accident has happened and try to determine the causes of these accidents and then issue certain regulations to try to avoid a similar case. So far as I know, there hasn't been, in my experience, an investigation which brought out that someone was negligent to the extent some action should be brought against him.

Q: If this type of thing did occur, how did it affect morale, and how did it affect your attention to duty the next time you were out?

Rhodes: Generally speaking, if someone was negligent the general feeling was that if he hadn't done what he was supposed to do, he should be so-called rapped on the knuckles, because generally our spirit was such that everyone was very anxious to do a good job and it was hard to understand someone who wouldn't do everything possible when the chips were down and his services were required. I hadn't any feeling at all that if someone was negligent in the type of assistance they were doing, that everyone didn't figure that he should be punished depending on the type of offense. However, negligence is entirely different from slightly wrong judgement. Everyone has to use their own judgement in very bad situations, and no one can help them use good judgement. It's always easy to second guess someone after it's all over and say maybe you should have done it another way. I think if someone just used a little poor judgement in some cases, the feeling was if he had done the best he could under the circumstances, as he saw it, then he should be corrected but the punishment certainly shouldn't be severe.

Q: What about cases of "biting the hand that feeds you" type thing? I've heard stories when I was in the service about a Coast Guard cutter patrol boat going to somebody's rescue, saving their lives, and in the process tearing out the chock from the bow, or smashing up the super structure, and going ahead and causing bad publicity --saying things to the newspapers about what a sloppy job the Coast Guard did, or even trying to sue the Coast Guard for damages. In cases like that, how did that affect you? How did you feel?

Rhodes: That affected me very badly and especially that was being done during the rum patrol days. Many people felt that if they could give the Coast Guard a black eye during those days, they were doing a service to the country, so to speak. So we were getting it right and left where we were certainly not deserving. Many times people said things about us that we didn't deserve at all, knowing the special cases. However later on, there is always a case of where the Coast Guard is doing the best they can, still if the vessel they are trying to rescue is lost or damaged, then the owner is likely to sue the Coast Gurad or the government to try to get the value of the vessel back. There again, it's a matter of judgement whether everything was done that could be done. When you tow a vessel off a beach and it sinks, the question is --if the vessel stayed on the beach it would have been battered to pieces. You don't have time to put pontoons on it and so forth, when you do get it afloat, so one of the first things is, if it's fairly free of water, to bring it out into deep water and then take care of it so it doesn't sink. If it stays on the beach, it's going to be pounded to pieces and it'll be a total loss in a short period of time. That is a very tough decision to make. We had to make that decision on the West Coast one time. When we pulled the vessel off, it floated for about a minute and then it sank. It was our opinion and the opinion of the owner before we pulled it off that if we didn't get it off in a hurry, it would be all battered to pieces and certainly you couldn't save anything. So he gave the okay to pull it off, but after we had pulled it off and it sank, he was trying to deny that he did give his okay to pull it off. It's things of that type that you've got to cover yourself with. But you don't have too much time when you have to operate on split second period, and we didn't have that owner there to sign any piece of paper. We had to take care of it in a hurry.

Q: Did you get more-or-less gun shy after awhile with this type of thing?

Rhodes: You have to become somewhat of a sea lawyer. You've got to realize that there are some people that will take advantage of a particular occasion, and if you do not cover yourself legally, you might be held libel. I remember the Commandant saying one time when we did something in a hurry, I didn't personally do it but one of our Life Boat stations, and we wrote in the circumstances. The commander of the Life Boat station did what he thought was right and the Commandant wrote back and informed us if he acted in the way that he felt was right, and he had to act immediately, that it is better to <u>act</u> than not to act at all, "take action which you deem is proper than to just sit still and not do anything.

Q: During your entire Coast Guard career, you and your fellow Coast Guardsmen must have coined that many times. When you got out on a limb and got sawed off, did you feel that the service backed you up most of the time?

Rhodes: In all my service career I felt that the Coast Guard backed me up, backed my associates up, whenever they figured they were doing what was right. Even when it turned out to be wrong on second guessing, I felt that as long as the people did what they thought was right, we were invariably backed up. On the other hand, if through negligence or other means, they were wrong, they received the type of punishment which the occasion called for. The fact that we were backed up, I think, allowed us to take a lot more chances, not unnecessary chances but the chances that we felt were worth while, when we otherwise would not have done so if we were afraid we wouldn't be backed up if something happened. Many cases when I figured a fifty-fifty chance of coming through all right, it happened we did come through all right, but knowing that I'd be backed up if something slipped, allowed me to go ahead with confidence and do the best we could. I think the word went out long ago and it was pretty well accepted, that anyone who was doing a dangerous job, if he did the very best he could in his judgement, he could expect a well done instead of a slap on the wrist.

Q: Do you remember any times when you thought, and your associates thought, that someone got a raw deal in cases like this?

Rhodes: I can't remember any time that I thought that anyone got a raw deal, except temporarily. After a thorough investigation was made and the facts were on the table, generally the decision was made correctly. Whenever someone jumped to conclusions immediately, sometimes there are insinuations that someone is at fault. You're bound to have that. Never-the-less when all the chips were down, generally the right decision was made because the decision is made then by your fellow officers who might get in the same type of predicament that you got in. You'd have a right to explain why you did certain things. They could see whether, with the circumstances that you were aware of, you were correct, and their decision will be made accordingly. They might have made a decision differently than you would, but at least you have a right to your own judgement in a case like that. In their report, they can well say that you acted in your best judgement, then they can find fault with your judgement in their opinion. So it becomes a good piece of paper that's circulated around the services. You can see where one officer made a judgement, a group of other officers think that judgement was incorrect, and it allows all of us to take a look at it and maybe learn a little bit from that discussion. On the whole, as far as I know, no one was ever punished because of poor judgement on a case.

Q: What was the period of time that you were on the MOJAVE?

Rhodes: I was on the MOJAVE in 1929 and was transferred to the WAINWRIGHT in 1932.

Q: How many ice patrols did you have?

Rhodes # 3 - 97 -

Rhodes: Two. 1931 and '32.

Q: They were both more-or-less uneventful?

Rhodes: That's right. Although they were very interesting. We saw a lot of icebergs, a great many interesting events up there, so they were uneventful as far as anything unusual happening.

Q: Tell me about your transfer to the WAINWRIGHT.

Rhodes: I was assigned as navigation officer of the destroyer WAINWRIGHT, which was also located in Boston.

Q: This is one of the destroyers that was an ex- *World War I Navy Destroyer*.

Rhodes: That's right. We had one division of destroyers at Boston, one division of destroyers at New York, and two divisions of destroyers at New London, Connecticut which were engaged in anti-smuggling patrols off the New England coast, or north eastern United States coast.

Q: How many destroyers were there in a division?

Rhodes: Generally speaking, there were six destroyers in a division. I think we had twenty-five destroyers in all.

Q: You said it was the northeastern United States where these patrols were conducted. What happened to the South and the West Coast and the Gulf Coast?

Rhodes: They were protected somewhat by patrol boats and Life Boat stations, however, the north eastern coast was by far the greatest threat to smuggling activities probably because the population, density, up there was such that the smugglers could make a lot more money in that area. Also there was a very irregular coast line and there were many, many inlets, and so forth up along the New England coast and off New York, New Jersey, and so forth, that allowed the smaller speedboats to contact the larger vessels lying off shore. This was the center of activity. There was some smuggling going on in other parts of the country of course, but the great investment of the smuggling activity had been made to try to run illicit alcohol beverage into the northeastern part of the United States.

Q: If I were a smuggler and I was confronted with what the Coast Guard had available to fight smuggling, I think that I would turn my attention to the Gulf Coast or the West Coast.

Rhodes: It's true some of them did. We didn't have enough equipment to stop them. The only thing that we could do would be to try to make it costly to them so that there wouldn't be nearly as much of it done. Of course, as the years went by, we were able to do a much better job than we were able to in the beginning. Of course, they became quite expert too, as time went on. They were smuggling along the coast, for example, between Canada and Detroit. There was a lot of smuggling there. You had smuggling all over the place. Many people were dealing with that in various parts of the country. It wasn't neglected down in the Gulf. We had quite a few seizures down there —some interesting cases down there in Florida especially, but the main activity was up around the northeastern coast of the United States, around New York, Boston, and in between.

Q: When you were on the WAINWRIGHT, this was just before the end of prohibition. Were you on the WAINWRIGHT when prohibition was repealed?

Rhodes: No, it was sometime after I got off the WAINWRIGHT that it was repealed. However, there was a great deal of talk about it at that time --a great deal of agitation in political circles. I know that was the time Al Smith was very much in favor --he ran on the program of repealing prohibition. I believe Roosevelt ran on the same promise that he would repeal prohibition, and it was my recollection after Roosevelt came in that they got that under way. That was sometime after the time that I was on the WAINWRIGHT.

Q: When you were on the WAINWRIGHT and the writing started to become apparent on the wall that prohibition was going to be repealed, how did that affect your diligence?

Rhodes: I don't think it affected us at all, actually. We were at a point where we were having more success in those days than we were earlier, there was no certainty that it would be repealed, and actually the prohibition ammendment had nothing to do with our duties, anyhow, because our main reason to be out there was to see that no one smuggled anything. They couldn't smuggle guns, they couldn't smuggle people, they couldn't smuggle alcohol unless tax was paid for it --it had to go through customs. So if they were smuggling anything it was up to us to stop them from smuggling. It's just incidental that it happened to be alcohol that they were making so much money on. If it was dope, we were especially active against that. It made no difference whether or not the prohibition ammendment was going to be repealed particularly as long as the smugglers were out there trying to smuggle anything in, we were going to do anything we could to keep them from doing it.

Q: You actually had drug smuggling problems?

Rhodes: Oh yes.

Q: Did you have any seizures?

Rhodes: Not so far as I'm concerned. The fact that everyone was working on it, and of course, they were not running boats loaded with drugs --there were boats loaded with alcohol. Drugs occupy such a small spot that that becomes more of an intelligence operation than it does an off shore type anti-smuggling operation. You just can't tell by looking at a ship whether he has drugs on board, or not.

Q: Insofar as drugs were concerned, what type of intelligence did the Coast Guard use?

Rhodes: The Coast Guard has always coordinated very carefully with the Customs Bureau and the Treasury agencies such as the alcohol tax unit, the narcotics unit, secret service, and the other law enforcing agencies out of the Treasury Department. They tell us what to look for and we tell them what we find, and by working together, there were sometimes seizures made that would never have been made by one agency working by itself. By sharing intelligence, and so forth, we were able to help quite frequently. There again it seldom comes out just exactly what the background was, how much cooperation and coordination was made before a particular seizure or arrest was made.

Q: Were you breaking codes, during this time?

Rhodes: Not to any great extent at that time. I still was using it as a hobby but I was so busy when I was on the WAINWRIGHT that I didn't have much extra time to do anything. It just happened I was assigned as navigator there and I think it was over a year that I was acting executive officer because every time they assigned an executive officer to that ship, he became ill and had to go to the hospital. They would assign someone else and the same thing would happen. There was about four or five executive officers assigned to that ship but they all had to go to the hospital so I was navigator and executive officer for a great deal of time that I was on the WAINWRIGHT. So I didn't have much time to take care of any of my hobbies.

Q: What kind of illnesses did the executive officers have?

Rhodes: They would have such things as appendicitis, or suddenly would have pains, I don't know whether it was chronic or just what it was, but they'd have to go to the hospital for observation and perhaps have their appendix out. I wouldn't want to say exactly just how serious the illnesses were, but most of them ended up in the hospital.

Rhodes #3 - 102 -

Q: It must have been a funny feeling to see those guys come in and go.

Rhodes: That's right. I was hoping to unload my job onto them and just as I thought I was going to make it, something would happen to them. Very frustrating, to tell you the truth. The skipper on there, Henry Coyle, was very much a search light man. We didn't have very good search lights on the destroyers as regular equipment, but Sperry had developed some very fine search lights and we had two of them on there. One was a twenty-four inch diameter search light and the other was a thirty-six diameter search light. We were able to hold rummies at ten miles distance with those search lights and you could not do that with any of our others --about a half a mile was the most you could do with a regular issue type search light. We didn't have technicians to keep those search lights in operation so Capt. and I were doing our best to keep those lights in operation, and a couple of times he even had us bring it down on the ward room table and we all worked on it together on the ward room table --the ship was rolling around. But he was very, very much interested in developing proper search lights for use out at sea. There was no doubt that search lights were a big help in identifying vessels and holding on to them in bad conditions. However, they naturally were not any help in a fog.

Q: What else happened to you on the WAINWRIGHT?

Rhodes: I think one real interesting thing is that on the destroyer force, we went down to St. Petersburg, Florida each winter for six weeks target practice, and that was a real respite. We had large caliber practice of the ship's four inch guns, and small arms practice, pistols and rifles on Eggmont Key, Florida. We also practiced drilling in formation in accordance with Navy rules for destroyers, operating together.

One thing I remember about that was very interesting, the skipper Henry Coyle always took his motorcylce aboard the destroyer. He took me in the rumble seat of the motorcycle, both of us dressed up in white to a dance at the Tampa Yacht Club over in Tampa one night, and that was one of the highlights of that whole trip. He was somewhatof a rugged type anyhow and to have him driving that motorcyle was a sight to behold.

Q: Your exercise in St. Petersburg --what was that in preparation for?

Rhodes: That was to keep us up on naval requirements in case we should be called upon to operate with the Navy at any time, we had to keep up to their requirements. Of course, all of our ships had about a month each year that they devoted to target practice and cruising in you might say, war time formation. Merely practicing the regular maneuvers which would be called upon in that type of work. They maintained proficiency in small arms, crews, the officers, pistols, and so forth. This was a requirement but this is one of the highlights that I remember on the WAINWRIGHT. It was a real tough assignment having that six weeks down in Florida, one of the things that I really remember about it.

We were patrolling off the coast of New England and generally we had these experimental searchlights which the captain had installed on the ship --one was a twenty-four inch, one was a thirty-six inch Sperry high intensity searchlight-- and they were far more efficient than the usual searchlight supplied to the destroyers. We actually kept the rummie in view over ten miles on a good clear night with the thirty-six inch searchlight.

Q: Were they eventually adopted by the service?

Rhodes: No. There was a great deal of consideration being given to adopting them as a whole, but I believe that just when they thought that they might be adopted, the prohibition ammendment was changed and also the depression had hit and money was scarce. Probably the real reason they weren't adopted was the depression which made money scarce. We had to economize in every way possible from then on. Definitely we learned a lot about those searchlights. We learned about the use of them. I think if the situation had gone on as it was, probably we would have standardized the large searchlights at that time.

Q: Was there any talk about radar?

Rhodes: The only talk I heard about radar was that it was some kind of a science fiction type talk, in that we felt eventually they would be able to use something in a fog, such as infra-red beams or something of that nature. The electronic art had not been developed to the extent at that time that we felt there was very much hope of ever developing radar as such. We used sonar and we wondered if they couldn't have some kind of sonar that would work in the air, but so far as we could see there wasn't too much hope for it. But certainly we could

Rhodes # 3 - 105 -

see the need for it.

Q: Was the Coast Guard trying to develop new equipment, new ideas, or was the Coast Guard relying on the other services and private sources?

Rhodes: I don't think the Coast Guard was working with its own technicians in trying to develop something of that nature. I think they were hoping that the Navy might be able to develop something or issue contracts to some commercial firm that would do it. Whoever did it, it was going to cost an awful lot of money in experimenting and developing apparatus, and so forth, and the Coast Guard just did not have that kind of money, especially in the '30s.

Q: How did the depression affect you in the Coast Guard?

Rhodes: The depression affected us more later on. We're talking about the WAINWRIGHT right now, but I think the depression hit us much harder when Roosevelt came in because he froze all promotions in the Coast Guard, and even if you got a promotion, you couldn't get the raise in pay that went along with it. Also, he cut everyone's pay fifteen percent. Even a man getting twenty-one dollars a month, his pay was cut fifteen percent, and even if he was promoted he couldn't get a raise in pay, so that really hurt. It gave many people the feeling of what's the use, because your pay was cut and there was no use to work for promotion because even if you got it, you couldn't get a raise in pay. I remember that I was in flight training at the time and they discontinued my whole class, closed the class down, so that not only

Rhodes # 3 - 106 -

gave me a fifteen percent cut in my regular pay, but I lost flight pay at the same time. A very low ebb for the Coast Guard at that time.

Q: I've heard talk that there was talk about merging the Coast Guard with the Navy.

Rhodes: Yes, there was very serious talk there at one time. In fact several times there's been serious talk about merging the Coast Guard with the Navy. Sometimes the position of the Navy has been that they favored it, sometimes they didn't favor it. It all depends on the circumstances and generally, the Treasury Department wanted to hold on to the Coast Guard in each individual case and so it was a question of investigating and finding out just why it would be desirable to keep the Coast Guard separate from the Navy and still be a part of the Navy in time of war. I think it was pretty well recognised that the Coast Guard could be of more value to both the Navy and the United States by remaining separate. For example there's a few items that I might mention. When they had trouble down in Cuba, that would be in the early '30s, the United States didn't want to show too much force but they did want to make sure that our own people were protected so they sent down several Coast Guard vessels, cutters and destroyers, so the Coast Guard then could help, rather than if the whole flotilla of the Navy was sent down there they might feel that the Navy was more of a threat. Another time during the Spanish trouble, a Coast Guard cutter was sent over to Spain and our American ambassador lived right aboard the Coast Guard cutter so that he was out of arms reach for awhile and still --he could do that on a Coast Guard cutter much easier than perhaps a naval vessel when it was a very, very touchy situation.

Q: This was the Spanish Civil War?

Rhodes: Yes, that's right. So they have used the Coast Guard quite frequently when it was a very touchy international situation and they didn't want to get involved with the Army or the Navy for some reason that seemed obvious, you might say --that we didn't want to do that and they used the Coast Guard rather than send in the Navy which frghtens people sometimes. I think, generally speaking, the Navy could see there were certain reasons why it would be desirable under certain circumstances for the Coast Guard to be separate and at the same time, any time the Navy needed help from the Coast Guard, they could always call on us and we would be transferred to the Navy, whether it was peace or war. It was automatic in war time, but I have operated with the Navy in peace time, and all I have to do is report in for duty with the naval commander with my unit and we could operate together just fine, as though we had always been operating together.

Q: When this came up in the early '30s, did you as a Coast Guard officer, do anything to support the Coast Guards staying separate?

Rhodes: No, I didn't at the time. I don't know exactly what was done. I feel that the Coast Guard, as a general thing, were against it, although just what they did to indicate they were against it, I don't know. But I believe Secretary Morgenthau, at that time, was a pretty powerful member of the cabinet, and I think he did more than perhaps even the Coast Guard did to convince the President and the powers that be that it was best that he keeps the Coast Guard under his jurisdiction as Secretary of Treasury. It seems to me that that was what happened.

Q: I understand that at one point in this struggle that the Coast Guard Academy alumni association became involved and really that was one of the things that brought the alumni association into a body that mattered. Were you ever approached as --

Rhodes: I was a member of the alumni association but only as a dues paying member. I was not active in that particular phase of it.

Q: Did anybody ever approach you about it?

Rhodes: We talked about it, but so far as I know, I don't know just what was done. My recollection is very hazy and, as I say, I wasn't personally involved, although I remember various talk pro and con about it. I know there was some talking we would be better of in the Navy and some talking we'd be better off in the Treasury Department.

Q: What was your next assignment after the WAINWRIGHT? How long were you on it?

Rhodes: I was on the WAINWRIGHT '31 and '32, then I was transferred first to Hampton Roads for flight training.

Rhodes #3 - 109 -

Q: How did you get involved in flight?

Rhodes: I had always wanted to go into flight training and naturally I had been putting in for it and finally I passed my examination and they assigned me to flight training at that time, in 1932. We went to Hampton Roads first to fly in sea planes and that's where I first soloed.

Q: How long had you been training to become an aviator?

Rhodes: I believe I put in my request when I was on the MOJAVE, and then again on the WAINWRIGHT. They only started classes once a year so if you didn't make the class, you just had to wait for the next one. I almost made the class the preceding year but there was a slight defect in my hearing, one ear, and I had just gotten over a cold when I took my physical exams so I didn't pass the physical exam. But the next year I passed my exam fine and had no hearing defect. It was not a permanent thing. It just happened that my one ear was slightly stuffed up when I took my first flight physical. I would have gone the year before except for that one thing.

Q: How did the Coast Guard go about choosing potential aviators?

Rhodes: They had to request it and they had to pass their flight physical. What other rules they used, I just do not know. You had to have sea duty before they considered you at all, I know that.

Q: Can you tell me something about your training? Was it a Coast

Rhodes #3 - 110 -

Guard station?

Rhodes: No, it was Navy. First we did go to a Coast Guard station at Cape May just for indoctrination, for example. We went there for about ten days in which time we flew around in Coast Guard planes, but we did not practice landings because the field there was not safe enough for students to practice landing. Before they sent us on to Hampton Roads they gave us a check out to see whether they figured we had any aptitude for flying. I remember the commanding officer of the station, his name was Stone, had been a co-pilot of a Navy plane, NC-4, which made the first circum-navigational flight of the world, I believe. After Cape May, they assigned us to the naval air station at Hampton Roads where they gave us ten hours of flight training, and then we had to be checked to see if we were eligible to solo or not. Those who passed their solo tests went on to Pensacola. Those who didn't, went back to sea.

Q: And you passed?

Rhodes: Yes, I passed my solo test and went on to Pensacola. We practiced in sea planes there at Hampton Roads and then went on to sea planes at Pensacola.

Q: It doesn't sound as if you received that much training.--that much time. Is that true?

Rhodes: Yes, ten hours at Hampton Roads, we soloed in that time. Then I think they gave us about three hours solo before we were

Rhodes # 3 - 112

transferred to Pensacola. Then we took training at Pensacola in sea planes --the regular naval course. We started out in sea planes, that was what they called Squadron 1, then when we got through Squadron 1 we went over to land planes, Squadron 2. It happened that my class was just Coast Guard and Marines. I think there were three Coast Guardsmen and three Marines in my class at Pensacola at that time. We were going along fine in Squadron 2, which was land planes, and had all kinds of stunts and formation flying, and so forth, and then the whole class was kicked out one by one, just before we got through Squadron 2. The whole air station was closed down for financial reasons --to save money. It was opened up some time after that but there for a while, in order to save money, the whole station was closed down.

Q: So you were closed down with it?

Rhodes: That's right.

Q: You never became an aviator?

Rhodes: No. Two of my classmates went back --one Marine and one Coast Guard-- in another class and they got through fine.

Q: Why didn't you go back?

Rhodes: I was assigned to the West Coast and then an ice breaker and, although I had asked to go back, I was still on the West Coast and they would have to get a relief for me out there so they got other people to go in my place. The big reason that I didn't get back was

Rhodes #3 - 112 -

because by the time they opened up again, I was on the West Coast.

Q: Were you disappointed?

Rhodes: I was at the time. Very much disappointed. As I say, when we were cashiered out, we lost our flight pay plus fifteen percent cut in our regular pay, besides losing out in the fun of flying.

Q: What was the state of Coast Guard aviation when you were involved in it?

Rhodes: Coast Guard aviation was coming along very well at that time. They had already started to make long range landings at sea to Rescue sick people off of larger vessels. They were using planes a great deal to scout out at sea --search at sea. They had special planes developed and built for the Coast Guard, special sea planes, amphibious planes. So they were coming along at that time very nicely. There again the limit of money was such that you couldn't expect any great expansion of any service.

Q: Did the Coast Guard use any air craft for fighting the rum Runners?

Rhodes: They did to a certain extent but the old planes at that time were so poor at navigation, and so forth, that it didn't do a great deal of good to use the planes of that vintage in the rum patrol. If they had the modern planes that they have now, it would have been a great help. Of course, navigation on the plane was very poor. The

Rhodes #3 -115-

ability to search was not too good at that time --no radar. It wasn't too safe to fly long distances over the sea, and that's where they would have been needed, especially under poor visibility conditions. So they were used at times and they were tested and it could be seen that if they just had more ability, seaworthiness, and so forth, it certainly would be a great boon to rescue and helping the floating vessels in locating the smuggling activity. They were used a little, but not, I would say, effectively.

Q: This is before helicopters and the Navy was developing aircraft carriers. Did the Coast Guard ever consider developing a small carrier for planes for search and rescue?

Rhodes: The Coast Guard did carry some planes on the cutters at sea, but the only way you could get it off the cutter was to hoist it off with a crane and the only way you could get it back aboard was to hoist it back aboard. So you would have to lower it in the harbor, let it take off, and it would have to land in the harbor and you'd have to come back and pick it up in the harbor. So that was very ineffective. So far as I know, the Coast Guard never thought of developing a carrier that a plane could land on board. We thought mostly of sea planes, where you could lower a plane into the water and take off, do scouting for you, and it would come back and we would hoist it aboard. When the helicopters came along, that was just the answer to the needs of the Coast Guard because we could easily build a small flight deck where a helicopter could land aboard a ship. The helicopters could do so many things a plane could not do such as hoist people aboard from a small boat or from the water, or from another ship without even landing. That one thing is a great help, especially when they are operating in rough waters or when they're operating in ice up in the Arctic. I had a couple of helicopters up there that we could transfer from one ship to another ship, but you'd never be able to do it when you're operating in ice unless you did have a helicopter.

Q: Where did you go after you left Pensacola?

Rhodes: I was transferred to the one hundred and sixty-five foot patrol PERSEUS in New York. I was the executive officer on the PERSEUS and that would be in 1933. That was the spring of '33 and we engaged in anti-rum patrol out of New York, but a great deal of our time was put in in patrolling regattas of various kinds. I do remember that was the time that Italo Balbo from Italy flew his planes over to Chicago -- wasn't that the Chicago World's Fair? -- and they came back through New York and our squadron was given the job of patrolling the waters off Floyd Bennett Field where they had landed. They were sea planes and they landed on the water there. We were there to protect his planes from curiosity seekers or vandals, and so forth. That was a very interesting assignment. While we were there, Wiley Post landed from his around the world solo trip, so that was doubly interesting.

Q: When you were on your rum patrol, were you a picket boat or were you chasing the speed boats?

Rhodes: Mostly we were a picket boat acting somewhat as a

destroyer at that time because these one hundred sixty-five foot patrol boats were very maneuverable. They were only a hundred and sixty-five foot long compared with three hundred feet for the destroyers, twin screws and twin rudders, and you could turn on a dime with those vessels. You didn't have to be afraid of losing them. Destroyers would lose them every now and then in the poor visibility at night. With these vessels you could stick right to them. They were really maneuverable and actually they turned out to be excellent assistance vessels because you could maneuver them so well.

Q: They were developed for rum patrol?

Rhodes: They were definitely designed for rum patrol but there was so little rum patrol at that time in '33 and early '34 that we were used for many other purposes, search and rescue as well as patrolling regattas. They were good vessels regardless of what you used them for. We went way out on the Grand Banks of Newfoundland to rescue a man with appendicitis on a trawler. We had to take him aboard in very rough sea. I was the exec at the time and, of course, the extra duty of the exec on the ship is to be the doctor so I had to keep this man alive until we got into Boston to transfer him to the hospital. We had all kinds of jobs and we cruised a long ways at sea. This was off past Newfoundland in the middle of the winter.

We had things pretty well under control as far as the rum war was there, but they were having trouble off the southern California coast. They had these great big steamers that would just anchor out there perhaps for months at a time, and the speed boats would come out

Rhodes #3 - 116 -

and contact them and run in when no one was there to stop them. So they sent a group of these one hundred and sixty-five footers out to the Pacific, early '34. We went through the Panama Canal and there again the maneuverability of these vessels showed up very well. Five of us went through locking together and the pilot was supposed to handle the vessels but first he hit one side of the locks and then the other wall --they were too quick for him. So he turned them back to us and had us handle them because he couldn't handle them. They were too maneuverable. He was used to handling large vessels and he'd give full speed ahead and they'd jump right out from under you. He said, "I can't handle this." So he had us handle them in locking through the locks there at the Panama Canal.

Q: That's sort of the way with driving a car with regular brakes and then power brakes --you go through the windshield. What was your home port?

Rhodes: San Diego was our home port. They had a couple that were assigned to San Pedro, also. One went up to San Fransisco. They gave us four boats at the southern California BASE and we had no trouble at all. Within a week after we arrived there the vessels left and so far as I know, they never returned again. They knew that we had them licked.

Q: You scared them off and you were out of a job.

Rhodes: That's right. There was no use in them staying there if they couldn't land anything.

Note. There is no page 117.

Rhodes #3 - 118 -

Q: What became ~~of~~ your function then?

Rhodes: Well, we had to stay there or it would have started again, but in the meantime we had search and rescue off the southern California coast. We even had to go off the coast of Baja, California --we made some rescue there. I had to rescue a whole barge load of sport fishermen. The tug that brought them down there had broken down so I had to bring this whole barge load of sport fishermen in. There was many things that we had to do out there. The people out there were very glad to have us. It just happened that the whole Pacific Fleet was transferred from the Pacific to the Atlantic just before we arrived out there, so we were doubly welcome because the Navy was practically gone.

Q: Even now the Coast Guard has been an East Coast oriented service. Most of the ships are based on the East Coast, and most of the people. Do you know any reason why this is so?

Rhodes: There is one good reason --any smuggling that would take place generally would take place on the East Coast. There are so many countries near-by here on the East Coast, including the Gulf Coast, that you could expect a lot more smuggling on this coast. Also the population centers are far more numerous on the East Coast. The shipping and fishing interests, pleasure boating always have been far greater on the East Coast than the West Coast. There are very few harbors on the West Coast, and the population, up until recently, has been very small. Your weather is generally much more severe on the East Coast, except when you get up to the Oregon, Washington coast. When you get inside the Straits of Juan de Fuca at the entrance to the harbor in the state of Washington, you're in generally sheltered waters. It's an easy harbor to enter, whereas the harbors on the Atlantic Coast are somewhat narrow and tortuous compared to the wide entrance such as that. Even after you enter the harbors on the East Coast you still have close harbors but out there there's lots of room to maneuver. There isn't nearly the call on a service such as the Coast Guard --it hadn't been previously at least. Of course, now the Pacific Coast is getting very well settled, population has increased, and you see a lot more need for the Coast Guard out there. On the other hand, southern California, you practically never get a storm there, so you don't have the sudden storms that you have on the East Coast. When we speak of the East Coast, we can also speak of the Great Lakes because we have a lot of Coast Guard activity on the Great Lakes. That is much closer to the East Coast than it is to the West Coast. For many years we've had activity up in Alaskan waters and all throughout the Pacific so the western coast activities are almost as great as the eastern coast activities. But it's mostly population and the fact that our Pacific Coast is great distances across the ocean from other countries that made smuggling activities very few. It's quite hazardous to hover off the coast of a country that's several thousand miles away, whereas the Atlantic Coast was very near to foreign ports.

Interview # 4 with Capt. Earl Rhodes, USCG (ret)

Takoma Park, Maryland
June 14, 1970

Subject: Biography
by Peter Spectre

Mr. Spectre: Captain, the last time we talked you were on the Coast Guard cutter, PERSEUS, which had been transferred to the West Coast to seek out rum-runners, and shortly after you got there the rum-runners left because of the power that you had on hand. What did you do after that? What did the PERSEUS do?

Capt. Rhodes: The PERSEUS remained in San Diego and performed regular Coast Guard assistance and patrol duties, mostly assisting pleasure craft and fishing vessels in that area.

Q: Was there a lot of rescue work required in that --?

Rhodes: Not a great deal of rescue work was required, however, every now and then some vessel or small pleasure craft would break down and have engine trouble, and it's very dangerous on that coast because the Pacific Coast is rocky, it's deep, it's hard for them to anchor to keep from being swept ashore on the rocks. Quite often when something like that happens, it's important that you get there as soon as possible before they drift ashore.

Q: The people that I have met and talked to from your age bracket, most of them have stayed on the East Coast or the West Coast. There are very few people who have served on search and rescue duty on both coasts, there was very little transfer in between. Nowadays it's quite a bit different. What would you say was the difference between working, speaking in search and rescue terms, on the West Coast versus the East Coast?

Rhodes: The West Coast has very predictable weather especially southern California. You can almost be sure there'll be no severe storms off the coast of southern California. It is very pleasant out there most of the time. It's on the cool side, rather than being warm. You think of southern California as a nice warm, sunny, climate, but actually, out at sea, especially, it is quite cool. The Pacific Ocean is much cooler than the Atlantic. However, you could always be sure that you'd have a morning fog. It would come in sometime during the night and last until ten a.m. or noon, and then the sun would burn it off. Generally during the summertime, you could be sure you wouldn't have any rainfall. You have your rain during the winter time and when you do get your rain in the wintertime, it generally rained awfully hard, and maybe you had a flood, though you had very few rains during the year. I suppose that's one reason they call it sunny California --certainly the sunshine does prevail and it's very pleasant on the whole. In the Atlantic the weather is very changeable --very severe weather in the winter time, and you have sudden, severe, storms in the Atlantic. There's a lot of harbors and inlets in the Atlantic and there's very few in the Pacific. If something happened in the Pacific, it's very difficult for a vessel to reach a harbor. You have sandy beaches in the Atlantic and rocky beaches in the Pacific. I said that southern California is free of storms, however, northern California, Washington and Oregon are known for their severe storms. You take a severe storm on a rocky beach, it's a very dangerous condition for vessels to be near the beach because if anything happens, they are bound to be blown up on a rocky shore. That's far more dangerous than being blown up on a sandy beach.

Q: You hear a lot about these bars that are out at the entrances to the harbors and the rivers on the West Coast. Was that true of southern California, as well?

Rhodes: No, it was not true of southern California. They had practically no bar off San Diego or off San Pedro, which is the harbor for Los Angeles. Perhaps that was because there were no great rivers there. You take up at Oregon where the Columbia River comes down --it dumps it's silt at the entrance to the river and that is really what makes the bar there.

Q: Have you ever had occasion to cross the bar in a bad storm?

Rhodes: Yes. Right after the second World War, I had command of a Navy AKA and we were coming back from Japan and it was too rough to take a pilot on board, but I had gone across the bar with Coast Guard vessels before, however this vessel was light. We were not heavily loaded --this was mostly passengers that we were bringing back but we had a heavy deck load of boats, landing craft. So I filled all the tanks possible, fuel tanks and water tanks, with salt water to give us ballast, and came across. However, there was a time coming across the bar that I wished I had not decided to come across. It's difficult to see how bad it is until you get into the actual breaker there at the bar.

Q: How deep is the water at the bar?

Rhodes: I would have to depend on my memory now, but it seems to me that it's probably about thirty-five or forty feet right where the channel is.

Q: How deep is it on either side?

Rhodes: On either side it's much deeper than that because the Pacific Ocean goes down very rapidly from the shoreline. It gets deeper very rapidly as you go out.

Q: What do you do when you crossed the bar? What makes it so tricky and dangerous?

Rhodes: As the large waves come in from the ocean they suddenly reach this shallow water and they break. In other words, the under part of the wave slows up when it hits the shallow water and the top part overtakes it, so that causes a break, and then tumbles. When a ship gets into that, it often throws the stern out of water and you have no propulsion --your screws are out of water and your rudder is out of water, so you can't stear and you have no power. That's only for a short period of time but it might be enough time for you to lose control of the vessel. It will broach broadside to the waves and you

lose complete control with those big waves breaking and curling over--
they could even swamp a pretty good size vessel. They are very large
waves coming in from the Pacific. Much larger than the Atlantic.

Q: They don't have anything to stop them.

Rhodes: That's right. Of course, the Pacific Coast is a windward
coast. The prevailing winds generally come from the westward. Therefore when you have a storm out there, you're on the windward coast and
being blown ashore. There's no way that you can seek shelter. On the
Atlantic Coast, your prevailing winds are still from the west, so if
you come in under the land, you do get shelter from the wind and the
waves. That is one reason why the Pacific Coast is much more dangerous
than the Atlantic Coast. If you get in trouble, there is no way you
can seek shelter except get into a snug harbor, and it's often dangerous to come in over the bar to a harbor under those conditions.

Q: From the way you describe it, I get a picture of the West Coast
that there are periods when nothing happens as far as the Coast Guard
is concerned. Nothing happens and then all of a sudden everything happens all at once.

Rhodes: That's very true, but of course, in the meantime you should
be patrolling out there so you will be there when something does happen.
You'll be a lot closer to it. As a result of that, even though you're
not actually accomplishing anything by rescuing someone, you are on the
scene in case something happens. You're much closer to where it's

Rhodes # 4 - 125 -

likely to happen if you are patrolling out there.

Q: Do you remember any of the cases that you were involved in?

Rhodes: Actually, I was involved in very few cases. One case, back on the PERSEUS, in San Diego, they had barges towed by tugs where they would take as many as a hundred sport fishermen out and fish for tuna, and so forth. That tug broke down out there and they sent word in that they had an awful lot of seasick sportsmen on this barge and there was no way at all for them to get in. I checked --there was no commercial tug around. I went down with the PERSEUS and towed this barge in with all these seasick people on board. They aren't used to going to sea. They are people down there on vacation that never have been out to sea before, so they were definitely sick. Since there was no tugs at San Diego, I had to tow them in, then drop the hawser and get alongside the barge, lash it alongside the PERSEUS, and put it up alongside the dock, and act as a tug myself, which is quite unusual. Generally when the Coast Guard tows a vessel into port, they have a tug standing by to take over the tow, but in this case they didn't have any tugs in San Diego Harbor. The one they did have that towed the vessel out, was broken down.

Q: What was your relationship to commercial salvage companies? If you get a vessel in distress, there's two types of people that could help rescue the vessel --the Coast Guard and commercial salvage FIRMS who make a living towing other vessels. I know that now, supposedly, the question has been settled, but during your time if both of you were on the scene, who actually did the work? How did you decide?

Rhodes: Actually, we would help regardless, whenever there was danger of loss of life. We would do anything we could until there was safety and no danger of loss of life. Then if there was a commercial tug available, we would stand by and allow him to bargain with the owners of the vessel in trouble and if he could strike up a resonable offer, generally he would go ahead and tow the vessel in. The Coast Guard never, even in those days, wanted to interfere with the salvage operation of a tug boat company which was in business for that type of thing and it was very important to the maritime interest to have those salvage companies available, because there are certain types of work that the Coast Guard doesn't get into anyway. We only bring it as far as port, at the most, and then call a salvage company or a tug to come out and get it. A commercial one would come out and bring it into the harbor proper. So we always had a feeling of cooperating with the salvage tugs, and quite often the Coast Guard would assist the salvage tugs because often you need two vessels or three vessels to help another one in trouble. For example, if a large vessel loses its rudder, one vessel has to tow it and the other one has to hang on behind as a rudder to steer the vessel. Otherwise, it's almost impossible to tow a vessel especially in a storm where it's unable to steer. So we've often helped commercial vessels in that way. Wherever there's danger of loss of life, we and any commercial vessel available will work together. There's no question of how the commercial vessel's going to get paid, he helped just like a Coast Guard vessel would, on the scene, then after there's no danger of loss of life or property, then he will dicker with the owner for the price of towing it in.

Q: What would happen if you were on the sea and a commercial tug was on the sea, a bargain couldn't be struck, if the owner of the distressed vessel says, "I can't pay", or, "I won't pay. There's a Coast Guard cutter right here and I want to be assisted by the Coast Guard." Then what would happen?

Rhodes: That would be a real tough question in the old days before radio. However, when I first went to sea, we did have radio which allowed us to get in touch with land. We had district commanders and the Commandant. Those cases would be referred to the district commander, who would, if necessary, refer it to Coast Guard headquarters to make a decision as to what we should do on the spot. Generally speaking, where there is no immediate danger, the Coast Guard vessel would hold off until he got direct orders from a higher command on shore to take action. I don't know of any case where they couldn't reach an agreement between the tug on the scene and the owner of the vessel --I'm not aware of any. Generally the Coast Guard favored the commercial tug who came all the way out to help rescue, they favored them towing it in, and the Coast Guard would generally hold off so that they could reach a reasonable agreement. However, the tug boat organization also knew that they couldn't charge salvage on this vessel, because if he wasn't there, the Coast Guard was there to save it and therefore the vessel was not in danger of loss. So he had to be reasonable in his charge.

Q: So he was really charging them for a towing fee.

Rhodes: That's right. He was charging them a reasonable charge for towing fee --his trip out there and his trip towing them back into the harbor, so he would not charge them salvage as though he had saved the ship from sinking. Therefore, to my knowledge, I never found a case in my own experience where the tug boat company was not able to make an agreement with the owner of the vessel.

Q: When you were in ~~were in~~ San Diego, what was the condition of the pleasure boat? Now there are yachts everywhere. What was it like in the early '30s?

Rhodes: There were very few compared with the number there are now. However, as I mentioned, this was very pleasant cruising out there so people with money, movie actors, and so forth, many of them had their pleasure craft. Generally speaking, people who liked pleasant cruising, would cruise off the southern California coast. You have the islands off there, you also can go down to Mexican ports, so there were quite a few pleasure crafts and there were several fishing vessels in that area. All the tuna fleet was down there, also. As a result of that, there was quite a lot of activty even in those days, but definitely there's a great deal more activity now than there was in those days.

Q: What happened to you after your tour of duty in the PERSEUS?

Rhodes: I came there in the winter of 1934 and I was transferred to the ice breaker cutter, NORTHLAND, in the spring of 1935, assigned to duty as the navigation officer on the NORTHLAND.

Rhodes # 4 - 128 -

Q: Where was the home port of the NORTHLAND?

Rhodes: The home port of the NORTHLAND was Seattle, Washington. I got there in time enough to make preparations for the Arctic Alaskan cruise in the summer of 1935. These cruises lasted a period of six months.

Q: Was this a normal rotation for you?

Rhodes: No, normally I would have remained on the PERSEUS at San Diego longer than that. However it just happened that for some reason they had transferred a navigation officer off the NORTHLAND and they needed someone right away. I was not necessarily available but it was probably considered easier to replace me on the PERSEUS down in southern California, as executive officer of the PERSEUS, than to find someone who was qualified and immediately available as navigator of the NORTH-LAND, who was due to leave very shortly on a six month Arctic cruise.

Q: You were a lieutenant then?

Rhodes: Yes, I was a lieutenant then.

Q: What was the NORTHLAND like?

Rhodes: The NORTHLAND was built to relieve the cutter BEAR, which was built as a commercial whaling type vessel for Arctic waters. It was primarily a sailing vessel with a steam engine to be used in emergencies when there was no wind or an unfavorable wind. Therefore, the BEAR had been so successful for many cruises in the Arctic, they decided that a steel vessel should be designed and constructed with similar characteristics of the old BEAR. In other words, the only thing in this case, it would be primarily a power vessel with auxiliary sails, figuring that at any time you might lose your propeller or lose your ability to use your engines up there in the Arctic where there was ice conditions. So here you had a very heavy steel vessel with heavy diesel engines and they did put sails on it. We would run up the sails every now and then and try to sail but she never did prove out as a sailing vessel. She had to have a strong favorable wind to make any headway at all.

Q: Was it designed by the Coast Guard?

Rhodes: It was designed by the Coast Guard, that's correct. She had diesel electric engines and that made her very heavy. Then of course, her steel ice breaking hull also made her very heavy. The amount of sail you could put on a vessel like that just was not sufficient to make her a sailing vessel. It's very doubtful that if she had gotten in trouble that her sails would have helped her.

I believe it was my last year on the NORTHLAND we decided that it was no use to kid ourselves -- she just was not a sailing vessel. Her masts were redesigned and her sails and yards were removed and she was converted to a power vessel only.

Q: Were there other ships in the same class?

Rhodes:	No, she was the only ship designed at that time for ice breaking and the Arctic cruise. She was the only ship the Coast Guard had at that time to replace the old BEAR. They never, at that time, figured they could have two vessels for that purpose. It certainly would have been advisable, in case one got in trouble, the other one could help it, but they did not have anything to assist it in case it got in trouble.

Q:	How about the Navy? Did the Navy have ice breakers?

Rhodes:	Not at that time. Not until the second World War were there ice breakers, designed as such.

Q:	This was just before the war. Do you know if anybody, from your experiences with ice breakers, if anybody saw the strategic importance of ice breakers for war time?

Rhodes:	Yes. Actually Russia showed what she could do with ice breakers. They kept the Arctic channel open across northern Siberia so she could run cargo vessels across the northern part of Russia from the Atlantic to the Pacific and vice versa. She had large, powerful ice breakers, and it was brought to our attention because in those days there was quite a little bit of experimental flying in that area. American flyers would be going around the world, such as Wiley Post, and so forth, and Russian flyers were also making experimental flights. When we were up there with the NORTHLAND, Russian flyers came up missing up in the northern Alaska section, and Russia sent one of their

Rhodes # 4 - 131 -

famous ice breakers over to help us search for the flyers. We were up there searching for the Russian flyers, and the Russians did send this very large, powerful ice breaker over to help search. At that time she did damage herself,--just what the damage was, they wouldn't tell us, but when she came over she was able to make great speed and go through the ice, and so forth. When she headed back home, she was limping along so we could make more speed than she could.

Q: Do you remember the name of this ship?

Rhodes: I'm trying to remember the name. I have a picture tucked away somewhere. I remember she was a two stacker and painted black. I believe it was the KRASSIN, but that has been a good many years ago and I couldn't be sure.

Q: Did you have a chance to go aboard this ship and look around?

Rhodes: No, they tried to avoid direct contact with us. We tried to communicate with them but there was no communication with them. We would have liked to coordinate our scouting activities -trying to locate these Russian flyers but we couldn't get any reply directly from them. We knew in advance they were on the way over to help look for the Russian flyers, but we only could communicate with our own people and the only real contact was with our headquarters in Washington, D.C. and we could not get any direct contact with the vessel itself. They wouldn't answer our signals so there was no possibility of coordinating our search.

Rhodes # 4 - 132 -

Q: Was Washington anxious for you to do the work?

Rhodes: Washington ordered us to search for the flyers, which we were doing, and they were very anxious for us to coordinate the search. We tried but we were unable to coordinate it with the Russian vessel directly.

Q: Now that the Coast Guard is designing new ice breakers and the Russians evidently, ever since ice breaking was invented, have been way ahead of the United States in design and actual operations, and from what I understand we have done a lot of intelligence work in finding out what makes Russian ice breakers tick, and to see if there's any features that they have that could be incorporated in our designs. So this is going on now, was it also going on when you were in ice breakers?

Rhodes: Oh yes. We were supposed to find out anything we could but since the important features of an ice breaker are below the water line, there's very little that you could see with a ship in the water. Of course, our people had seen the Russian ice breaker in Russian ports many times, so they were able to have a great deal of detailed information about them. At first the Baltic countries also had good ice breakers. Sweden, Norway, Poland --they had fairly good ice breakers but that was mostly for inland waters. Russia had the big ice breakers for the Arctic, and therefore we, and the other countries, were also anxious to see just what developments the Russians had made. I'm quite sure that we had very good information on the Russian ice breakers but it was not obtained by we on the NORTHLAND

Q: What could the NORTHLAND do?

Rhodes: She could do very little, actually. The main thing was, she could cruise among scattered ice and if she hit the ice it generally wouldn't hurt her. Her plating was heavy enough so she could hit it and she could be pinched by the ice, and generally it would not damage her unless it was quite severe. We also had mines on board so that if we got in an ice pressure ridge we could set off these mines and blow up the ice so it would ease up a little bit on us. We used those mines quite often when we got in a tight spot in the Arctic. They still do use them. But she could rescue other vessels that might get into trouble. They had the old whaling vessels and sailing vessels still up there ven when I was up there. The schooner HOLMES was a very famous one. She always made a summer cruise in Alaskan waters and the skipper would barter for furs with the Eskimos, and so forth. That was about the only large trading vessel that went up in the ice country. The regular steamers never went farther north than Kotzebue. Most of them ended up at Nome, therefore there were very, very few vessels which went north of Nome and none but the HOLMES went north of Kotzebue, which is just above the Arctic circle. Of course, we and the HOLMES went well north of that, Point Barrow and beyond.

Q: How did the Coast Guard, the United States, justify ice breaking in Arctic waters? What was the purpose?

Rhodes: The main purpose was, Alaska was a very sparsely settled country and most of it was Eskimos. We had explorers going up in those days and many times the Coast Guard was sent up to help locate missing explorers --to help any way we could. Also the whaling fleet always was on the edge of the ice, and at one time the whaling fleet was crushed by the ice, and that left all the men up there to starve to death unless you could get food to them. That was before the time of airplanes.

Q: When you say the whaling fleet, how many ships are you talking about?

Rhodes: It might be about twenty ships.

Q: Would they all stick together?

Rhodes: They would all stick pretty well together because they stuck where the whales were and the whales would generally stick to the edge of the ice because that's where the other life was. As the ice receded, the whales receded and the whaling fleet would then follow them. When the whaling fleet was caught in the ice, that put all the men manning the ships ashore, and there wasn't enough food up there to feed them --no shelter or anything else to speak of. So they put a Coast Guard officer ashore who had the job of bartering for reindeer and he hired some herds- men and they drove the reindeer overland to provide food for these whalers and then you could get them out next spring. That was a very famous rescue. I read about the whole thing and, of course, it's been discussed many times but I can't remember his name right now, but it's well documented.

Q: Did you have pretty close contact with the whaling fleet?

Rhodes: We did at that time, but when I was up there, the whaling fleet had almost disappeared. They did have a factory ashore down in the Aleutian Islands when I was there. I think that was Akun Bay at that time.

Q: How did they operate? Did they stay out for long periods of time?

Rhodes: Yes. The whaling vessels would sometimes stay out for years and actually, I believe they made the Hawaiian Islands one of their main headquarters. These sailing vessels used to sail out of New England, New Bedford, and so forth, and maybe make a two, three, four year cruise.

Q: These are still sailing ships?

Rhodes: They were sailing ships, yes. But, of course, steam was coming in and foreign vessels were getting in to it and the American whaling fleet just about disappeared. There was very little left of the American whaling fleet and there was discovery of petroleum which eliminated the urgent need for whale oil. The whale bone was used in the old corset stays and they became somewhat out of date in the Roar-

Rhodes # 4 - 136 -

ing Twenties, so there was not nearly as much money in whaling as there used to be and it just about put the American whaling fleet out of business.

Q: What was your relationship to the Bering Sea patrol?

Rhodes: We had direct relationship to the Bering Sea patrol in that we were somewhat under the command of the commander of the Bering Sea patrol. However, we operated north with our headquarters at Nome and his headquarters would be at Dutch Harbor in the Aleutians.

Q: Who was your over all commander?

Rhodes: We generally reported direct to headquarters because the things that we were doing were of primary interest to the Coast Guard headquarters and quite often we would get direct orders from Washington on the NORTHLAND. For example, when Wiley Post and Will Rogers were killed up there off Point Barrow, we got direct orders from Washington to help in any way we could. The Bering Sea patrol really had their interests in the Aleutians and as far north as the Pribiloffs. Their real interest did not go as far north as Nome and farther north into the Arctic, therefore when we were north, we did not go through them at all --only when we came down once a year, did we come under direct control of the Bering Sea Patrol.

Q: You brought up Wiley Post and Will Rogers and their death in Point Barrow. What did the NORTHLAND do?

Rhodes: We had just been to Point Barrow. In fact, we had been driven out by the ice coming in so when we got the order to go and help any way we could, we found that the ice was so heavily packed in that there was no way for us to get back up there. By the time we could have gotten back, all arrangements had been made for the bodies to be flown off, and therefore there was nothing for us to do and we were relieved of further activity. However, we did go back the next year and saw the remains of the plane.

Q: Did the NORTHLAND break ice the way ice breakers nowadays do it --riding up on the ice and breaking it by the weight?

Rhodes: She was built to do that. You could break thin ice but she didn't have the power. She was not any where nearly as large as a present day ice breaker.

Q: How big was she?

Rhodes: I think she was about two hundred and six feet long, but her beam was somewhat narrow. I'm guessing now but I would think that her beam was probably around thirty-five or forty feet. She just did not have the power to break ice. As soon as we'd hit she'd be stopped and we'd have to back down and try to ram it again. She only had a single screw, therefore it was difficult to maneuver her. As soon as she would hit ice, she would glance off and you couldn't control her like you can the large ice breakers nowadays. About the only thing you could say, she was protected from the ice but as an ice breaker

Rhodes # 4 - 138 -

she certainly couldn't break Arctic ice.

Q: What was the primary mission?

Rhodes: The primary mission was to take care of all the Eskimos as far as medical and dental treatmnet for them. Where a village would be starving, you would furnish food enough to get them by and make arrangements for transportation of food for them if the Bureau of Indian Affairs would furnish it. We also furnished transportation to school teachers. They had school teachers in all the Eskimo villages up there. The federal government provided those.

Q: These were not Eskimo school teachers?

Rhodes. They were regular white school teachers sent up there by the States. They had to be man and wife to go into an Eskimo village. That's the only way they would permit them to operate --as man and wife. They had several missionaries of various nationalities up there and we would help them. We also took the nurse --the public health nurses would go around and visit the Eskimo villages. They used dog sleds in the winter time and they would hop on the NORTHLAND and we would take them around with us so they could visit each village in the summertime. That's really the ohy transportation that these people had up there in the summer time, the Coast Guard vessel, the NORTHLAND. We just had to help in any way we could, either in transportation or providing food. Actually the NORTHLAND one time took a group of Eskimos out --the ice had gone off, they had no food, so we took them off and they took their boats along with them. They got the walrus and seals and then we transported the walrus and the seals and the boats and the Eskimos back to their villages and they were very happy about it. That is the type of thing you would do --anything necessary to help them out where they were in trouble.

Q: You always hear it said that the Coast Guard was the Eskimo's, and the people who lived in the northern areas, only contact with the government. Is that true?

Rhodes: Not completely. That was fairly true in the early days, but in the later days, when I was up there, they had school teachers which were government people. However, they would stay right there. The same school teacher wouldn't go around. Of course, the government when I was there, also had these public health nurses there, but that was a fairly recent thing. They didn't have them in earlier days. Each year they were adding a little bit of service for the Eskimos. The Coast Guard, I understand provided reindeer for the Eskimos. In a visit in the early days to Siberia they found these reindeer and how the natives there herded the reindeer. It gave them food and the hides made good clothing, so the Coast Guard, the old BEAR, transported reindeer over to Alaska, and that was the beginning of reindeer herds in Alaska. It's that type of thing that the Coast Guard did provide the natives up there. They did everything they could to make life better for them because civilization for the natives was killing them off. We were carrying diseases up to them. It wasn't the Coast Guard that was carrying the diseases but the whalers and everyone else who was visiting these Eskimos up in these remote villages who were carrying diseases, and as a result when they would get a disease such as the measles, many of them would die because they had no immunity against diseases they had never had before. It was very serious --they were losing many of the population because of diseases which they had never been exposed to before.

Q: This is why the public health service was there?

Rhodes; That's right. That's why we were furnishing as much medical attention as possible to try to alleviate the thing and also to give them immunization to certain diseases which we were able to do.

Q: What about law enforcement? What did you do in that area?

Rhodes: Traditionally the commanding officer of the NORTHLAND would be appointed a U.S. Commissioner and the executive officer would be appointed a U.S. Marshall. In this way, any place that we visited, if there was a case where someone went beserk, or something, the executive officer has the power to make any arrests and bring him before the commanding officer who is the commissioner, and the commissioner could hold him, send him to any prison for safe keeping, and so forth, depending on the circumstances. So we had a practical authority to arrest anyone in an emergency and hold them. Then we would carry the court around on the NORTHLAND where they could hold cases in various localities. That was another one of the NORTHLAND's duties.

Q: It sounds as if the NORTHLAND was crowded with extra people.

Rhodes: That's right. We were always crowded. And then, of course, besides that we always had a scientific expedition of some kind taking samples here and there and studying. The NORTHLAND always had some kind of scientific people aboard.

Q: It sounds as if it would be very difficult to work with all these various elements all calling for attention to their needs. I imagine the nurses probably wanted to go one place and the missionaries wanted to go somewhere else and the scientists had their own mission. Did you have conflicts?

Rhodes: You had continual conflicts, there's no doubt about that, but one thing about it, the commanding officer always had the power to resolve those conflicts. He could listen to everyone and then he would make the decision, all right we'll go here first and then go to the next place. He would set the priority and decide where they were going and also he could say who he would take aboard and who he wouldn't take aboard, so they knew they could present their case to him but they couldn't demand anything. He had the full authority to make the decision as to exactly what would be done. AS a result everyone got almost all their needs taken care of, but quite often they weren't happy they didn't get there as soon as they wanted to. They didn't get everything they wanted but their urgent needs were taken care of.

Q: It sounds as if the commanding officer of the NORTHLAND at that time, maybe even ice breaker commanding officers now, has to be a man of all seasons.

Rhodes: That's true. Also, I think, he has to have a great desire to want to help people. That's the only way that you can really do a good job is to want to help all these people. You have to want to help the Eskimos, you have to want to help all these people who were providing services for them, you want to help the scientists who were trying to discover more facts about the great Arctic which we knew very little about in those days, and still we know that there's a great deal more that we must learn.

Q: Was the commanding officer picked especially for his qualities? Who was he when you were there?

Rhodes: My first commanding officer, when I first went to the NORTHLAND was Commander William K. Scammel. He was, what I would say was the best skipper I ever had. I feel that he set a great example to everyone around him. I think many people who knew him would like to pattern themselves and their own actions after him. He was a very kind and gentlemanly person and yet he was very capable. He never got excited. He always took things easy, apparently, yet he was always very timely in everything he did. It just seemed that it happened that he was in the right place at the right time. He handled things which an ordinary person would make a big to-do about just as if it were the regular course of duty. He didn't get excited about it and he always handled things very well. Going on a six month cruise having a skipper like that was a wonderful thing. I do think that probably they did try to select people with somewhat serene dispositions to be commanding officer on a long cruise like that, because there's bound to be irritations among the officers and crew, and unless you have a very well balanced commanding officer, the irritations can lead to serious difficulty.

Q: What about the next commanding officer?

Rhodes: My last year I had Commander Zeusler. We started off in a very bad situation. We had a new commanding officer and a new executive officer, and the commanding officer had just been on board where the executive officer was found lacking on another ship, and as a result, on this long cruise, the commanding officer and the executive officer were practically not speaking to each other. They had no like for each other. I was the in-between man. That shows me how important it is to have a commanding officer who keeps everything running smoothly. That last year on the NORTHLAND was a nightmare to me because I had to be the middle man all the way through and try to keep the other officers and crew calm, The executive officer can't have very much authority over the other officers who are aware,--he has no influence with the commanding officer and they know it. It is a very difficult situation on a cruise like that. That type of thing should not be permitted. It certainly taught me a lesson, or it confirmed my own opinion that I knew a thing like that shoudn't be permitted. As I say, it was just one long nightmare as far as I'm concerned.

Q: How did this come on again? The executive officer --

Rhodes: The executive officer had been the engineer officer on either the INGHAM or the SPENCER up in Port Angeles, Washington, and the assistant engineer officer committed suicide --shot himself in the shaft alley. Commander Zeusler was one of the investigating officers on the board who investigated the whole case and there were some statements about the commanding officer, the executive officer, and the engineer officer on that vessel—that was quite a mess. As a result they feel that the situation that developed on the ship had something to do with this officer committing suicide. Uncovering some of these things, caused Commander Zeusler to have a very poor opinion of Commander Sarratt who was the engineer officer and the new exec on his ship.for the next cruise of the NORTHLAND. It was a result of that investigation that caused the hard feelings between my skipper, Zeusler, and my exec, Sarratt.

Q: Couldn't the skipper say, "Hey look, I'm going on a six month cruise in the Arctic and you've assigned an executive officer on my ship that might be a fine man but I can't get along with him personally." Couldn't he have done --?

Rhodes: He should have done it and he could have done it. That's what should have been done. You should never leave on a long cruise with that type of situation.

Q: As far as you know he never did?

Rhodes: As far as I know, he never did, but he might have and I wouldn't know it. Certainly that should not be a situation that they would allow to exist on a vessel operating by itself in an isolated place for a period of six months. It's a good example of what you should never allow to happen.

Q: I can just imagine what it must have been like.

Rhodes: It was terrible. We certainly were happy to get back because everyone suffered from it. Everyone aboard ship suffered from it.

Q: Has anything ever happened before or after that, and was this brought to anybody's attention after the cruise so it could be avoided later on?

Rhodes: To my knowledge, nothing like this ever happened before or since. Certainly not for the extended period of time where everyone would be affected by it over a period of time. You always find cases where there might be a little hard feeling now and then, but they can be glossed over, and if it was going to last any length of time generally there was a transfer made --give each officer a chance to work with someone else. Quite often you can have two perfectly fine officers who just can't get along with each other. It's just inherent. They take an immediate dislike to each other and the best way to do is arrange a transfer so they can find someone they can get along with. Generally they can get along with most people but they just can't get along with each other. Headquarters has always been quick to make transfers of that type. Why they didn't in this case, I just do not know.

Q: After they came back, did they learn of the situation and try to prevent it?

Rhodes: I believe that was broken up but also that was my last cruise on the NORTHLAND and I had orders by radio before I ever got back to Seattle, so I knew that I was leaving the ship. What the details were after I left, I don't know. I should say I don't remember but I do know that it was brought to the authorities attention and I believe that the whole thing was straightened out. After this investigation they had to immediately arrange transfers, or split up, the captain, the exec, and engineer of this other ship. So that was one reason why they put the exec over on my ship, because they had to split them up. This happened just before we were ready to cruise and we needed an exec and that's what happened. Timing perhaps brought this about where it would not have happened otherwise. If they had a couple of months to prepare for it, it wouldn't have happened this way. Of course, in those days, once you sail, you sail. There isn't any plane service or anything else that could take care of a thing like that later on.

Q: What was the services attitude and your attitude toward ice breaking? Was it considered good duty or lousy duty or what?

Rhodes: In those days it was considered somewhat romantic duty. And it really was because no one of us ever had had any experiences of that kind. Outside of the long cruises, the six month cruises, this was choice duty. If I hadn't gotten it, I would have put in for it. If you are an explorer at heart and want to see new places, strange places that very few people have ever seen, that's the place to go. It's probably the most beautiful cruising going up there and back that anyone will ever experience and then going and observing all the Eskimos and the northern people. You meet many people up there, very friendly. It's a real experience. I never would want to miss. In fact, I like it so well that I've gone back several times.

Q: As a Coast Guardsman?

Rhodes: Yes. I went back during the war as an ice pilot and then I had command of the ice breaker NORTHWIND for two years, and that was at my request. I like it up there.

Q: What about the men in your crew --were they volunteers?

Rhodes: Many were. Many were old timers that had spent many years on there and they looked forward every year to that trip up north. They all like it.

Q: Were there any holdovers from the BEAR?

Rhodes: Yes, there were. Of course, enlisted men. Officers were not allowed to stay year after year on a ship. Some of the enlisted men have been on this annual cruise for twenty years and they would look forward to it every year. They really like to go up there. Especially the men of Swedish and Norwegian descent. They seem to like the cold up there and to have all that ice in the middle of summer --it was really something.

Q: What was the Lighthouse Service doing up there?

Rhodes: At that time there was very very little being done by the Lighthouse Service. You had some of the main locations with lighthouses but it was very little.

Q: Were there any buoy tenders there?

Rhodes: I believe there was but they would be based back around Juneau in southeastern Alaska. There was nothing farther north although they would have a contract with someone living at Nome to go around and -- what they had there were more land beacons for the dog sleds in the winter time. Up there in the summer time they don't need light houses so much because it's light day and night, so they had beacons that they would put on the points of land for the dog sleds to head for these lighted beacons. The trail, of course would be covered up in the winter time and they wouldn't know where the land was and where the water was in the winter time. So they did have these lighted beacons on shore but that was about as much as they had. They also had lights on break water at Nome, the harbor entrance, but there was very, very little in those days where they marked. There was no navigation in the winter time and all you would need was just enough so the dog sleds could move around.

Q: You mentioned the midnight sun. What was it like living in total sunlight?

Rhodes: You had to cover up your port hole to get any sleep because it would be broad daylight when you turned in. Of course, when you're at sea and standing watches, you'd often have to be on watch at night and get your sleep in the daytime, so therefore it doesn't make nearly as much difference to us as it might to a person who sleeps at night and works in the day time.

Q: Did it have any psychological effect on you? Did you get so that you hated that damned sun because it just stayed there?

Rhodes: No, not at all, because actually when you would go up there the days would be getting longer and then before you were coming down the days would be getting very short. So you have the midnight sun in the middle of June but it would soon start receding and when you stay up there until October you have an awful lot of darkness. So it's changing all the time. June is a marvelous month up there. It's beautiful weather, beautiful sunshine, everything just seems fine. Then after that, then the weather starts coming up and you start having miserable weather. When you get up around the ice in August and September up around Point Barrow, you often have very miserable, foggy weather.

Fog is very prevalent up there.

Q: You were the navigator on the NORTHLAND and from what I understand polar navigation is quite a bit different from mid-latitude navigation.

Rhodes: Yes. It's very, very difficult. One of the big difficulties is with your compass. The farther north you go, the less your horizontal magnetic force becomes. It becomes vertical force but the needle of your compass is horizontal and therefore you need horizontal force to keep your magnetic compass pointing in the right direction. Therefore any slight deviation will pull the needle of your compass way off. If you're down near the equator, you'd have to have a team of horses to pull your needle off the course. Now your Gyro compass had the same difficulties and therefore any slight thing wrong with a gyro compass it would start going in circles up there. If you had been down near the equator or down off the coast of the United States probably the gyro would have kept right on its heading.

Q: When you had compass problems did you know you had them or was it something that just fooled you?

Rhodes: YOu couldn't always be sure and you had to keep checking it all the time. I could always check it, of course, if the sun was out or if the stars were out. It was constant checking to see whether the compass was still where it should be. Every now and then we found that we had been steering the wrong course because the compass had gone out on us. It sometimes would go out temporarily --just something that would disturb it temporarily. But if someone stood alongside the compass with a jacknife in their pocket, the magnetic compass would be way off to one side. We often checked the *gyro* compass with a magnetic compass, and if they didn't jibe we knew immediately that something was wrong, either with one or the other. We checked them every fifteen minutes to make sure that something unusual hadn't happened.

Q: Did you have standing instructions that nobody shall come near the compass with a jacknife in his pocket?

Rhodes: Of course that is always standing instructions but we even made it more mandatory, you might say, and they all were quite aware of how bad it was. We showed them what would happen if they stood even three or four feet away --just put a knife out there it would pull the compass way off the course, and by demonstrating that way, you got the cooperation of everyone because none of them wanted to go on the beach and be stranded up there.

Q: How did you navigate celestially if the sun was out all the time and you couldn't see the stars?

Rhodes: You can always navigate by the sun. If you can see the sun you can keep your position very well because you can take sun sites in the morning for your longitudes, take noon sun sites for your latitude, take afternoon sun sites for your longitude. But also if the moon is

Rhodes # 4 - 152 -

out even though it's somewhat dim, it might be out in the day time, you can still take moon sites also. There's only a very short period of time when you can't take star sites because that's only the middle of June.

Q: If you're navigating just by the sun, you have to know your dead reckoning plot very well in order to advance your sun line and if your compass was questionable factor there, weren't you sort of uncertain?

Rhodes: That's so. The only thing is up there you were generally in sight of land most of the time. Unless it was foggy you wouldn't have too much trouble and we used our fathometer for sounding. When we came into close quarters we always used the leadline so we were having men swinging the lead taking exact soundings. Generally on the Arctic coast it is very even bottom. It does not shoal rapidly, so therefore if you had five fathoms, which is thirty feet, it wouldn't change very rapidly and the tides are not very different. High and low tide is very little change. There is some change but comparatively little because that whole area up there is somewhat land locked. The Bering Sea and Arctic Ocean are somewhat landlocked. They're not open to the main Pacific Ocean to any great extent, so your tidal affects are minimal. If you take a sounding one time of the day, the chances are it isn't going to vary more than six feet for the whole twenty-four hours.

Q: Did you get any special instructions for navigation before you went out to the NORTHLAND?

Rhodes: No, the navigator had already left. However each navigator over the years had left a notebook. We all added to the information that we found up there. So I had to study all that they had found. Then, of course, my skipper, Scammel, was a very fine man who knew a great deal about Alaskan waters. He had been skipper the year before and he knew pretty well what the score was. He gave me a lot of pointers. He taught me a lot and I respected him very, very highly. I must say that he helped everyone on the ship and to everyone who ever served with him I think he was a great help. But he especially helped me because he knew a great deal about Alaskan waters.

Q: How did you feel about just navigating up there? Were you worried a lot of the time?

Rhode: You are inclined to be because there's so many places that aren't marked at all and you've just got to have local knowledge. You've got to be able to recognize head land, and so forth, so you know where you are just from recognizing the point. There's so many places that look the same but they're just a little bit different --if you know how to recognize them, you can. As I say, there's no light houses, no nothing compared with what there are other places. Of course, there's many more now than there were in those days and there had not been any regular surveys up in those waters. The only surveys that had ever been done were the Coast Guard --previous navigators. So if we would find out something, we would always add to the knowledge so the next navigator that came along would have some information. As a result, our charts were inaccurate and we just had to depend on local knowledge from what our previous navigators had found and what we could add to that knowledge.

Q: You said that a lot of the enlisted men who served on ice breakers just stayed on and on whereas the officers changed constantly. It would seem to me from what you just told me that it would be more logical to have everybody who served on an ice breaker, if they liked it, to serve there for a long period of time because probably the first year or two of being on the ship was just learning about the Arctic and the conditions that surrounded you. You no sooner learned all that, than it was time to leave. This wasn't considered at all?

Rhodes: The big thing is the Coast Guard had very sad experience on special duty. In other words they had had what they called line and engineering groups. The engineers would have nothing but engineering duty and the line would have nothing but navigation and command duties. That right away creates suspicion and hard feelings which last throughout their career. This was apparently admitted by the higher-ups and they saw it was getting worse rather than better. That's why they amalgamated the service back in 1926, when I was a cadet at the academy. I came in as an engineer officer and then they changed it all to both line and engineer in 1926. Perhaps they figured in a small service there wasn't really any place for strict specialists. Everyone had to be qualified for general duty. They could have a speciality but they could only serve on it for a certain time and then be assigned to general duty and then perhaps go back to their speciality. But they couldn't just stay on that special duty.

Q: If it worked for enlisted men, why wouldn't it work for officers?

Rhodes: Because the enlisted men were not in power to create ~~this~~ hard feelings. The enlisted men are all specialists. You have your engineer, your quartermasters, your boatswain mates, your various ratings, so they are all specialists anyhow. But they don't have power as commanding officers to form prejudiced decisions because they are specialists. The commanding officer should be able to look at the over-all picture. He should have had experience as an engineer officer as well as a navigator, as a gunnery officer. Also he should have experience on the East Coast, West Coast, ~~Artic~~ Arctic, wherever, so he can pretty well make good judgements that are not generated by looking at it as a specialist. I think that is generally the reason why they transfer officers around much more than they do enlisted men. And they insist on transferring them around because just because he's awfully good at that one is all the more reason why he should have experience on another job so he doesn't look at himself as strictly a specialist.

Q: On the NORTHLAND what did the scientific party concern themselves with?

Rhodes: There were some from Smithsonian Institute, for example, that would go and dig at some of the old Eskimo settlements and unearth bones from both humans and animals to show what had been going on for several hundreds and thousands of years in these old villages. They apparently built up layer after layer through the years. Another thing would be taking sounding and samples of the bottom in various locations and seeing how the temperature of the water and water content and plankton, that's the microscopic sea life, what type it was and whether it was plentiful.

Q: Were these people from the Smithsonian as well --

Rhodes: Quite frequently they would be from the University of Washington in Seattle, or the University of Oregon, or some university in California. Sometimes they would come from eastern universities. We could generally only accomodate one or two groups for each cruise so there would be a scramble to see who would be on the list to be approved for the cruise up there. We not only were limited in our facilities for them to use their scientific instruments but we were also limited on the number of beds that we could turn over to their use.

Q: Who decided on who was going to come?

Rhodes: Sometimes headquarters would make the decision and just send them out there. Of course first they would ask the commanding officer for his approval. Sometimes they would come to the commanding officer and make preliminary arrangements and he could request an o.k. from headquarters to take them along. Sometimes, for example, right up there in Alaska proper there might be people working scientifically and they would want to be transported to another location. The commanding officer could make that decision on his own if he was able to accommodate them. In that case, you see, he didn't have to worry about interfering with private enterprises --people just couldn't get there unless he took them. No one else could take them, so if he could do it and he figured that it

Rhodes # 4 - 157 -

represented a good legitimate cause, he could go ahead and make the arrangements and take them himself. We often did that. We would have passengers for a short period up there, scientific and otherwise. Often the Navy research had people up there that we would transfer from one place to another.

Q: What was the Navy doing?

Rhodes: The Navy let out contracts to various groups generally the university groups, for general research that did not have to pertain to anything that the Navy might be definitely interested in, but they were getting a lot of basic information which the Navy could use, and in the meantime, the Navy was supporting research of matters in the Alaskan area which, of course, it's nice to know a lot of different information about a country like Alaska. These researchers could pretty well pick their own subject. If they wanted to learn something about Alaska, the Navy, if they had the funds, might support it.

Q: Who payed the bill if a scientific party came on board for six months, the people ate and occupied space, took up your time, took you out of your way? Did they have to pay for that?

Rhodes: Generally the only charge we charged those people was for their meals. We did not charge them for the room they occupied, we did not charge them for transportation. All we charge them for is their meals, unless it is a commercial venture. It's just possible that we might have to transport someone who's got to get from one place to another and he might be representing nothing but a commercial company. In that case he would be charged transportation and we would ask our headquarters to send a bill to his company. We wouldn't set the price, it would be up to our headquarters to set the price. But we would report that we had given him transportation from here to there --it was the only transportation available-- and recommend that they bill his company for it. In the meantime he would sign a statement that he had received this transportation, and that would go along with the bill.

Q: What about search and rescue? What type of cases were you involved with, if you were at all?

Rhodes: Most of it would be for medical cases or among the natives. Sometimes someone would be injured --you'd have to get help to them right away and, of course, we had the doctor right with us. There were a lot of those cases. One time a man was shot and we had to rush him to the hospital. In that case I had one of these little bush planes come out from Katzebue. The closest we could get there was ten miles from the harbor, so this plane came out and took him aboard and flew him to the hospital at Kotzebue. He was accidently shot in the village. We have often been called on to supply food, either carry it up there or supply it right from the ships stores in an emergency where a village is practically starving. We take care of it temporarily until the Bureau of Indian Affairs can arrange to get food up there otherwise. It's their resposibility and we only take care of the emergencies. We don't take care of the years supply, we only tide them over until they can get it from somewhere else. Often, I suppose, a bill is sent in to the Bureau of Indian Affairs. If we furnished so much food we would report it and our headquarters will mail a bill and there will be a transfer of funds. Those things can always be arranged. The main thing is we don't let them keep on starving, we take care of the emergency and report the emergency and someone else takes care of them the rest of the year.

Q: Were there Indian agents that came with you or did they have their own network?

Rhodes: No, they were mostly at the headquarters at Juneau or Fairbanks, places like that, at main headquarters. We would have to report to our headquarters down in the States and they would get in touch with the headquarters of the bureau resposible, who would in turn get ahold of their people in the field. We had no direct contact, generally, with other agencies up there. The only people we might deal with would be the military if they were around and the school teachers, and so forth, that were right there on the scene. The rest of the people would be missionaries and business people, and so forth, scientific people who had no relationship with the government directly.

Q: People selling refrigerators to Eskimos.

Rhodes: Yes, they always had the Sears and Roebuck catalogue --they could order almost anything out of the Sears and Roebuck catalogue. One Eskimo had a brand new electric washer and he had that right in the middle of his main living room and he called that to your attention. He wanted you to come and visit him so he could show you his electric washer.

Rhodes #4 - 160 -

Of course, it was never used for washing and I don't think they washed very often anyhow. I think they just sewed themselves into their clothes and have one outfit for winter and one outfit for summer.

Q: What about vessel assistance?

Rhodes: Very seldom were we called upon to assist any vessels up there because there were so few vessels. There was the schooner HOLMES that I mentioned --we always made it a point when she was around the ice to be ready to assist her in case she needed assistance, but I will say that she had a fine skipper aboard and if there was wind, he'd be able to take care of it all right. As far as I know, as long as I was on the ship, she never had to ask for assistance.

Q: Was it a wooden ship?

Rhodes: A wooden sailing ship, a schooner, fairly good size, three masted. He was a marvelous seaman.

Q: Do you remember his name?

Rhodes: Johnny Backland. It's a long time to remember back, but I think that was his name.

Q: He had been doing this for a long time?

Rhodes: Yes. Now in later years there was a Bureau of Indian

Rhodes #4 - 161 -

Affairs ship that went up there to supply the school teachers, and so forth, in various villages. That was the NORTH STAR and we would see her once in awhile but they didn't stay up there very long because all they did was go to these places where they had to supply the school teachers and then got out of there.

Q: Was the NORTH STAR a former star boat from the fishing fleet?

Rhodes: No, I think it was built especially for the Bureau of Indian Affairs for that purpose because they transported teachers and their supplies.

Q: Did you have any contact with the star boats?

Rhodes: Yes, The NORTH STAR, the Bureau of Indian Affairs ship, we always had contact with the commanding officer of that ship because we would help them quite frequently. If he was on a tight schedule, we might take some of his passengers and take them over to certain villages so he wouldn't have to make that extra stop, if we could arrange to do it. So we always had contact with him but there was very little commercial fishing going on up in the northern waters. There was Eskimos, and so forth, and we were always around to help in case they needed assitance. Down south the Bering Sea patrol took care of the commercial fishermen.

Q: It's funny to hear you say down south in the Bering Sea patrol. To me that's way up north.

Rhodes: That's right. But to us it was way down south. There was a lot of commercial fishing down there for salmon, and so forth, and that is one main reason for the Bering Sea patrol was all of the interests --you had foreign vessels over there --Russians, Canadians, Americans, Japanese, all out there and you could have minor feuds among these different fishermen, so you needed a strong Bering Sea patrol down in the southern part of the Bering Sea and along the Aleutians and up around Kodiak and places of that type.

Q: Do you remember any particular incidents that happened to you up there that would be considered unusual or exciting?

Rhodes: There are so many incidents that I can't remember any one. I remember the terrific job of navigating in fog up there. When you're in the inside passage and the water's too deep to anchor, and you've got to keep going, and the aids to navigation are very few and far between. I think that is almost horrible sometimes when you're caught right among all this rocky coast, you could go ashore any time and most of the time, a great deal of the time, you have to navigate by blowing your whistle, listening for the echo and timing the time it takes from the time you blow your whistle for the echo to come back to find out how far you are off these cliffs on both sides. It's quite a feeling. You can't tell when there's other vessels around either, especially small ones. But you've got to keep moving because the currents are fairly strong in those waters, and they are deep and you can't anchor. If you're caught in a fog under those conditions, I think that is the thing that I remember most.

Perhaps another thing is visiting some Siberia villages. When I

Rhodes # 4 - 163 -

was on the NOTHLAND, we went over and visited several Siberian villages. I remember one, the Russian inspectors came right out to the ship as soon as we dropped anchor and they weren't going to let us go ashore. I invited them in and we had coffee, and although they couldn't speak English and I couldn't speak Russian, I showed them around the ship and they decided we were all very friendly so they let us go ashore and we played volleyball with the local people over there. They had quite a few native Russians as well as Eskimos. To see those little children, all in uniforms, marching to school, it was interesting to see the way they ran their schools over there, even right on the coast of Siberia.

Q: What were the Russians doing in the sections of Siberia that you visited?

Rhodes: Mostly they would be fishing and trapping and to make sure the area was settled. It is hard to tell exactly what they were doing because we couldn't speak their language. We would find an interpreter somewhere but it was very unsatisfactory as far as getting everything across. But we did have very pleasant visits with them wherever we went, although the tendancy wherever we went was to run us off. As long as we were friendly, and so forth, they finally got around to trusting us. Now we had had authority to land at various villages up there for scientific reasons and, as I say, we did have these scientist aboard who wanted to take these soundings to see what the content of the water looked like and so forth. We had reason to be there for scientific reasons and we had been given authority through the State Department and Russian foreign office to visit these places but apparently word had not gotten to the local people, and we got the idea over that we did have authority, and we were completely peaceful and just wanted to visit. Invariably they would allow us to go ashore. Generally some kind of a game was gotten up between the crew --they were very friendly people and our people, of course, are very friendly and they got along fine.

Q: I remember Captain Capron telling me, he did some ice breaking work in the Hudson, that they had more-or-less a floating basketball game going where every night they put into a port on the Hudson River on the way up the river and back down again and challenge the local teams to a game of basketball in their gymnasium.

Rhodes: It's very interesting. I think that sailors gradually have a knack of being friendly with people wherever they go ashore, and the people seem to reciprocate. Quite often --it's just contagious. As long as people are friendly, you can always find friendly people who step up and really enjoy fraternizing with each other.

Q: Were the Russians doing the same thing in Alaskan waters? You mentioned that they came over to search for some downed flyers, but did they ever come over to do scientific work?

Rhodes: We know that their scientific ships were out all the time. We would often see them. We don't know of any coming into American waters, American ports, without permission, but they often do come in with permission. This was merely reciprocating. In those days it was just a short time after we had established diplomatic relations with

Russia, and therefore it was somewhat touch and go as to what was going to happen to us if we did go ashore. However it was very pleasant once we established the fact that we were only there for friendly relations.

Interview # 5 with Capt. Earl Rhodes, USCG, (ret.)
At his home, Takoma Park, Maryland   July 26, 1970
Biography   by Peter Spectre

Mr. Spectre: Captain, in our last interview, which was quite a while ago, we covered your tour of duty on the Coast Guard cutter, NORTHLAND, and I believe that we ended with the end of your last voyage on the NORTHLAND. Could you tell me what happened after that? How did you hear about your new assignment?

Capt. Rhodes: I recieved my new assignment just before I arrived in Seattle. I believe it came in in a radio message. So I was transferred off the NORTHLAND shortly after I arrived back in Seattle and I was assigned to what was then the Chicago Division of the Coast Guard. We had headquarters in what we called the new post office building in Chicago. It was right near the Union Station.

Q: Could you explain to me the difference between divisions and what's now districts?

Rhodes: Generally the Coast Guard used to call their outlying headquarters divisions. They generally coincided fairly closely with the naval district, however, instead of numbering them by district, they called them such as the Chicago Division, the Boston Division, San Fransisco Division, New York Division, and so forth. Lateron when we coordinated very closely with the Navy, especially at the approach of the second World War, we decided to call them districts, and numbered them the same as the naval districts.

Q: So when you say the Chicago Division, you are really talking about the mid-west?

Rhodes: That's right, although at that time we had a Chicago Division and a Cleveland Division and the area of the mid-west which was the 9th Naval District was split up between two divisions.

Q: So about what area was the Chicago Division?

Rhodes: The Chicago Division had Lake Huron, Lake Michigan, Lake Superior, and included the states of Michigan, Indiana, Illinois, Wisconsin, Minnesota, North and South Dakota, Nebraska, Kansas, Iowa.

Q: Was this a normal rotation for you?

Rhodes: Yes, this was the first real shore duty that I had had. This was in 1937, so therefore, I had been out of the Academy for about nine years. Outside of my aviation training I had had no shore duty up until that time.

Q: Do you think you were assigned there because you were born and brought up in that area?

Rhodes: Yes, I think that had a lot to do with it. I had, in my fitness reports where you are given an opportunity to state your preference for assignment, I had always put the Great Lakes area.

Q: Tell me a little bit about the state of the Coast Guard in that particular area. I've talked quite lengths with Coastguardsmen who have had a lot of experience on the East Coast and the West Coast, and the Gulf Coast, but I haven't heard much about the Great Lakes.

Rhodes: The Coast Guard on the Great Lakes were mostly known for the Lifesaving Stations on the Great Lakes. There were very few vessels in the old days, however there were some patrol vessels and small ice breakers based at Escanaba, Michigan when I arrived there. However there was a reorganization taking place, in the wind so to speak, and later on, shortly after I arrived there, we somewhat amalgamated the Lifesaving Station districts into the office of the district commander or division commander, so that the Lifeboat Stations, generally, were somewhat autonomous even after 1915, between 1915 and 1937. The district commanders, who were old Lifesaving Station men, pretty well ran the Lifesaving Stations themselves. Shortly after I arrived in Chicago, those district commander offices were transferred into Chicago, right into the office of the Coast Guard division commander.

Q: This was happening all over the service?

Rhodes: That's right. There was somewhat a consolidation because even though they had been part of the Coast Guard, they had operated somewhat by themselves. They coordinated with the rest of the floating Coast Guard but they hardly knew each other --they had very little direct contact. This gave them direct contact because this coordinated all activities right in the district commander's office.

Q: With something like that I envision a lot of problems right at the beginning and large power struggles to prevent it from happening and to make it happen? Is that true?

Rhodes: That is very true. I can still remember some of the old timers struggling to maintain their own power, you might say, and actually they felt very strongly about it because they knew their job very well and they felt that the outsiders couldn't possibly do the job as well as they could. Of course they didn't realize that by coordination, the ships, the planes, the sea-going Coast Guard could help the Lifesaving Stations a great deal, and vice-versa, the Lifesaving Stations could help the sea-going people a great deal if only the efforts were coordinated at some central point. That turned out to be correct.

Q: How did you feel at the time?

Rhodes: Well, of course, I was at that time communications officer for the whole district and also personnel officer for the whole district so I had to do a lot of consolidating personally and organize the whole thing. At that time all we had in the office in the way of officers were district commanders, chief of staff, chief engineer, and myself as communications and personnel --somewhat public relations also. The chief of staff handled a great deal of public relations but naturally I was concerned with it a great deal with my work. Those were the only commissioned officers. Then we had a radio electrician, a machinist, and a couple of pay clerks, and that comprised the whole office at that time.

Q: That's really a small organization. What kind of problems do you have? Do you remember any specific things that came up when you were trying to bring about this reorganization?

Rhodes: Well, of course, small-boating was getting quite active on the Great Lakes at that time and we had to escort a lot of regattas. That was one of our main activities. These squalls would come up and that's where our communications were very important, to rescue alot of people when these yachts capsized. I remember one time we had over a dozen yachts capsize just outside of Chicago and we managed to save all the people, then went around righting the yachts and towing them in. I still remember the owner of one yacht who was very, very angry because we hadn't righted his yacht immediately after we saved the people from it --we went around saving the other people first before we started righting any yacht. There was some damage done to his yacht which he did not think would have happened if we had righted it immediately and put his people back aboard. But our main objective was to pull people out of the water, and then we did right all the yachts and get them in safe anchorage. That is the type of thing that you would have. You would have these sudden storms out there on the lake, and this is where the floating units of the Coast Guard could help the Lifeboat Stations along the coast and vice versa. It was by having control directly from the office there was far better efficiency obtained by coordinating the efforts of all those available. One of the big things that happened out there, I believe it was the winter of 1938, when we had to install radios at certain strategic Lifeboat Stations in the middle of winter so that we could have two way radio communications from those stations, which would cover all of the lakes.

Q: This is voice radio?

Rhodes: Yes. All of the ships on the lake, then, would be equipped with this same radio come spring, so we would be listening on distress frequency for all of them. This is the first time established, and that frequency I remember was 2182 kcs. This gave the Coast Guard communication with all the large vessels on the Great Lakes. We had to go out there right in the middle of winter to these island stations. We installed one on Thunder Bay Island; Mackinac Island; Grand Haven, Michigan; Charlevoix, Michigan; Three Rivers, Minnesota, on the north side of Lake Superior.

Q: These were all Lifesaving Stations?

Rhodes: Lifesaving Stations, yes. There was another one on the Copper Peninsula, our Lifeboat Station right out in the southern part of Lake Superior --the peninsula juts into Lake Superior.

Q: What kind of commercial shipping was going on in the Great Lakes at that time?

Rhodes: Most of it was the ore boats. The car ferries ran right through the winter, but these big ore boats were the most important vessel on the lakes for many years, including that time. But there were many other vessels also --specialized cargo and passenger vessels. Fishing vessels also --they were not compelled to carry this radio, but generally they did when it was available. They could see the advantages of having it, so if they could afford to put it on, they would. They were informed that it was available and someone would always be listening to them if they had a question to ask or if they got in trouble.

Q: In other words, the radios weren't supplied by the government or the Coast Guard for the ships --just for your own stations?

Rhodes: That's right. The Coast Guard installed and maintained the radios on their own station and, of course, their own ships were also equipped with this same radio, but the commercial vessels had to supply and install the radios on their own vessels. The fisherman would have to install his own radio if he wanted the advantage of having it.

Rhodes # 5 - 173 -

Q: What about the ice problem in the Great Lakes? How did that affect you?

Rhodes: The ice problem was pretty severe at times because the lake generally would not freeze over but there would be a lot of slush ice on the lake, and the wind would blow that slush ice from one side of the lake to the other depending on the direction of the wind. Say there were a bunch of fishing vessels out on the coast, this wind blowing the slush ice against them would tend to force them ashore. Then our vessels would try to help them and tow them through the ice. The great difficulty with slush ice is that it would pile up and go almost all the way to the bottom so you were operating in slush ice. That was not difficult, you can operate in slush ice just like in water, but the trouble is, as you try to cool your engines with sea water and you suck in the slush ice, that clogs up your pipes and so your engines heat up and you can't operate until you clean out your strainers, so it was a very, very difficult job operating in slush ice because it tends to go all the way to the bottom. Ordinarily we wouldn't have any difficulty operating up in the middle of the lake, but when you get into harbors, often they would be protected and they would freeze over and we'd have to continue to keep them broken out so that the smaller fishing boats, and so forth could operate. We never tried to keep Lake Superior open in the winter time, at that time. I was talking about Lake Michigan and Lake Huron. It was always a big time to open up Lake Superior to shipimg as early as possible in the spring, although we didn't have any large ice breakers at that time, still our smaller vessels could help a great deal. The Coast Guard was also charged with handling traffic through the Soo Canal. Although the Army engineers operated the canal, the Coast Guard actually handled the traffic up there.

Q: Was the slush ice problem the reason why they built the special ice breaker for the Coast Guard in the Great Lakes rather than use one of the WIND class ice breakers?

Rhodes: No, the reason it had to be a specialized ice breaker was because of the shallow water in the Great Lakes. An ice breaker of the NORTHWIND class could draw close to thirty feet of water and that is far too much to navigate some of the harbors on the Great Lakes. So they had to have a shallower draft vessel in order to get into many of the harbors and still be effective on the Great Lakes. Generally, the large ice breaker, ESCANABA, that they built for the Great Lakes had been able to open navigation about a month earlier and keep it open about a month later than they ever could before that.

Q: Are there tides in the Great Lakes?

Rhodes: There might be but not enough to measure at all. There's such a small area compared to the world as a whole that they just say there are no tides on the Great Lakes.

Q: When you amalgamated the Lifesaving Stations with the floating Coast Guard on the Great Lakes, you were personally involved, and so forth. What kind of oposition did you get and what form did it

Rhodes # 5 - 175 -

take? Personally, what kind of problems did you run into?

Rhodes: There were naturally many problems for us all to solve. I got along fine, at least on the surface, with everyone involved. One of the Lifeboat Station commanders cooperated fully and he was designated operations officer when he moved into the office, so he coordinated the operations of the Lifeboat Staions and the floating Coast Guard. The other one did not cooperate and he retired shortly thereafter. He was older and the man who stayed with us was younger. I think that makes a great deal of difference --where you've served your whole tour under certain methods and you get over sixty years old, you're not about to want to change anything. If you're about thirty-five and the whole future is before you, you can see the way the wind is blowing and you can decide that you are going to be effective, and, of course, the only way this officer could be effective was to cooperate, and he was an outstanding success. I should say, though, that about this same time, the Lighthouse Service was also transferred to the Coast Guard, so we had the job of coordinating the Lighthouse Service in our office in Chicago --it formerly had been at Milwaukee. We moved all the officers from the Lighthouse Service down there. I had the job of inducting all Lighthouse personnel who wished to come into the military service of the Coast Guard, inducting them into the Coast Guard. We had to interview all the people in the Lighthouse Service and also inspect all the facilities --all the lighthouses, all the lighthouse tenders. But we did then get some additional vessels which were quite capable on the lakes the lighthouse tenders, so as a result of that we had to coordinate the services between the lighthouse tenders, the Coast Guard vessels, and the Lifesaving Stations. Then the lighthouses could be tended by Lifeboat Station personnel. Also the Coast Guard vessels could help the tenders take care of some of the buoys and the lights, maybe get the mail to the isolated Life Stations, which was a morale factor -- our Lifeboat Stations were especially good at that. The tenders were very able vessels and they could help us a great deal in assistance, ice breaking, and things of that nature.

Q: When you talk about a lighthouse tender, do you mean what is now called a buoy tender?

Rhodes: That's right. They have to operate in almost any kind of weather, and they have to be able to carry buoys on their deck, put buoys on station, and also take up old buoys that are in need of repairs. They have to put batteries, and so forth in the buoys, and keep them lighted. So a vessel of that type is quite able at sea. They were built to operate on the Great Lakes, therefore they could operate under almost any condidtion and they were a great help to the Coast Guard in emergencies. At the same time under normal circumstances, the Coast Guard was a great help to them in helping take care of a great many smaller lights and buoys, also personnel-wise if someone got sick out on a station, we could put one of our men in in a hurry and keep the light on the air, so to speak. It gave us strategic points for communication, and so forth, lookout, our communications were consolidated, so on the whole, after we consolidated that whole operation --and this, by the way, included the Coast Guard telephone line, then cables. Up at Green Bay they always had the office of the telephone lines and cables. The Coast Guard maintained a great many cables off to outlying lights and islands --that was the only communication to those islands. In some cases we had a good size cable out to an island and rented circuits to the telephone company, who would then supply telephone service to the natives of the island. Every now and then we would have to have a cable ship lay cables around the Great Lakes. In order to consolidate the whole operation, we also brought the office of the telephone commander into the office. We had then, radio communications, telephone communications, and Lifeboat, Lighthouse, everyone consolidated right in one office, and we were able to go next door and talk to each other and find ways that we could consolidate the whole thing. It was very helpful in all of our operations from then on.

Q: The district office must have gotten pretty big.

Rhodes: It was. Actually they had to build two extra floors on the customs house and kind of spread out over there. We first got some extra space in the post office and then it was decided to build two extra floors on the customs house, which was nearby. It was a new customs house, also, and that, then, was given over to the Coast Guard. So they consolidated the whole thing. Then, of course, on top of all this, the disturbance in Europe was coming about and we

were required to recruit a great many extra men out there to
and training them --we had to have a training station, and so forth
because this was about '38, '39, '40 and we started to get additional men for our own purposes out there but also the sea-going Coast Guard was being beefed up. The middle west was, of course, a very good place to obtain good men who had a romantic interest, if nothing else, in going to sea. So that kept us quite busy.

I could go back there and give you one of the other great interests out there. Just before I arrived, I believe it was the spring of '37 that they had one of the worst floods up in the Ohio, Mississippi River that they had ever had. So I was called into Washington --we had a conference there in Washington-- and I was designated as communications officer for flood purposes for the whole area. No matter what happened, I was to handle communications out there. So I recommended that before things happened that we send two mobile radio stations out there, which would move to wherever location I told them to and get information. In the meantime I would keep in contact with the Army engineers and other people in the area. This way we were able to get direct reports ~~of the situations~~ of the situation in the various areas --trucks moving around and setting up communications and also keeping in touch with the local people. That always gave us a jump so that instead of having to ask for trucks to be assigned out there, we had men already there who were familiar with the terrain and also familiar with the poeple who they would be operating with.

Q: You're talking about planning before a flood ever took place?

Rhodes: That's right. So your key people would be familiar with the terrain and also familiar with the Army engineers, and others, say mayors, police department, fire department, who they might be called upon to operate with. They've got to set up their radio stations almost anywhere --it's a mobile, self contained on a truck. They can operate very well for awhile, but still they've got to be able to get the information they get by radio to the proper hands locally. Also they've got to get the local information and get it to us. Since they were familiar with the police department, the city government, the Army engineers --I'd keep sending them from one place to another so they would become familiar with them. They would actually set up their station in each place and then make themselves known and become familiar with all the people. I would go down with them and meet the local people, so we had a good set-up. It just happened that we didn't have any bad floods while I was there. However, the organization was set up and later on, when they did have one, I learned that was a big help to be in touch with all the people like that.

Q: You talked about taking in new people because of the coming war and also took people in from the Lighthouse Service. What did that do to the service?

Rhodes: Of course it enlarged the service a great deal. There was a great many officers taken in, say, in the Lighthouse Service. Also the former district commanders from the Lifeboat Service were taken in. I just mentioned one of the commanders of the Lifeboat Service retired rather than move to the office of the division commander. That, of course, makes vacancies for young officers coming up and you can assume, generally, the officers from the Lifeboat Station and the Lighthouse Service were on the whole, fairly elderly. They were excellent people, they knew their job but never-the-less, as they gradually retired that gave the regular Coast Guard an opportunity to fill them as regular officer billet. This eliminated any conflict of interests gradually as the old officers retired and the officer billets were filled by general duty Coast Guard officers. Any conflict that you might have found between the Lighthouse officers, Coast Guard officers, and Lifeboat Station officers generally, of course, that disappeared, and coordination and cooperation increased every year.

Q: Before the Lighthouse Service became part of the Coast Guard, did they transfer around within their organization or were they static? In other words you joined a lighthouse crew and stayed on that crew?

Rhodes: Generally speaking the crew would stay on that tender. They wouldn't transfer from one place to another. Also the Lighthouse engineers, although there was some transferring around, generally you wouldn't call it rotation --it was transferring to fill a billet because someone had retired or something of that nature. Once they were almalgamated with the Coast Guard, there was more transferring although the older men that we took in from the Lighthouse Service, generally were pretty well left where they were familiar with the jobs that they were doing, and they were left in charge of that particular phase of it. They ran what they were familiar with but after they were retired it would be pretty well consolidated as a single operation with the rest of the district office.

By the way, it might be interesting to mention here that probably one reason that the Coast Guard offices were called division offices is because the Lifesaving Station offices were called district offices. They were Lifesaving districts and the Lighthouse offices were called district offices. Once they joined the Coast Guard division, that was when the Coast Guard called their main offices district offices.

Q: Was this about the same time that an enlisted man in the Coast Guard could expect duty on board ship in a Lifeboat Station and a Lighthouse Service Station?

Rhodes: That is correct. That is when we started transferring them around and that is one of the big jobs that I had as personnel officer in the district office --starting the amalgamation of the men in the various services. For example, if we gave all the men on lighthouse tenders military rank, if one of them retired or took a discharge and left, he would be replaced by a military man who had been trained maybe on a cutter, and gradually, then, all those men manning the tenders would have been trained at some Coast Guard training station and perhaps have seen service on a cutter. The same way in the Lifeboat Station. Generally we would fill vacancies there with men who had been trained at a regular Coast Guard training station, went through boot camp and perhaps had had a little sea duty before he would be sent to a Lifeboat Station. Previous to that, the officer in charge would just go off and get someone locally to fill a billet in his Lifeboat Station. As a result, sometimes those men would stay in the same station all their life. This is the first time we really got rotation, and I believe it was very good for the Lifeboat Stations and very good for our floating units also.

Q: From what I can understand from listening to you and other people that I've talked to, the Coast Guard might have been the Coast Guard in name in 1915 but it wasn't until the late '30s that it actually became a real organization.

Rhodes: Exactly. It hardly had anything to do with the Coast Guard as a whole. The Lifeboat Station and the lifeboat districts were quite separate from the division commander's office although they would operate under him. Still he would operate through the lifeboat district commander, and the district commander would give the orders to all of his people. They would not come from a ship or an airplane. Now, after that, we could put a senior officer in charge of a certain distress operation and he would be in charge of all the ships, planes, Lifeboat Stations, and perhaps even lighthouse tenders that might be on the scene, so that you would have local command but you'd never have that under the old system where all orders had to go through the Lifeboat Station district commander. It did not give close coordination between Coast Guard ships and Coast Guard Lifeboat Stations.

Q: Another thing that occurred at this time was the formation of the Coast Guard Auxiliary. In talking to Admiral O'Neill, who was the first director of the Auxiliary and who more or less organized it, he said that a lot of his initial support came from the Chicago area. Could you tell me something about that?

Rhodes: I would be happy to because we take credit out there for the Coast Guard even thinking about it. Several yachtsmen and I got together discussing how much they could help the Coast Guard in various ways. They were interested in doing it. By the way, Mr. Caliendo was out there and he was very much interested in it and there were other Chicagoans in the yachting fraternity who also were very interested. I informed the chief of staff of district commander of this and we wrote a letter to Admiral Waesche explaining what our ideas were, he was Commandant at that time, and a very short time later Admiral Waesche told us that he would like to come out and talk to us. So we arranged a meeting with these particular people in yachting fraternities, including Mr Caliendo. Admiral Waesche came out and he was very favorably impressed. As a result of that meeting, the Coast Guard did introduce a bill in Congress for the voluntary, what we called at that time the Coast Guard Reserve --we had no Reserve at that time so that was what it was called. It was agreed that they would voluntarily assist the Coast Guard in educating the yachting public in assisting in distress cases and keep in close touch in communications with the Coast Guard, all voluntarily. That, surprisingly to us, went over very, very, easily. When you say that they got support from the Chicago area, this is really where the bug hit and where it spread. They did do a lot to go around and talk to other yachtsmen in other parts of the country, trying to get support. Once it was explained, everyone was very much interested.

Q: What kind of opposition was there against the idea, against people joining, against the idea in the Coast Guard and against the people who you would like to recruit for the organization?

Rhodes: Generally you get opposition to anything that's going to cause more work and more trouble. Once you explain to the people just how it will work, there generally was no answer to it. They say it would sound good in theory, but how would it work out? They just couldn't believe that all these people would voluntarily put in their time and effort to do all these things. Even if they didn't do all they said they would do, still it was a good way to keep in contact with them, and the Coast Guard would have a lot more information on how to handle their distress cases, anyhow, if we could talk to these people. No one could say that it was so bad that we shouldn't go into it and everyone would say if it works the way they

Rhodes # 5 - 185 -

say it will work, you can't afford not to go into it. It was the real answer to many of our problems. As it turned out, it turned out far better than even those who were in favor of it visualized it because, as practical people, it was hard to believe that all these people would go out and volunteer their service and help the Coast Guard in the many ways in which they have helped the Coast Guard through the years.

Q: What about the people you were recruiting for the Coast Guard Auxiliary in the Chicago area --if they opposed the idea, what were their reasons for opposing it?

Rhodes: They thought that there would be too much politics in it. They thought that they should organize their own thing and they were also afraid that the military might try to cram things down their throats. It was merely afraid of trying something new. They were satisfied the way things were. They weren't so much interested in trying to improve things because they liked it the way it was. I think that was mostly the opposition. Of course, they could give all kinds of arguments but those who opposed, and they didn't oppose it very strongly, generally, were the ones who just liked things the way they were --they didn't want to see any changes. I learned a lot in Chicago --you'd see all kinds of things out there.

Q: What other type of work did you find up there? Was there any spectacular distress cases in the Great Lakes when you were there?

Rhodes: No, not what I would call headline type action, although they all hit the local headlines and they were very serious as far as the local people were concerned. Still, when you manage to save them from precarious positions, it is not what you call spectacular because a lot of people just expect it to happen that way. They don't realize how touch and go these things are in many cases. We had a lot of assistance cases out there. The Great Lakes are known for sudden changes of weather so that is one thing that gave emphasis was the Coast Guard Auxiliary, Coast Guard Reserve at that time, out there, was the fact that so many people would go out on boats just like a person will go out in an automobile. The only thing is, they didn't require license, they didn't require anything. In good weather anyone could steer a boat, but let a squall come up and then something happened, they would be in very serious trouble because they had no idea what to do about it. These people who were concerned about that type of situation were the ones who wanted to teach these poor innocent people how to sail a boat before they ever bought a yacht or went to sea in it, if possible.

Q: A couple of years ago when I was in the service there was a big tragedy on one of the Great Lakes, I think it was Michigan, where a whole fleet of boats were out fishing and a big storm came up unexpectedly --there were very few advance weather reports about it and what was put out in advance didn't help because the people were already out on the lake, so quite a few people died and many boats were destroyed. After that there was a lot of talk about some sort of a regualtion that prevented people from going out in bad weather. Was this ever considered when you were there?

Rhodes: Yes, it was, and the Coast Guard did a lot about it. That is one reason why we installed these radio stations around the Great Lakes and certain large vessels were compelled to have radios, whereas the smaller ones were encouraged to have one, but there was no law to force these smaller boats to have one and we would advise strongly against vessels going out but there was no way of stopping them from going out. Also while I was up there, it was brought out that definitely there should be some way of warning these vessels up there. We had no air station in that area. I was called into Washington and asked to locate the best possible place for an air station. I went around and I figured Traverse City, Michigan, which already had Penn Central Airlines up there. That was about the most centrally located place in the whole Great Lakes. I negotiated with the town people and they accepted my recommendation, and shortly thereafter we did have planes stationed there.

Q: You were the father of the Traverse City air station.

Rhodes: That's right. By the way that's about fifteen miles from where I was born so I was that familiar with the place up there. This way, if we knew that something was coming up, the planes could always go off and drop warnings to the boats. We've done that many times in the Gulf where hurricanes would be approaching. These isolated boats without radio, the only way to get them would be to drop a warning tied to a cork float, or something of that nature. These fisherman would never stand for Uncle Sam telling them it's too dangerous for them to go out. They figured they could handle it themselves. On the other hand, we certainly should be able to tell yachtsmen that they can't go out, yet there are as many yachtsmen that feel they are far better seaman than the people who are telling them that they can't go out. So you are really getting into serious politics when you tell someone that they can't go out; you can advise them that it's unsafe to go out, but I certainly wouldn't advocate passing a law telling them they can't go out. I don't believe the Coast Guard ever has advocated such a law because you'd have a terrible time enforcing it.

Q: In this particular case, the recommendation came from the National Transportation Safety Board, who investigated the case. There was quite an uproar about it, I remember, and I was curious to know whether that type of thing had happened before. I was curious to know whether anybody had ever thought of that idea.

Rhodes: We had discussed it many, many times, because even if they went out, if they could keep us informed of where they were, we could go on and advise them that they had better get in if they didn't. At least we'd know where they were so that we could go and help them when they capsized and needed help. Much of our time was taken in searching for people who reportedly went out in a storm and they were overdue. If there was someway of keeping us informed of their location and how they are, that would be a big help. We've often discussed the advisability of keeping people in when we know that it's real hazardous for them to go out, but when you stop to think of the practical methods of trying to enforce this and the political repercussions that would come from keeping people from sailing when they wanted to --it's just like telling someone they can't go in their automobile because it's dangerous to drive on this particular day.

Q: It's also a matter of opinion as to whether it is a bad day.

Rhodes: That's right, you're definitely dealing in opinions and knowing the weather forecasting as it always has been, it's always possible to be a little bit mistaken in the forecast because weather plays some funny tricks on all of us. Therefore, you keep someone in the harbor, they can't sail, and it turns out to be a beautiful day outside. You'd have a lot of explaining to do under those circumstances. So from the parctical side of it, we warn them all we could, but we always use the official weather forecast. We never made our own forecast to put out to the public. All we could do was pass the information along and let them use their own judgement. We might add our own advice that they had better stay in but if they still went out, there was nothing we could do about it.

Q: Nowadays all you hear about the Great Lakes is the pollution problem, that the Lakes are dying, and so forth. You hear every time some oil is spilled on the Great Lakes or any body of water now, you hear a lot about it and it sounds as if all of a sudden oil is being spilled, whereas it wasn't before. When you were up there, were there oil spills?

Rhodes: Yes, there were and there was already laws on the books forbidding oil spills. We were enforcing it along with the Army engineers and port authorities. It's a lot more difficult enforcing a law when the public practically knows nothing about it and is not greatly concerned about it. We would find a lot of stumbling blocks proving a case, and so forth. The public weren't nearly as interested in helping you prosecute a case in those days as they are now. I would think that with public opinion as it is today, they can progress very much faster than we could in those days because we didn't have enough forces of our own, in those days, to investigate all these things, and follow through. It takes a great deal of investigation sometimes to find out who spilled the oil. Unless you have help from the local people, you just don't have the man power, and so forth, to go out and investigate all these things in order to make a case for prosecution.

Q: Were the Lakes polluted when you were there?

Rhodes: They were, but nothing compared to what they are now. Each year they're worse. I was stationed there before 1940, I left there in 1940, and that's over thirty years ago. It wasn't nearly as crowded then, there weren't nearly as many boats as there are now, but there were a lot of them even then. All those boats make pollution. Many cities were discharging their waste directly into the Lakes without doing anything to prevent it, even in those days. So since that's kept up, and the population has increased, and all these boats are throwing stuff over the side, and of course, the chemical industry is --industry of all kinds, the steel industry, all of them are putting pollutants into the water. That just adds up. I would think that in the thirty years since I left, it must be very, very, bad because very little has been done about it in all those years. We've had the second World War and certainly nothing was done about it then except to add to the pollution, because ships were built on the Great Lakes then --there was a lot of industry established on the Great Lakes. Nothing was done to clean up the place nor even thought about probably.

Q: Was there anybody when you were there who would come in and demand action or any pressure group, or anything?

Rhodes: No. About the only thing that you would hear then is about the same as you hear now that people shouldn't throw tin cans along the street. In other words, it was practically never heard of. The yachtsmen would kick about it, the fishermen would kick about it, but there was no organization or anything of that type who was anxious to do anything about it. Certainly the people weren't concerned, the newspapers weren't concerned, the news media was not concerned. Very seldom would you hear it mentioned and yet we all knew that it was bad.

Q: Maybe there is hope then because if people were aware of it, as you say ---

Rhodes: It's the old saying, "Where there's a will there's a way." If people are concerned, they're going to find a way. They don't care how much it costs, it can be done. I'd certainly like to see it. I think most people when they consider the beauty of those lakes and what a terrible thing it is to think that all the fish are getting poisoned, they in turn poison the people if they eat them. It's hard to believe that we would do that type of thing to great bodies of water like that. There again we're polluting our oceans, too. New York Harbor back in the '20s and '30s -- It doesn't seem possible that anyplace could be as polluted as that was. I remember it very well. I've never seen anything as bad as that.

Q: It still is.

Rhodes: It still is but I think, there again, that they could do something about it, but it's going to take an awful lot of money and quite a little time.

Q: What happened to you after Chicago?

Rhodes: After Chicago I was transferred to Washington for a course of cryptanalysis in the Signal Corps. That was the old Munitions Building. I understand now it has been demolished ~~is in it~~ and I think we're all pretty happy about that. It certainly has served its purpose through many years.

Q: Temporary buildings are temporarily around for fifty or seventy-five years --

Rhodes: That's right.

Q: You were involved briefly in decoding messages when you were assigned to the destroyer --

Rhodes: The PORTER, yes. We were working quite a little on that and then again I was interested in it when I was assigned the PERSEUS as executive officer in New York in '33 and '34. I was interested and quite friendly with some of the people working on it and got into quite a few phases of it on my own.

Q: Did you keep your hand in it?

Rhodes: No, I could not when I was away from the source of information, you might say. It's much more interesting when you can be working with people who are working with it and you can see your results. Unless you can prove your results, it's pretty hard to keep your interest up. Although I was always interested in it and I always read anything I could get on it, and solve problems on it, I wasn't involved in the real thing like I was when I was based in New York.

Q: How did you get that assignment? Why were you sent to that school?

Rhodes: I applied for it. They asked for applicants of those who were interested. One of the people, my shipmate on the old PORTER, who had been working with me had already graduated from the school. I have a hunch that he might have put in a good word for me knowing that we worked together, knowing that I'd been very much interested in this.

Q: Will you tell me something about the school, how it was run, who ran it?

Rhodes: I can tell you this, which is pretty well known: Mr. Friedman --we had his wife, Mrs. Friedman working in our outfit right along, and Mr. Friedman is known nation wide and world wide, actually. He was really the head of the school. Then they had quite a few expert scientists, and so forth, working there and they also had military who actually were running the whole set-up. There were only three of us in the class, two Army officers and myself. So you can see they weren't going into it in a big way, and they were only choosing certain individuals. I think probably one reason they took a Coast Guard officer in was because of the close association made possible by Mrs. Friedman being the wife of Mr. Friedman. Of course, Mr. Friedman is generally referred to as Colonel Friedman because during the war he was a colonel.

Q: What was the purpose of the school?

Rhodes: The purpose of the school was to learn all the methods of reading secret messages, decoding them. So that you got so that very, very few things couldn't be deciphered if you worked on it hard enough with enough imagination. Sooner or later somebody makes a mistake that gives you a break, and you have to reckon they will make a mistake. Generally, that is no secret whatsoever --there's lots of books written about   but it takes quite a little bit to train someone to actually do these things and be in charge of an office and teach other people how to do it, and make a success of it.

Q: Were you also taught how to encode?

Rhodes: Oh yes, but anyone can do that just by following instructions.

Q: Devise codes?

Rhodes: Yes, you could devise them, and you also knew the safe ones and the unsafe ones, and how dangerous it is to use an unsafe code and think that you are safe. Many people will use a type of a code which an amateur can break down. For example these rummies were using things that didn't take real brilliance --an amateur could do it. That's what made it so interesting. It's very, very important to know what makes a code safe and what makes it dangerous. Also to know how to be careful in the use of it because if you know what the cryptanalysis are looking for, then you will know what you shouldn't do. For example, supposing you encode a message and send it over the radio, and the guy can't decode it so you send it in plaintext --you've got to get that message to him. That means that I've intercepted both of those messages. I've got the coded version and I've got the plaintext version. That's the break I've been looking for. That's the simplest type of break.

Q: How would you know that --there must be thousands of messages that go out in a day from any one place-- how would you know that you had intercepted a plaintext version of an encoded message?

Rhodes: That is the big thing that they taught us, how to catalogue coded messages so you could classify them all together. One of the big jobs there is to classify the things and, of course, when you get machines working for you, that's the whole secret, like the IBM, and now you've got the computer. With a computer, you can do almost anything. I would say over a period of time a computer can solve almost anything if they have a good brain behind it because a computer can go over a vast amount of messages which you've intercepted and notice any similarity between them all. In true comparisons, and so forth, a well trained cryptanylist could probably handle almost anything along the line.

Rhodes # 5 - 197 -

Q: How many cryptanylists were there when you began? Were there a lot of them?

Rhodes: Very few. There's a lot of clerks working on things and of course, sorting them out, cataloguing them, but for the people who were actually working on the solution of these things, very, very few people are engaged in that kind of work.

Q: What did they expect you to do? You went to the school, learned the trade, what did they expect you to do when you got out?

Rhodes: They expected me to work in our classified methods department. In other words, whatever is necessary, that particular group would handle, and probably I would be in charge later on. Of course, the Coast Guard got out of it later on and therefore I didn't have any particular need for it but my first job when I graduated was to be in charge of all classified communications, and also in charge of the school which taught officers to handle classified communications. It was up to me to see to it that none of our people jeopardized the security of our classified communications. Of course, by that time, we were in the Navy and working with their communications and if we jeopardized our communications, we also jeopardized the Navy's communications. I was in charge of this from '42 to '44.

Q: What was the procedure that they used to teach you?

Rhodes: There were written courses and then there were problems. They will assign you right along with an expert working on real problems, so in that way you advance as you learn these problems, then you go into the practical experience. Practical experience is much more difficult to get into than just solving problems out of a book, especially when you get the tougher types. In other words, if someone is using an Orphan Annie-type cipher, that's pretty easy. My grade school daughter sent for an Orphan Annie code, and I was taking the course at the time, and I asked her to give me a message in it. About a half an hour later I gave her back the plaintext. She didn't understand how anyone could possibly read that. That was a very simple type code, a substitution code. I was sure it would be simple or they couldn't send it out like that.

Q: How did you know that you had broken something? This is the thing that has always puzzled me about the whole thing. Couldn't a highly intelligent person devise a code that would translate, that would come out in plaintext saying different things depending on how you cracked the code? You could think that you had cracked the code. It says one thing and now it says something else that you think is perfectly understandable but it really would also translate into something else using a different combination.

Rhodes: The big thing is when you solve, you know you've solved it on that particular message but then if the same solution will enable you to read all other messages of that day, then you know that you've got it because you know already which messages were sent in that code. You're able to look at the coded text and decide which code it's been sent in. There are indications. There have to be indications there so that the man knows which code to set up. When we say code, it's generally in ciphers. There's substitution, transposition, or machine ciphers, so there's many different ways and you've got to have an indicator on it to indicate what code they're using. Once you've solved someone's code, you know their habits. It's just like an Indian tracking down an animal. A lot of it is learning a person's habits, finding out just what type of things they do. If you can solve one message, you can read everything he's sent that day. Now if it has to be a code, then it's just like substituting one word for another. It takes a lot longer to solve that than it does an enciphered message because you only get a part of it. Maybe there's five thousand code groups meaning different things. If you have five hundred you can probably read about ninety-five percent of everything he sends. Even though you have five thousand possible meanings, most of his messages will be sent in not more than five hundred, so you will read it except for a few unknown code spaces, and then you can guess what that means. If you've got quite a few messages where you guessed, you can pretty well come down and say this is exactly what that means.

Q: You talk about your practical experiences. Where did you practice?

Rhodes: You can practice on each other, as far as that is

concerned. Send each other messages. Whoever it is, they have developed certain habits, and what you get in studying it is messages which maybe were sent many years ago, and it's up to you to solve them and if you know that --in the first place they let you know that these messages were sent by the same people-- you solve one and then you know what to look for in the other one.

Q: Another thing that's always bothered me about it is around this period of time we were tackling the Japanese code, and I could see where it would be a problem just tackling the code but you're also confronted with a foreign language at the same time. Were the people fluent in Japanese who were also working on these codes?

Rhodes: No. Actually you work on probability. Almost everything is probability and as soon as you get the correct probability, the machine you're working on will probably stop and lay it out. You see, it's mathematical as much as anything.

Q: In other words you weren't striving to understand what was said, you were just trying to figure out what the essence of the code was?

Rhodes: Oh no. We were trying to make the code come out in the probability of plaintext. You know the probability there of plaintext. What you try to do is get this lined up in such a way that it has the same probability as plaintext. That's difficult because you've almost got to recreate the machine to put it out. There's where you—where a lot of intelligence, and when I say intelligence I mean information, can be a help. The more information you have, what someone's using, how they're using it, and so forth, the more likely that you will be successful. You can't just go in cold on something which is very difficult. As I say, you've got to watch for mistakes that somebody makes, and when you catch the mistake, you've got to make use of that information which you get. It's generally a long drawn-out process before you can really go into something that's real difficult. They are a race of brilliant people, so don't think that it was easy for those people who were working on it.

Q: What kind of people, from your experience, were involved in cryptanalysis?

Rhodes: I would say that they were somewhat of the scientist type. In fact they would be satisfied to work by themselves, and work on problems for long periods at a time before they finally made the solution. Generally they are mathematicians because all of this type of work deals in probability, and if you reach the proper mathematical formula, that's what you're looking for. So you've got to have a person with a scientific bent who'se just interested in solving a problem.

Q: Was it a game to the people that you were associated with? I mean was it sort of like playing horses, or chasing women?

Rhodes: It's mostly a feeling that you will not accept defeat. You might be rebuffed, but you're going to work on it and there's a certain stubborness along with it because it takes an awful lot for a person to keep working and working on a problem when it appears that they are no nearer a solution than they were a long time ago.

Q: When you talk about time, what kind of time is involved? Is it days, weeks?

Rhodes: On the simple ones, of course, a days time is a long time. A difficult one, years may be spent before you really get a break.

Q: If it takes years, what good has come of it because everything is probably water under the bridge by the time you solve it.

Rhodes: If nothing else, a person like that would get satisfaction out of finally solving a very tough problem. And really, that's about all they're working for is satisfaction, as far as they are personally concerned. A person of that type derives a great deal of satisfaction from solving a difficult problem. When they are so tenacious, even if they are doing it only for a hobby, they're probably the best type of person to put on a problem like that because, generally, they have to have very much of a scientific bent as well as a mathematical. They have to study and catalogue everything they have, and get information from every source possible, then study it in a scientific way. It's strictly a science but the tools of the science are mathematics. You have to have an orderly brain and a mathematical brain.

Q: Were you a chess player before you --

Rhodes: Yes, I did an awful lot of chess playing --anything that has to do with probability I've always been interested in.

Q: If you broke a code, discovered the secret, was there any way that the people that sent the code knew that you broke it other than the fact if it were something like they said they were going to invade a certain point, but you were ready for them when it came, was there any other way that they had of knowing?

Rhodes: No, unless you were so elated that maybe you would send a message to your higher headquarters informing them of that, and they had already broken your code and they read it. That's the danger of that type of thing. If you can break theirs, you can assume that they can break yours.

Q: Did people know that you were doing this kind of work?

Rhodes: They knew what school I was going to. There was no secret about that because I was designated that right in my orders which were not classified.

Q: What I'm getting at is if there were very few qualified people in the country at this time which was the beginning of the war and during the war, and obviously this type of work was one of the key things of our war effort, were you in jeopardy? If the other side could get to you and your associates, then it would solve the problem to get rid of the mind that figured all this out, and they're safe. Were you ever in jeopardy?

Q: I would say that a great many people are in jeopardy at the time of war, if a person could get to them who wanted to do them in. For example: me being in charge of all Coast Guard classified communications, if they could get the information I had or cause me to have an accident of some kind, naturally it would be a real feather in their hat. Generally speaking, when you're in a war like that, we don't have very many people in this country who would be interested in doing that. If they could get me off by myself, they probably would. But there's a great many people who they would like to have accidents. Of course, communications, especially classified communications are the most important of all because if you can read somebody's thoughts when he thinks he's perfectly safe, it's very dangerous for him. That is one reason why it's good to be able to tap someone's telephone when he thinks he's perfectly secure because you are reading things that he would never say to you to your face and you are finding out a great deal about him. That is one thing that you learn when you read somebody's communications, you not only are finding what he is saying in that message but you are also learning a great deal of what his thinking is, what his plans are, and why. You're learning a lot more than just the information in that particular message.

Q: When you were selected for the school, I imagine it takes more than desire. They can send out a message and say, "Who wants to go to this school?" And I could say, "Gee, that sounds like it would be interesting." But that doesn't mean that I'm qualified. How did they determine that you could do the work? Did they test you in any way?

Rhodes: No, except that they knew people who I had worked with and we would make up problems for each other just for fun, as a hobby. If you are able to solve their problem and you're willing to spend your off time doing that kind of thing, that's the kind of person they are looking for. He's got to be willing to do all this work as a hobby. No one would ever do it just to get payed for it. They've got to want to do it, they've got to enjoy it. It does take a particular type of person, there's no doubt about it. There were a few of us together who would make up problems for each other. One of them, as I say, went to school ahead of me. Another one took special courses and then went to the Academy as a permanent instructor. He never went to sea again. He was the scientific type who wanted to do nothing but scientific work and deal in scientific subjects. So that is the type of people who go into that kind of thing.

Q: How long did the school last?

Rhodes: Two years.

Q: That's a long time. Did you have any other duties at that time or were you solely devoted to --

Rhodes: No, I was solely devoted to that and, of course, it required a great deal of study. I studied at night practically all my life and weekends were taken up with it as well as the time at the school itself. Anyone who wants to go to school must study outside of school, in this type of work especially. It takes a great deal of time.

Q: If there were only three people there when you were there, and it took two years, were there only three cryptanalysis that were produced in a three year period? How many were there before that?

Rhodes: Very few. A place like that doesn't graduate very many students --very few graduates.

Q: If there were so few, how did they let you get away? You went back to the Coast Guard. I would think that during a key period like that they would lock you up in a room and start shoving messages under the door.

Rhodes: Probably the work that I was doing to protect our own classified communications was considered more important than trying to break down some other messages and also perhaps they felt the people assigned to that work were pretty well qualified to handle it. In fact, the Coast Guard officer who I said preceeded me on this work was in charge of Coast Guard work at that time. So there wouldn't have been a vacancy for me to move in. We were both about the same rank. There was one graduate protecting our own communications, the other graduate looking into any possibilities of using information from other communications which would be valuable. It developed that a lot of information was gathered in that way.

Q: As far as protecting communications, which you were doing, as you say there were different grades of safety and dangerousness of a code. Did you use different grades of codes according to how vital the material was?

Rhodes: Yes. The big thing there was small commands didn't have the complicated code. If you were sending a message, say, to a Lifeboat Station, you'd have to send it in the very simplest code because that's all that he has available but you probably wouldn't expect any enemy to intercept it or be able to decipher it either. But if they did, it wouldn't be very important, otherwise you wouldn't send it to him.

Q: They wouldn't take one of their key men to decode it?

Rhodes: Exactly.

Rhodes # 5 - 208 -

Q: Were you sending all your messages in code?

Rhodes: No. There was a great deal of plaintext that went out even during the war but there was a terrific volume of coded messages that went out and you had to handle that. I had to handle all the coded messages and all the decoded messages. We had to take care of that. I had to see to it that every one in the Coast Guard handled them properly so they wouldn't give the enemy an opportunity to break in on them.

Q: How did you go about training the people who were actually going to handle the information and actually take care of the codes. I imagine there must have been some way that you taught them.

Rhodes: Of course, our Academy graduates were pretty well trained ahead of time, and also every now and then they had practice where you make sure that everyone, higher echelon as well as lower, know how they must be handled. For example: everyone knows that when it's a classified message, it doesn't make any difference what anyone's rank is, only those who must know the information, gets it. So you narrow the possibilities of that being compromised by seeing to it that no more people know the contents of this message than must have it. That's the type of training that you would give to people who were handling it. Then make sure they get a signature every time they give someone a message, make sure they sign for it. They keep track of every copy that they make and then if the officer who got it doesn't want it any more, it's up to him to give it back so they can cross his name off the list. He knows it but he doesn't have a copy of it anymore.

Q: Did you get buried in a morass of paper work?

Rhodes: You're inclined to do that but that's something you've got to avoid because in a thing like that, you can't get buried in a morass of paper work because you've got to know where every paper is. There again that's one reason for keeping the classified communications as small as possible. You should not send a coded message if the thing can be sent in plaintext --that's one of the worst things you can do. It's got to be real important information in order to justify putting it in code in the first place. That's why you definitely should have most of your messages in plaintext --nothing that might help the enemy but it would bog you down so much if you sent all of it in code. You'd jeopardize your code and you couldn't operate that way because a lot of messages you have to get through so they can take action on it in a hurry.

Q: How many people were working with you in the Coast Guard when you were doing that?

Rhodes: I had about twenty or thirty people most of the time. We were training SPARS at the time, women Coast Guardsmen, and those that were being sent as classified communication officers throughout the district, I gave them about a month extra training. They would actually handle messages, coding and decoding, and so forth, and I made sure that they knew all the details of the work because they were going to replace officers who were trained in doing that when they got out in the district. There was comparatively few of them. I would say there was about an average of ten a month, for a while, until we filled all the billets.

Q: You must have been a popular man in headquarters. You certainly knew everything that was going on.

Rhodes: Yes, but on the other hand I was probably the quietest man. I didn't dare to talk because it was hard for me to remember which was classified and which wasn't.

Interview # 6 with Capt. Earl Rhodes, USCG (ret.)

Takoma Park, Maryland　　　　　　　　　　　August 2, 1970

Biography　　　　　　　　　　　　　　　　by Peter Spectre

Mr. Spectre:　Captain, in our last interview we talked about your experiences at signal school and also your assignment to Coast Guard headquarters in Washington. What was the name of the school that you went to?

Capt. Rhodes:　I've forgotten the proper name for it. I will have to look that up.

Q:　It's name signified something else than what actually took place. Was that intentional?

Rhodes:　No, I think that definitely the name was quite general in order to keep some curious people from asking questions.

Q:　About how many people, during the war, graduated from this school, say from 1940 to '45? I know there were three in your class.

Rhodes:　After I graduated from the class, we somewhat lost contact with the people there. The war was going on and, generally speaking, anyone who didn't have to know, didn't need to know, was not informed, therefore we did not have access to the people working with that organization any longer, and I was not informed of future

Rhodes # 6 - 211a

developments.

Q: Could you make a guess? Do you think maybe ten or fifteen?

Rhodes: Of course, during the war, you can imagine that there were several schools going on in various places in the world. The experts were sent to different places where their services could be used to best advantage.

Q: Was there any question in your mind, or anybody's mind that after you attended the school that you might not be assigned to Coast Guard headquarters, that you might be assigned somewhere else?

Rhodes: It was almost sure that I would be assigned to Coast Guard headquarters as soon as I graduated. That was assumed right along. We weren't quite sure what particular job I might get over there, but necessity determined that. I was assigned where they felt that I could be the most value, and I believe that they were right. That's my own conclusion.

Q: What was your exact title?

Rhodes: I was Officer in Charge of Communications Security. I believe that's what they called it at that time.

Q: Did somebody have that position before you or was this a new--?

Rhodes: This was a new title.

Q: How was it done before that? Was anything done or was it a new concept?

Rhodes: Yes, they did it but it was generally an additional duty of the assistant Chief of Communications. He just saw that he was not able to handle it. It was one of the most important things that there was at that particular time because if it wasn't handled properly there was going to be a great many mistakes made and certain publications lost, perhaps. You worked very, very, carefully to see that everyone was aware of the proper handling of communications publications at that time.

Q: You started there in '42?

Rhodes: That's correct.

Q: I know that the Coast Guard became under the administrative control of the Navy in '41, but I would imagine that when you came it was still in the state of flux as to the channels that were used and how you'd reorganize --this would be the Navy. What was it like? Were there problems in working with the Navy in the beginning?

Rhodes: There were many problems involved because we had to work very closely with the Navy and maintain communications with them all the time. We were manning naval ships; we were expanding all the time, therefore we had to keep training new officers because every ship had to have a qualified communications officer, at least, and others qualified as his assistant. They all had to handle these highly classified devices, therefore it was up to us to issue them to all the Coast Guard units and at the same time, make sure the people you issued them to were properly informed and instructed. That was a tremendous big job because we had to keep very closely involved with the Navy at all times, and at the same time make sure that we were instructing our people how to take care of naval publications and highly classified devices.

Q: Were Coast Guard procedures in communications similar to the Navy's before the war? We talked before about the matter that the Coast Guard engaged in a different type of communications than the Navy. Was it significantly different before the war so that during the war you needed time to catch up?

Rhodes: The devices we used in communicating with the Navy were generally naval devices and therefore somewhat different than we would normally communicate with when we were just sending messages back and forth between Coast Guard units. However it wasn't so difficult to learn to use these devices, but the main thing was to see to it when we received so many additional devices that we had proper storage for them and that we took very good care of them. In peace time the people got to feel that if something happened, only the illicit operators would learn what our plans were, but in war time, it's far more important to guard all these communications and devices because if anyone just gets one of those devices then they have the whole system. So we had to tighten up and make sure that all our people understood not only the communications officers but the commanding officers, that the most important thing of all was to protect classified communications devices.

Q: How did you go about doing this for actual practice?

Rhodes: We would send directives out and also go around visiting the various district commanders where we had communications officers to make sure that their communications officers were aware of how important it was to handle these new systems that they were being issued, and also they would have direct contact with the commanding officers and the communications officers of various ships that they would be issuing these devices to, to make sure that they understood how important it was to guard these devices and to follow the instructions that went along with them.

Q: Did you have any problem cases?

Rhodes: There were always problem cases. Some were much more serious than others. So far as I recall, we had no real serious loss or compromise that came to my knowledge. However, there were many minor cases where people slipped up in not following directions to the letter, and we had to see to it that whenever anything like that happened that there were proper disciplinary action taken. At least we recommended it and they followed through with it.

Q: I remember when I was studying the whole business, they scared us to death about what was going to happen to us if we slipped up in any area.

Rhodes: That's very true. No matter if it's your best friend, you've got to make an example to make sure that others are very, very careful that something like that doesn't happen to them. It's too bad but this is the most important thing you can have. If your communications are secure, you're in a good way to be able to fool the enemy. If he knows everything you're saying and you don't even know that he knows it, it's very, very dangerous. You've got to be sure that all of the instructions are carried out all the way through.

Q: How did the Navy determine what the Coast Guard was going to have? Did you have any say or make any recommendations?

Rhodes: Yes, actually though, this was decided more on operational level than it was on a communication level. In other words, if they wanted to send certain type messages to a particular ship, and they wanted all ships of that type to receive the message, they had to make sure that they had the proper equipment. So it was the Navy

Rhodes # 6 - 216 -

that determined what our ships would have, because it was the Navy that was sending messages to them. If they wanted our ships to get those messages, they had to see to it that they had the proper devices.

Q: What was the over-all function of Coast Guard communications? If the Navy has it's own communications organization, during the war if they, the Coast Guard, were working directly with the Navy, in other words, messages are coming from the Navy to the Coast Guard as if the Coast Guard ships were Navy ships, then what they, in essence, have done is eliminated the Coast Guard headquarters communications organization because they are going directly to the units which before were under Coast Guard communications. So what happened to headquarters communications?

Rhodes: Actually, it was greatly built up. We took in a great number of commercial vessels, fishing vessels, yachts, and so forth, who were out along the coast watching for submarines, and ready to rescue people in case a vessel was sunk. We had to communicate with them.

Q: The Navy didn't?

Rhodes: The Coast Guard did that. In other words, this is the type of communications that the Coast Guard had to handle that the Navy was not at all involved in. We also had our Lifeboat Stations up and down the coast and our small boats that we had to communicate with. We also had to maintain search and rescue along the coast because that was very important with the submarines sinking our ships along there. Then we had the beach patrol orders and so forth. We had telephone communications, radio communications all the way along. So it was a great deal of communicating that the Coast Guard had to do with their own units along the coast. That's where our radio stations and air stations and Lifeboat Stations and small vessels were located. We still had our buoy tenders, and so forth, that had to maintain the lights and buoys along the coast.

There were many small operations that the Coast Guard had to beef up its communication to handle them. Also the Coast Guard had to communicate with their own ships as far as certain personell matters, maintenance matters, financial matters, and so forth were concerned. They would have to send a message every now and then and we had a direct tie in with the Navy ground system so that if we had a ship operating with the Navy, we would send the message to the Navy and the naval radio station would get the message to the ship, and vice versa they would come back to us and it would be delivered to our Coast Guard headquarters for deciphering and delivering to whoever needed it.

Q: The Navy was primarily concerned with large seagoing ships with the Coast Guard.

Rhodes: That's true. Operating with the fleet, you might say.

So our vessels assigned to the Navy would receive their messages as other vessels in the fleet would receive them, whereas we had many operating directly under the supervision of the Coast Guard so we had resposibility for the safety and patrol of the coastal areas and also search and rescue, and we had both land and sea items that we were very much involved with. Of course, we were responsible for port security and navigational units that we were installing. So we had a lot of communications going directly to Coast Guard units.

Q: How did all this work at the beginning? It was a drastic change to switch from autonomy, more or less, under the Treasury Department to a second class status, more or less, under the Navy Department. Before, under the Treasury, you operated, more or less, as you needed to and really didn't have to speak to higher authority for day to day operational decisions, whereas it was just the opposite in the Navy. How did you feel and your collegues?

Rhodes: Actually, individuals had a lot more authority than they had back in the Coast Guard because there was rapid promotion, you received a great deal more responsibility and authority than you would have at the same age if there hadn't been a war and you stayed in the Coast Guard and Treasury Department. Therefore the responsibilities were far greater and there was nothing arbitrary about any orders issued. They were standard orders. You were generally in command of your own unit, the vessels would be manned by Coast Guard right from the captain on down, but of course, many of the people you'd have in your crew had just come in to the Coast Guard, they were pretty well greenhorns and you were so busy training your people that you just hoped that you could operate successfully. I would say that, generally speaking, we were very glad that we were with the Navy because they were having the same kind of problems we were. They were having to expand and man their vessels with people who had not been at sea very long. On the whole we got along very, very well with the Navy.

Q: Was radar considered communications?

Rhodes: Some types of radar was, but on the other hand, at the beginning of the war radar was so undeveloped that very few ships had it. It wasn't until close to the end of the war that we really got real good radar on board.

Q: Were you involved in any way in the testing and developing of radar?

Rhodes: No, I wasn't in that. I was interested but I wasn't in the actual working out of the radar.

Q: When did Coast Guard cutters first receive radar?

Rhodes: That was generally towards the latter part of the war.

Q: Were there any ships that had experimental sets?

Rhodes: I'm not sure. At that time, during the war, the Coast Guard was operating with the Navy and they might go into a Navy yard and the Navy install it without my knowledge. It strictly was not handled through communications, that was mostly through engineering and operational requirement. That would not be really a communication MATTER. However there are signals that you can put on radar that you can identify yourself with. That would be the only type of communication device that you could use on it.

Q: There's always things that come out of wars, unfortunately, that turn out to be good things in the future, later years, which is always the thing you hear about most. They say, "Well, it might have been a bloody war, but we learned this and this." What did you learn in communications during that period that was an asset to the Coast Guard and to all communications in general?

Rhodes: Probably the most important was the use of very high frequencies. As they experimented with very high frequencies, then they would go on to higher frequencies, radio frequencies. They had to learn the characteristics of them and they developed some very excellent communications gear. At the end of the war we were using miniture voice radio equipment of very high frequencies that gave us a great deal more communication with small units, between ships and airplanes, and airplanes and the ground that we never could have done if it had not been for expanding the spectrum, so to speak. Of course, radar was one of the developments in these ultra high frequencies and without knowing how to use frequencies in these higher bands, many of these developments could not have been made. I would say that the expansion of the radio spectrum into the high bands were one of the greatest developments of the war. For example all your commercial television, all your mobile units are in the high bands. You never could have had those if it hadn't been for exploring the utility of those bands.

Q: What drove the research people into this? Was it a lack of channels to operate on?

Rhodes: It was a lack of channels on the lower bands. Actually they didn't really know the higher bands were there in many ways. You had to be able to transmit on these bands and receive on them before you could prove that they were there. The old equipment, you never could have developed these bands without developing new equipment that could transmit and receive on these shorter frequencies. Therefore it cost a lot of money to develop communications and equipment that could utilize these bands, which probably would not have been available if it had not been for the war and the need to develop them real rapidly. They were developing them slowly, of course, before the war. They were experimenting, you might say, in a labratory and they would have eventually been developed but it may have taken twenty-five years where it took three, or four, or five years at the time.

Q: There's a question about communications that I've never been able to understand. You're at sea during the war in a Coast Guard cutter, and you're operating in an area where there's not only your side's ships but there's also the enemies' fleet. Everybody's communicating. How do you assign frequencies? I understand how our side does --we say, okay you're going to use that and you're going to use that-- but the enemy, I would assume, would disregard every law and regulation that we would have in favor of their own. If it comes to fighting, then anything goes and that means violating the frequency assignment that might have been worldwide before the war. Were there problems where a ship would be on a frequency and being interferred with by an enemy ship on the same frequency?

Rhodes: The first thing is that out at sea almost all of our ships and the enemy's ships practiced radio silence, whereas in peace time they would be yackety-yacketing all the time. We had methods of sending messages to our ships so that they would not be required to answer back, to maintain radio silence, because just as soon as they opened up on their radio the enemy would know right where they were through radio direction finding, and so forth. We had the same type of equipment, radio direction finding equipment, where you could be listening on various frequencies and immediately locate anything. This was mostly for search and rescue so if they sent a distress signal you could get a location, but you can also locate an enemy ship if he starts operating his radio at sea during war. Generally speaking, then, these ships were quiet at sea, and they had their instructions as to what frequencies to listen to, the frequencies where they would get their messages. Therefore the enemy, without prearrangement with all the ships, couldn't change in frequency because they would be listening on a different frequency and he'd have to order them to shift to a different frequency in order to send on that frequency. Some times they might send a coded message and tell them to shift to a different frequency and we'll transmit you another message on that frequency. Since people are listening on both sides to the whole radio spectrum to intercept anything that is going on --they have special equipment where you can listen to many frequencies at once. It's somewhat of a standard.

Q: I understand your concept there, but say a battle arose. Then everybody would be talking amongst themselves getting a battle line, and so forth because you've already been discovered --you know where they are and they know where you are. Would that problem come up then?

Rhodes: Yes, the only thing is that that's where the development on using the very high frequencies came in. We always communicated among ourselves under these very high frequencies which were only good for line of sight. If a fleet was out there, no one would be able to hear it beyond the horizon. You take the chance that if someone were in sight, he'd know you were there anyhow. So if your radio didn't carry beyond the line of sight, you were fairly safe in using it. This is voice radio where it's perfectly plain. You can get your message across, one captain can talk to the other directly. You get rapid communications and fairly safe communications because of the fact it doesn't go beyond the line of sight, whereas the lower frequencies which they had been using before, there was no limit to how much they might bounce around. That was the big advantage of these very high frequency radio bands --you could have this equipment and talk directly by voice radio to all the ships in sight, but those out of sight would not be able to hear you. It was not only convenient, it was also fairly safe.

Q: You mentioned that you had ways of sending messages to your ships so that they wouldn't have to be answered. How was that worked out? How would you word a message like that?

Rhodes: That would be strictly in code and they would have to decode all the call signs. There would be a call sign to each message and that also would be coded. Every ship would have to receive every message that was sent on this particular frequency. Then they would decode the call sign. The radio room would send these messages to the code room and it would be up to the code officer, communication officer, to decode the call sign and they were only supposed to decode the message that was addressed to them. In that way, no one would know, unless they had the code, who these various messages were addressed to. You would only know after you had received it, after you had decoded the call sign.

Q: Were the call signs in one code and the body of the message in another?

Rhodes: Yes. You'd have a call sign code and you'd have to decode the heading of the message first. Then you would put the message in cipher. In turn the people off the ships and so forth, would have to decode the call sign. If the message was to them, they would have to determine what cipher it was sent in and then decipher it in this other method.

Q: When you're in Washington and sending a message to a Coast Guard cutter in the middle of the Atlantic, how do you know whether they received it? It might be an important message. You don't want them to reply because you don't want their position given away, but how do you know they've got it?

Rhodes: You don't know that in the first place. There's no way of telling without them opening up on a radio until they get into port. It would have to be a very important message that would require that they open up on their radio.

Q: Were there many cases where they didn't get it and you never knew it?

Rhodes: Let's put it this way. There were some cases but in the great majority of cases, a high percentage, they did receive the message and if it was a real important message, you would ask that it be transmitted, or broadcast, several different times. If they didn't pick it up one time, they would pick it up the next.

Q: What's the difference between a code and a cipher?

Rhodes: A code will have a group of letters which may mean a phrase, or may mean a word, or may mean just one letter. You have, say, a group of five letters at random and opposite that in your code book you have your meaning. A cipher means that you generally have one letter or character representing another letter or character in the message. When you cipher it you have the same number of letters in your coded message as you do in the original message itself. It's just a scrambled up bunch of letters and you've got to find out what letter in the code means a certain letter in the plaintext.

Q: What's the hardest to crack?

Rhodes: I would say that the hardest to crack is an enciphered code. First you code your message, and then you encipher that code so you scramble up all those coded --they're no longer in five letter groups. They're all jumbled up. So to decode it, first you have to decipher it using the method they use to cipher it, and then you would have to go to your code book, once you got your regular coded figures and look that up in the book.

Q: Ciphering and deciphering is done by machine, is it not?

Rhodes: It often is, but a great deal of it is done by hand. For example transposition is one of the oldest forms of cipher there is, and also substitution cipher—they have sliding alphabets. You just let one letter equal another letter. That is the simplest type of cipher, the sunbstitution transposition. Then when you go to machines, and so forth, then you make them far more difficult to solve. For example in your regular substitution ciphers, probably "r" will equal "a" all the time. If you say "r" equals "a" then all through the message "r" equals "a". But in machine ciphers, it runs at random and "r" won't equal "a" at all times. In fact it won't equal it any more than once in twenty-six times. It's pretty much at random.

Q: It amazes me that you could figure something like that out. Were they broken that often?

Rhodes: Perhaps sometimes they would forget to encipher their coded message and the guy on the other end couldn't get it, or they found out their mistake, so first they would send it on the air as a regular coded message, and then send the same message as an enciphered message.

Q: Like the Rosetta Stone.

Rhodes: That's right. So if you could solve the one message, you might also have solved their encipherment in another way, and from then on you can read everything they sent.

Q: Is this the type of code that you had to have? Could you sit down with an enciphered code with nothing else, no mistakes made by the other side, no secret document that you picked up somewhere, but just that message, and sit down and come up with an answer?

Rhodes: It's very difficult to tell. You probably couldn't. But you could study it and in studying it you can recognize the mistake. Remember, with as many people that are handling that, there's going to be a mistakes made. There's always mistakes made. Then when they correct their mistakes, you can notice that, and you start to see what they're doing. It's correcting their mistakes often that gives you a clue to what they're actually doing. In the first place, a code has no rhyme or reason to it, it's just an arbitrary coded group representing something else. So when they encipher these coded groups, you couldn't possibly be sure what was going on if you just got the enciphered messages. There isn't any way that you could study just one message. You've got to have a great volume of intercepted messages in order to study them. Then you take the ones that are different from the others, and you find out why they're different. That is really how you break into these things. If everyone did everything right, you'd never get anywhere, except the very simplest type of messages.

Q: What kind of --what's the term that you would use for something that is not a garbled series of letters, but instead of calling a person a man, you'd call him a dog, and a house is a car, that type of thing?

Rhodes: That would be a code.

Q: Were there   that you use recognizable words.

Rhodes: No, they normally would be just five letter groups at random to represent some other thing. On the other hand, what you just said, we had substitution ciphers where one letter represents another letter. Perhaps what you just gave an example of would be a substitution code, where you have one word means another word. That's probably a substitution code.

Q: That would be just about the only thing you could use in voice communications. Did you code and encipher in voice communications?

Rhodes: Generally you didn't, except where, say, you were talking between airplanes and between groups, they would give a code name to the skipper of each ship or plane. Or supposing you were on an operation, talking plaintext all the time, you would give a code name to that whole operation, but everyone in your group knew what it meant, and if the enemy was listening in to it, he would soon be able to tell who was who, and he would know that this other code name was the code of the operation. If he could understand English, he would soon be able to do that.

Q: Were any of your codes broken? I don't mean you individually. [*"Were" crossed out, "Were" handwritten above*]

Rhodes: You can always be suspicious that they were broken. In fact, we worked on breaking them ourselves. If we could break them, we could assume the enemy could.

Q: In other words, you would listen to your own messages?

Rhodes: That's right. When I was going to school in the beginning, before the war actually started, we were assigned the job of trying to break down our own encipherments to our own vessels at sea. I remember one case, it took me about a day before I could break down everything that was being said to a ship, in code.

Q: What did they say?

Rhodes: They changed it in a hurry. To get into it within a days time, they knew that it was not safe to send classified information. And what the ships were doing was sending their positions in this code. It was a cipher, really. You can see, it's that type of thing —you've got to try to break down your own code as well as enemy encipherments to know just how safe you are.

Q: When you were at Coast Guard headquarters from 1942 to '44 how often were you able to break down your own code?

Rhodes: I was not doing that at that particular time. We had another unit that was doing that.

Q: How often could they do it?

Rhodes: So far as I know, they didn't do that at all, unless they came over to the office and got a little bit more information. That's what you've got to watch out for --just how much information do they start out with if they're trying to break your code? If they've got the code book in the first place, and they probably have --

Q: They have to be honest about it though because if they get something the enemy has, and they break the code, they really haven't proved anything.

Rhodes: Actually, they've got to be completely honest or they're no good. Therefore, just how much information can they use? The enemy gets a lot of information that we don't know where he gets it or how, so that helps him a great deal in breaking a code.

Q: You're talking about spies?

Rhodes: That's right. Also we don't analyze all of our messages.

It would take a tremendous amount of time, but the enemy will analyze a great many of our messages and find these mistakes that have been made. When we find a mistake that has been made in our own method, we study that mistake to see if the enemy might have been able to get some hints on it. We definitely do that. But we don't know all the information he has and therefore we don't know where to start from when we try testing our own code and ciphers. If all you have is just what goes over the air, it's very difficult. But if you have some other information on the side, it might be fairly easy to solve these things. Our people, in breaking down our own code, have a great deal of information that the enemy shouldn't have and therefore it's hard to say just how much information you're going to let your own people have before you see whether they can break down your own codes, or not.

Q: How did you protect yourself against spies in your own work?

Rhodes: We always kept all the doors locked. We never let anyone in except when they identified themselves. Of course, anyone in my group had to have the very highest clearance in order to get in or be utilized in my group. We did everything you could think of to play it safe. On the other hand, you could never be sure. You were always watching to see whether there was any hint that someone might be careless or otherwise let out certain information. You had to be continuously on the alert even though all the people you were using had the very highest clearance.

Q: Did you have any problems?

Rhodes: No, I didn't, except through carelessness. Of course, carelessness is just as bad as deliberate --just as soon as you saw anyone do anything careless at all, you'd have to call that to their attention immediately. Then perhaps even use that as a horrible example to teach the other people that is something they've got to be careful of.

Q: What would you do?

Rhodes: It all depends on how serious it is.

Q: What would happen on an average case?

Rhodes: The big thing is, you would call them together and point out how dangerous it is just to let this safe be open for an instant longer than it should be open --you don't dare turn your back on it.

Q: Could anybody go to the brig?

Rhodes: If it were serious. I didn't have serious enough cases because my particular people were very highly trained and you made sure that they got in the right habits all the time. It was nothing really serious, it was merely these little things that would happen that I would give them object lessons as to what might have happened

Rhodes # 6 - 234 -

if the person next to them happened to be untrustworthy. In other words, we had a very strict rule that no one could know anything unless they had need to know it. Even among our own groups we handled it that way. That's the type of thing --if one person was handling something, he couldn't let someone working next to him know what he was doing. You don't want everyone to know everything. They could only know what they must know and they've got to be quiet about that.

Q: If the enemy broke your code, your cipher, is there any way of knowing they've done it other than if a ship's position is discovered and they bomb the ship --do it by an act that shows that they know that something is going to happen at a certain time. Is there any other way?

Rhodes: One of the easiest ways --if you are reading what he is saying, reading his code and ciphers, and he informs another ship of his group that they've found out that your ship is going to be in a certain location at a certain time, and so forth, and practically quotes what they have learned from one of your messages, that is one of the best ways of finding out. And that is generally the way it is found out. The great difficulty is if you don't find it out that way, you go along, dumb and happy, thinking that they don't know what you're doing and all the time they're reading your messages. That is the worst type of false security there is. You keep feeding them information because you don't know they've broken the cipher.

Q: Do you ever send false information to see what they would do? Like tell them the biggest ship in the fleet was going to be in a certain place at a certain time to see if somebody showed up.

Rhodes: We didn't indulge in that particular phase of it, not as high as we worked. That would be perhaps done in operations in the fleet out at sea. They might possibly initiate something like that. On the other hand, you've got to go to great lengths to fool the enemy because the chances are he knows a lot more than you think he does, and it takes more than a message to fool him. For example, when the Japanese came over to Pearl Harbor they transferred all their radiomen off those ships that came over, and put them on other ships around Japan, and had them transmit just about the same as they had been transmitting before the fleet left for Pearl Harbor. So we knew that those ships were still over there at Japan. We kept hearing the radiomen transmit all the time, the same ones. You can get used to hearing a particular radioman transmit on a key, just like playing a musical instrument he has a certain key, and a good radioman will know who they are, in the intelligence game. It's that type of deliberate confusion that they throw into something. That's far more important than just transmitting a message because here these people had been transmitting for months over there and they continued to do it just exactly as they had been before, but they weren't on their own ships. They had been taken off their own ships which were heading toward Pearl Harbor, and they kept up this communication back and forth, making us think that those ships were still over there.

Q: That's a wild trick.

Rhodes: It's that type of thing that is very clever and quite often it works out.

Q: What was life like in Washington at that time? We've spent a lot of time talking about the work that you did, and what was happening in the war. What was it like in Washington for you, how did you get on, how did the war affect your private life?

Rhodes: For one thing, I didn't have very much time that I could devote to social functions, so as a result, my social life outside of my home and my office, was practically nil. I just bought my own home, just off MacArthur Blvd, between MacArthur Blvd. and Foxhall Road on 49th Street --so between my home and my office, and I practically lived in my office a great deal of the time, it was very simple. Of course, due to the fact that I had to go to my office at all times, I always had a parking space right down there so I would drive back and forth. I wasn't troubled too much about the gasoline ration because I had to use my car therefore I was able to get what I needed. On the other hand, I wasn't making trips so therefore I didn't need anything extra. At that particular stage there was very little rationing or anything of that sort, but of course, there were a lot more people in Washington every day --it was starting to get crowded.

Q: How many hours did you work?

Rhodes: I would generally work maybe ten or twelve hours during the day at the office and often I would go back at odd hours just to make sure that things were going all right, and to make sure that they would never know when I might pop in on them.

Q: Here comes the old man?

Rhodes: That's right. Then I also would take home problems that I had and do certain paper work at home. It was more than a full time job because my office had to operate seven days a week, night and day. It kept me plenty busy, there's no doubt about that.

Q: What kind of rules did you use on how much you were going to work? I would imagine that depending upon each person that you could interpret the work that you were doing. It was either an eight hour day, or a twelve hour day, or a sixteen hour day. You have to compromise somewhere. How did you arrive at --

Rhodes: I didn't do it deliberately. I did it as the work called for it. As I say, I would maybe wake up in the middle of the night and decide this was a good time to go down to the office. That way it was at random. I didn't want to fall in any pattern. I didn't have to be in my office all day. I could spend part of the day and part of the night with each group. I'd have different watches and watch officers on at various time of day and night so I'd make a point to be there for awhile during each one.

Q: Was it divided up into three watches?

Rhodes: Yes. In that way my assistants had to be there during their particular scheduled time but if I got down there and found out something that I didn't like what they did, or didn't understand what they had done, I would call them in even though they were not on watch, to explain what had happened.

Q: How did Coast Guard headquarters run?

Rhodes: They had just moved from the old Liberty Loan Building to new quarters down at 13th and E, the old Southern Railway Building.

Q: The Liberty Loan Building is down by 14th Street?

Rhodes: 14th Street Bridge, right near the Mint down there.

Q: How many people would you say?

Rhodes: They expanded greatly when they came over from Southern

Railway. It gave them, perhaps, five or six times more space than they had at the old building. They kept filling it up and filling it up and finally they had to expand into other areas. However, I never knew the details of all that because I was behind locked doors a great deal of the time down there and although I could see the expansion and see the results of it, so far as numbers was concerned, I was not involved in that at all.

Q: What about Washington itself?

Rhodes: There again, Washington was expanding very, very rapidly. They were occupying all different types of buildings at that time. They built the Pentagon and many other buildings they completed, and all of the temporary buildings; and they had all the builders who were building these buildings plus the people who were coming in to work and so forth, it made Washington very over crowded at that particular time. It was not what you'd call a pleasant place to live at that time, because of the over crowded conditions. On the other hand, very seldom did you hear anyone kicking in those days. They were all anxious to do whatever they could, so it was pleasant, as far as I was concerned. I never heard any grousing about these conditions.

Q: Did you enjoy the kind of work that you were doing?

Rhodes: Yes, I did. One thing, I felt it was of supreme

importance, and regardless of how tough you think a job is, it's a lot easier to put yourself out and work long hours if you think it's important, and as a result I really enjoyed it or I wouldn't have asked for that type of work in the first place. You're looking for problems all the time, and as long as you keep your eyes out for things that are out of the ordinary, it's a lot easier to catch them, and as long as you like it --work that you like is not hard work.

Q: Were you one of sailors who couldn't wait to get back to sea, though? Just about every person you interview says, "Well, I had a shore assignment and it was nice to get there and after a few months I couldn't wait to get back to sea."

Rhodes: No, I was not that. On the other hand, toward the latter part, where I figured I had things pretty well organized and we were coasting along, I asked to get to sea many times before they finally assigned me to sea. I didn't want the war to be over without my having any sea duty. So early in 1944 they did give me a sea assignment, but I asked for it many times before that.

Q: How were assignments made at that time? Before the war, a lot of it was rotation --stay here for a few years-- that's the way it's done now. You know, you get an assignment, you practically know how long you're going to be here. You might not know where you're going, but you know how long you're going to be there. During the war, was it done the same way or was it done by the needs?

Rhodes: It was done mostly because of the expansion. In other words, they would assign certain officers, say, to a group of ships, and after they had had experience on those ships perhaps in particular landings, then the junior officers, when they would start manning other vessels, take those with experience and make them in charge of the new vessels, and put other officers who were coming up to relieve those experienced officers. So there was a great deal of rotation but most of it was caused by expansion. Everyone, as they got a little bit of experience, they would also get a promotion and go up to larger ships and so forth.

Q: The way you explain that, I think I see a tendency to have real specialists. If you're a junior officer on a landing ship, for example, then the next logical thing would be exec on another landing ship, and then CO on a landing ship. Is that the way it happens?

Rhodes: No, it's really not. You might be exec on a landing ship, and then the next job you might be exec on a destroyer escort. The next time you might be navigator on a large transport. He would have different types of duty. In other words, we would have landing crafts, we would have destroyer escorts, we would have attack transports, both cargo and personnel, and then we'd have just personnel transports, operating them for the Navy. Each one of them would call for a great many different types of rank and experience and they had to mix up the reserves. People who came in from the outside were commissioned and the people who came up from the ranks in the Coast Guard and were commissioned, they had to consider what their experiences had been. At the same time they had to put general duty officers in command positions so that they could utilize all this cross section of experience to the best advantage. It was a very difficult personnel problem, but on the whole, with the pressures that were on, people did much better jobs than you'd ever think they were capable of doing. I was surprised; I know many other people I've talked to were pleasantly surprised to see how well people react when they have pressure on them. They will often surprise themselves and do a better job than you thought they were capable of doing. That was the pleasant part of the war ~~shore~~ experience of most of us was that we found that many of these people, not out of college very long, OCS, do outstanding jobs. You'd think it would require a great deal of experience for a man to do that, sea going experience. Maybe they hadn't been to sea very much at all before they proved that they were very capable.

Q: Since you spent so much time in Washington during the war, and you're also here in Washington during another war --it's hard to believe, but we are in a war-- what differences do you see? The differences between the second World War, the people's attitudes and how business was conducted, and so forth, and now. What lesson do you see?

Rhodes: Actually, when you come right down to it, there was

almost as much agitation against getting involved in the war before we got involved in the second World War, as there is now. There is great feeling against getting in any kind of war, but once we got in it, in those days, we were in it, and everyone was in the same boat. Of course, it was so serious that no one could be sure what would be the outcome. Generally, after we were in it, everyone was trying to do his best to make sure that their efforts payed off, working together. Now, probably as much due to the undeclared feature of this war, and many people thinking it was just a brush fire type of thing that no one that they would know would get involved in, and then find out that it developed into a much more serious thing, and many of them aren't called upon to do anything about it --they're just having life as usual with no rationing, no nothing-- as a result they go about their own selfish way. It's very distasteful to watch, the way some people react to it, and yet, when you realize that many boys are over there being killed and injured, it is a very distasteful thing to see the way some people react to the whole situation.

Q: Would you characterize Washington, during the second World War, as in a crisis frame of mind, whereas now it isn't?

Rhodes: It was to a great extent then because we all felt we had to build up to fight off the thing, in other words, there was a great fear among some people that the Germans might bomb Washington the same as we went over to bomb Tokyo. It would be possible. It was very personal among many people that they were in danger right here in Washington. Certainly there's no feeling like that now. I think that is one reason why people don't have the feeling that they have to buckle down and do everything they can. During those days everyone had doubts whether they would be living a few years hence.

Q: Tell me about your new assignment.

Rhodes: I was assigned as prospective executive officer of a brand new ship that was being built at Kearney, New Jersey. It was to be named the GENERAL MEIGS, after the large troop transport. It was to have a crew of about six hundred men, manned by the Coast Guard. It was our job to train the crew and have it ready to go aboard, everyone knowing their assignment and so forth, by the time the ship was ready to go in the water.

Q: How far in advance were you assigned there before it was actually in commission?

Rhodes: I believe I was assigned there around the first of April, and it seems to me that it went in commission around June. There was a nucleus crew assigned first and we went down, looked it over, and got acquainted, the captain, the engineer, the executive officer, and a few of the other key rank.

Q: Who was the captain?

Rhodes: George McKean. Then I, as executive officer, was sent up to Newport and given certain key ranks, and then they sent the rest of the prospective crew up there. I had to organize the crew, write up the ship's organization bills, and so forth, and we made sure that all the men had target practice on the type of guns they would be using up there, and knew how to maintain the guns. Engineers, in general, would go to engineering school on the type of engines the ship would have, and type of equipment. So we organized the ship, you might say, living in barracks up there, and went through our paces up there as though we were living aboard ship. Everybody knew where their assignment would be, what it would be.

Q: You said that you wrote up the organization bills for the ship. Where do you begin? How do you do something like that?

Rhodes: We had standard books that you could go on. It would differ a great deal from the ship you were going on but you would have, at least, a standard example to go on. With that you had to organize your own ship. You have to give numbers and names to each man. First you'd have the organization book and you'd assign numbers to each job. Then you'd have to assign rates to each number, and then eventually you'd have to assign names to the numbers, the names and the rates corresponding.

Q: It must have been really tough to do.

Rhodes: Yes. That's when I was in charge of assigning the men to the various courses of training, and so forth. I had to get all that done, ready to go aboard the ship. When the ship was ready for us to go aboard, we went from Newport down there, and went aboard, and they gave us ten days down the Chesapeake Bay for shakedown, and loaded up with troops for the European theater. A lot of people don't realize how complicated a ship like that can be -- a floating hotel-- you've got to take care of all the passengers, feed them, keep the place clean. At the same time you've got to be able to take the ship and navigate it.

Q: How well made were the ships? You're the first person I've talked to who stepped aboard a brand new ship built during the war. Were there bugs in it?

Rhodes: There were, but actually that ship never missed a lick. We were always able to make our cruises on time. I would say she was very well built. It had the most modern machinery and equipment. We would only have temporary failures and the engineer would generally be able to fix it up in very short order. On the whole, I think that, being war time, they did a marvelous job in building that ship.

Q: That was Federal ship building?

Rhodes: Yes. Federal ship building.

Q: It seems that a lot of shakedown cruises and a lot of invasion preparations were done on the Chesapeake Bay. It seems to me that the Chesapeake Bay is a unique place, that it might be the wrong place to go on shakedown cruises and to go on invasion practice landings, which was done all the time. Practically the whole Chesapeake Bay was used for the North African invasion practice, the Normandy, and Sicily, and yet the range of the tide is minimal there, there are only waves to speak of. How was it justified to use that as a training ground when it really didn't have the conditions that you would probably encounter?

Rhodes: One thing, you had to have a place to maneuver as though you were out at sea. You had to be able to turn around and make various maneuvers. With all the submarines off the coast, they didn't want us to do it out in the open ocean. So this was protected water and really it's about the only protected water on the East Coast where you can maneuver a large ship. Actually what we had to learn was make sure that each man knew his duties aboard ship, knew how to lower the boats and hoist the boats, knew how to fight fires, knew how to abandon ship or any other reason, make sure that all the guns would fire properly, and the men knew how to operate them. We had to hold all these drills and it made very little difference whether you had real rough weather or you had choppy weather in the Chesapeake Bay. You're really testing out your men and equipment. You had to anchor, make sure your anchor equipment was working, you had to screen your paravanes. If you had to go through mine fields, you wanted to make sure your men knew how to operate them, and that they would operate properly. You wanted to maneuver the ship to make sure that the rudder wasn't going to stick over to one side or the other when you make a sharp turn. There was all kinds of things that we had to do to test the men and the equipment and once everyone knew what they were supposed to do under certain conditions, then you felt that you could go to sea with them.

Q: I could see in your type of ship, it wouldn't be a problem, but I do remember talking to Admiral O'Neill, for instance, who was telling me that he was on a transport in the North African invasion and the Sicily invasion, and they did all of their boat landings in Chesapeake Bay before they went, and when they got to North Africa, they had entirely different conditions for landing than they had in the Chesapeake. There was very little tide change and there was no pounding surf on the beach, or anything like this, but they did land in North Africa in pounding surf. This is what always bothered me about the whole business --I guess it's really a trade out, whether you want to get sunk by a submarine while your practicing or whether you want --

Rhodes: That's right. If you had large vessels off the coast, with these landing operations, one torpedo could really cause a lot of deaths out there. I really think, along with Admiral O'Neill that after you practice in Chesapeake Bay, you probably should go then and land on a beach sometime in real tough conditions. But you can't expect to land on a beach in tough conditions if you've never experienced it in training. We lost an awful lot of boats and equipment, and some lives, I'm sure, because of not having rigorous enough training.

Q: He told me that in that first landing they lost every boat that they had. They got everybody ashore but they couldn't get the supplies ashore. They were very lucky because they captured Casablanca so they could unload in Casablanca when the troops landed. If they hadn't captured that city they probably would have been in a big jam.

Rhodes: Yes, because the men without supplies and ammunition could not have held off an attack of any severity.

Q: Where was your first voyage?

Rhodes: Our first voyage was to pick up troops in Hampton Roads and unload them at Naples, Italy.

Q: Was this during the Italian campaign?

Rhodes: Yes, it was while the Anzio beach head was going on, in fact. On our return trip, we took off a lot of people who had been on the Anzio beach head. I remember we had three Army nurses which had been on the Anzio beach head all the time and they were in a complete state of shock. I had them eat at my table to try to make it as pleasant as possible. I still remember how they might jump if they heard a noise or anything like that. It just seemed like every bit of life had been drained out of them from what they'd gone through. It was that time that we were over there when the Anzio beach head was still going on and they were evacuating the wounded, and so forth.

Q: You brought Army troops over?

Rhodes: We brought replacements of all kinds. They were never organized replacements, generally, just whoever they wanted to load the ship up with. For example, we had to over load the ship to such an extent that we had five hundred Air Force pilots, young second lieutenants who had just gotten their wings, over there that had to ride in troop quarters. There wasn't enough officer space to put them in. This was real urgent times in those days to send five hundred commissioned officers that had to live in regular troop bunks.

Q: You went over in a convoy?

Rhodes: No. We invariably ran by ourselves, singly. We had just escort enough to break us off our port, and then we would zig zag our way, singly, over there. They would pick us up then to get us through Gibraltar and then we'd run singly from there on to Naples.

Q: Why was that?

Rhodes: Because we had enough speed to outrun the submarines, and it would probably be safer and we could make faster cruises by going alone because they wouldn't want to assign too many submarines to get one ship. By zig-zagging with our speed, they would practically have to run on the surface to do any damage to us, and we hoped that our gun fire would be enough to discourage that.

Q: It must have been a lonely feeling.

Rhodes: It was. That's why I say with five thousand passengers and a crew of six hundred, and you're completely on your own --if you had to abandon ship, there wouldn't have been anybody anywhere near you. As a result of that, it kept us on our toes.

Q: Did you ever sight any submarines or get any indication that there were any around?

Rhodes: We had the hunter-killer groups quite active around Gibraltar a few times when we went in. We heard later that they had got a submarine right near us at one time. I know they were blowing up a lot of water around there with depth charges and so forth, but those hunter-killer groups apparently were very good because they kept them from bothering us. One time in the English Channel, going over from England to France, this was in a convoy, heavily guarded, and yet apparently some German submarines got underneath the convoy, and the escorts were running down the ranks of the convoy dropping depth charges to keep the submarines confused so they couldn't pick out a ship target to fire there torpedoes.

Q: You came from Naples and went back to --

Rhodes: Back to the United States with the wounded.

Q: Where was your home port? Was it Norfolk?

Rhodes: Part of the time it was Norfolk and later on it was New York, but we kind of alternated between Norfolk and New York. We had one of our sailors shot by a shore patrol, and it happened that he was completely innocent and the crew was quite upset. This happened down at Norfolk and from then on the tendency was to assign us to New York because there was a very strong feeling among the crew about this particular shore patrol who had shot one of our completely innocent men and there were several of our men with him, knowing that he was innocent.

Q: What happened?

Rhodes: It's hard to tell just what actually happened but there had been a fracas and our men happened to come along after the fracas was over and apparently the shore patrol said something to him, he might have said something back --anyhow it was a misunderstanding apparently, but a misunderstanding can cause a lot of hard feelings. That's about the size of it, so after that we generally went to New York.

Q: Where were your next orders?

Rhodes: I've forgotten just how many trips we took over there at that time but shortly after that first trip we were assigned to go to Brazil to pick up Brazilian troops to take them over to the Naples area. The first trip was made with our sister ship, MANN, which was Navy manned, a transport of the same type. We made two other trips besides that first one down to Rio to pick up Brazilian troops. One trip we took wounded back from the Italian theater down to Rio.

Q: It's probably a big blur because it sounds like routine work.

Rhodes: It was quite exciting as far as the Brazilians were concerned because we had to put up special signs in Portuguese what they should do. Many of them were not used to using the type of equipment aboard ship. They wouldn't know what showers were for, wouldn't know what wash basins were for, a toilet was for, so we really had a job keeping the ship clean that trip. They were generally much more sea sick than our own troops. If the sea kicked up they really stayed to their bunk.

Q: How much turn around time did you have?

Rhodes: We would have, perhaps, a week or ten days in the States, but over in Naples we had to completely unload the ship of passengers or cargo, clean up the ship, then load it with wounded, stretcher cases, and so forth, and completely load the ship and get out of there within twenty-four hours. That was a fast turn around.

Q: Did you carry a lot of doctors?

Rhodes: Yes, we had our own medical force. They were public health service doctors. I remember Dr. Griffey had the rank of a captain, Dr. Hoover who was a two stripper, and Dr. Tench who was a j.g. Whenever we took wounded back, several Army medical platoons would be assigned to the ship under the control of the chief medical officer, because we had to take care of the wounded stretcher cases, of course, We would always have at least five hundred psycho cases that would be assigned to the ship that generally had the run of the ship, but they'd have an arm band on so that we would all know that they required special care. We would often have American prisoners and German prisoners to carry back. It was always a conglomerous type of group. The only real organized group that we had coming from the States was the 10th Mountain Division, who were one of the most elite type of outfits that I have ever been associated with. Many of them were college men from New Hampshire, colleges where they had winter sports, they'd been training for two years up in the Colorado Rockies; they were real hard, tough, good looking men, very proud. They were given a great deal of credit for breaking through on the Italian front up in the mountain passes. A lot of them were lost. It seemed awfully sad to me because I can only remember them as such a wonderful group of young men.

Q: To me it would have been sort of depressing. You're bringing over fresh troops and in twenty-four hours you're bringing back wounded people, prisoners, and so forth. You see them going in and you see them going out; it must have been a lot more hard to get used to than if you were a soldier and went over there and fought, you would probably see a little bit less than what you had seen.

Rhodes: It was very, very sad. The only thing that compensated it was that there was nothing we could do about that part of it and there was a lot that we could do to make it pleasanter for those who rode with us. We tried to make it as pleasant for those going across as possible, and then for the wounded on the way back. They would get good steaks and fresh made ice cream on the ship, and all the attention that you could give them. To see their faces light up -- that was the big help. In other words, there was nothing we could do about the over all picture but at least we could make it pleasant for those who had suffered, because of what they had been through.

Q: What was the GENERAL MEIGS like? How big was it?

Rhodes: She was over six hundred feet long, I think they considered her a twenty-thousand ton ship, she was a two-stacker, large stacks, and she was designed as one of the big passenger cruise ships and when the war came along they built extra ones from that design and finished them off as troop ships instead of finishing them off as passenger cruise ships. They would carry about five thousand troops, and that's crowding them in a great deal to carry that many. The make-up of that ship in the way of crew, we had a mainly Coast Guard manned ship. Then we would have a hospital group manned by the public health service. We had Navy chaplain, Chaplain Hansen who was a very fine gentleman and helped greatly. He formerly had been founder and in charge of the Great Lakes Choir they had for several years on the radio. They had a very fine reputation. The chaplain would have organized entertainment—one night during the cruise, the ship's company would give the entertainment to the passnegers, and then, toward the end of each cruise, the passengers would give the entertainment for the ship's company and the rest of the passengers. He organized that very well.

Then we had Army Transportation Corp who would watch out for the passengers, and that was headed up by a colonel in the Army. Then we had a Marine guard, of thirty Marines, so we had pretty well a cross section of all the services manning that one ship.

Q: The thing that amazes me is just how you kept them all fed. It's hard enough to feed six hundred people on a ship, and then you throw in all these extra people. Of course the ship was probably designed that way.

Rhodes: Besides my own men, I had to organize a working force of fifteen hundred men among the passengers, each trip, or you couldn't feed them, you couldn't keep the ship clean, you'd have to have police guards all the way around. You could use passengers for this under the Marine guard because they would station them and check on the guard. Then you would have other groups of passengers who had to work to keep the ship clean. Others who had to help prepare the food and serve it, and keep the dishes washed, and so forth. So we not only had to organize our own crew, but we had to organize the passengers to the extent of at least fifteen hundred men each trip as a working force, guard force, and so forth. Having a completely unorganized passenger list, that was a very great difficulty to get those working forces detailed, organized, right in the beginning because unless you organized them you wouldn't be able to operate the ship internally. This was always a great difficulty. Kind of a touch and go thing especially when you were taking wounded and replacements on board in the European theater in your twenty-four hour turn around, then organizing them so you could operate the ship coming back.

Q: You say you needed fifteen hundred people and there's five thousand on the ship. How did you get them to cooperate? Say you picked me and I said, "Hey look, Mac, there's three thousand other guys over there that aren't doing anything. Why don't you pick one of them?"

Rhodes: The only thing that we offer them is three meals a day instead of two. The passengers that didn't work only got two meals a day. The passengers that worked got three meals a day and they'd also be in touch with the crew if they needed an extra snack --they'd probably be able to get that also. It also gave them something to do. If they were able bodied and we called for volunteers over the public address system --it was about the only way that we could get volunteers, over the public address system-- told the guards where to report, told those who wanted to work in the galley who to report to, told the clean up gang report up on the main deck so we could line them up and count them off. Generally, being volunteers, they would report each day when they were supposed to report, but there was no way of finding them if they didn't report so you'd have to get replacements. It was just touch and go. We had no discipline over them at all. A great many of them would rather be working than just doing nothing.

Q: I guess the old rule, "You're in the service, don't volunteer for anything." I guess there are people who violate the rule.

Rhodes: That's right. The worst trouble we had getting volunteers were among the Americans who had been prisoners in Germany. Apparently they had been promised that they wouldn't have to work on the way back. So we got a whole ship load of these prisoners and they weren't about to offer work.

Q: They were prisoners of the other side?

Rhodes: Yes, they were taken prisoners by the Germans and they were released finally toward the end of the war. As we were advnacing, they would release these prisoners and we would take them back. Toward the end of the war we got a whole shipload of these Americans who had formerly been prisoners of the Germans, and they weren't about to work. They were going on strike. I explained to some of their leaders that this was very bad because we wanted to beef them up. We knew that they weren't used to good American food, all they had was German food, we had the facilities, we certainly had the food available, but we needed someone to help us prepare it, keep the ship in order, and so forth. Unless we could get some volunteers, we just weren't going to be able to serve any meals. We got our volunteers and had a very happy group when we landed.

Q: How long were you in this line of business?

Rhodes: I was transferred from there right after the end of the European phase of the war, and assigned as ice pilot to escort some supply ships up in the Arctic, along the northern coast of Alaska.

Q: Were you involved in the Normandy invasion?

Rhodes: No. That came before. I was not involved in that but we were landing a lot of troops down there in Italy, who were used to invade the southern part of France. We were in on that although we weren't the type of ship who lands people on the beach. A lot of them that we had carried over there were in on the invasion on the beach.

Q: You needed a port for your ship?

Rhodes: That's right. We were equipped to unload on docks. We didn't carry boats to unload on the beach.

Interview # 7 with Capt. Earl Rhodes, U.S. Coast Guard (ret.)
At his home, Takoma Park, Maryland   Sept. 13, 1970
Subject: Biography   by Peter Spectre

Spectre: Captain, the last time we spoke you were serving on the USS GENERAL MEIGS and we went through that tour of duty. After that you had a new assignment. Would you tell me about that?

Capt. Rhodes: Yes. Actually I remained on the MEIGS until the surrender of Germany. I believe on the last trip coming back I received a radio message assigning me as ice pilot in Arctic waters so I got off the ship and proceeded to Seattle as I had been directed. However, when I arrived there I found that the expedition wasn't to leave Seattle until August and I believe this was about the first of June when I arrived out in Seattle. I called headquarters and informed them that I had a couple of months on my hands and they, after talking it over, decided that it would be a good idea for me to take a course in hearing and examining officers in the merchant marine because these vessels that I was going to take into the Arctic ice were manned by civilian crews, therefore it would be handy if I was trained in becoming a hearing or examining officer. So I proceeded to New York where the school was held and took that course for about five or six weeks.

Q: What kind of an expedition was it?

Rhodes: It was three cargo ships that the Navy was sending up to supply the expedition up around Point Barrow, which was investigating the possibilities of oil deposits and other important minerals that might be in that area. You can only supply that area by ship about once a year.

Q: Were the people already up there?

Rhodes: Oh yes, the people were up there year around working and they had quite a little bit of equipment but they wanted a great deal more and of course, the Navy was supplying people by air continuously but the heavy equipment and the fuel, and so forth, to operate their machinery had to go up by ship.

Q: What is a hearing and examining officer?

Rhodes: The Coast Guard had the authority and duty in case of accidents or in case of misconduct on the part of merchant marine officers or seamen, to investigate the facts and if they found anyone at fault, since the Coast Guard had power and duty to license all merchant marine officers and seamen, they had also had a right to take the licenses away from them for misconduct. Therefore the examining officer would investigate whenever a misconduct of any kind was brought to their attention, or in the case of rumor of any kind that would have to be checked out. Then he would have to bring the information before a hearing officer who would hear the facts and testimony on all sides and he could decide what the penalty should be, if any. He had a great deal of authority. That has changed somewhat now, but that is the way it was run during the war.

Q: Had every Coast Guard officer who conducted the hearings been previously trained especially for that or was it possible to have an untrained person hearing these cases?

Rhodes: No, generally they would not assign an untrained officer to that duty because first of all, you had to know what the law was, you had to have had some experience under other experienced officers. It was something new and we were dealing with civilians rather than military, therefore our military court procedure and investigation was not proper methods to go about investigating occurrences on ships operated by civilians. So it was very necessary to train an officer as to policies and laws, and legal aspects of the whole matter before you let him loose where he might do a lot of damage merely from a public relations point of view.

Q: What did your training consist of?

Rhodes: First we studied the legal aspects and policies were set out, the powers of the hearing and examining officers. Then we would be assigned to sit in on several cases --operate with examining officers making investigations. We were operating with someone else and then we would sit in on the hearing cases and see just what the procedures was. You went right through the whole thing and you actually had some experience before they assigned you to a certain case.

Q: In these days a lot of the people that deal with merchant marine affairs in the Coast Guard are former merchant mariners who since joined the Coast Guard. Was that true when you were in this aspect?

Rhodes: Yes, it was especially true in those days. There were few regular officers who had been in the Coast Guard for some time who had any experience at all with this type of duty because it was right at the beginning of the war that the Steamboat Inspection Service came into the Coast Guard, and therefore they were handling most of the duties. However, the expansion of the merchant marine at that time and a great number of new officers and men coming into the service required quite a few new officers so the Coast Guard had to provide that. The former Steamboat Inspection Service formed the nucleus of the whole organization.

Q: During that period were there a lot of merchant marine officers who joined the Coast Guard?

Rhodes: For example, the pilot service --all pilots became officers in the Coast Guard. They were strictly a separate group entirely. They were not paid by the Coast Guard but merely wore Coast Guard uniforms and had the power of the Coast Guard while they were actually on duty --at no other time. They were actually paid their regular pilot's fees, as they were previously. They came under the authority of the Coast Guard when they were on duty and in turn they had the authority of a Coast Guard officer in the performance of their duty, which was done for the safety of the ship and the navigation of the harbors. This was a special war time situation.

Q: Do you think they sent you to school to fill time?

Rhodes: No. It's always possible in an isolated place where you could have certain merchant marine officers and crewmen acting up and the captain wouldn't have enough authority to maintain discipline. These ships did have armed guards with them, therefore you could report any discipline which was adjudged properly. This was just one assurance that if something should happen, you could handle it judiciously on the spot. The Coast Guard maintains hearing and examining offices throughout the world so they were in a position to immediately take action as soon as the ship docks and maybe the captain makes charges against certain crew members. The case could be heard and decided right there rather than wait until the ship got back to the United States and having that hanging over the men's heads. Morale can get pretty low if you can't handle the case on the spot. I think it's somewhat the same as our lag in trying criminal cases now in the civil court. Probably the one great reason why we are not able to turn the tide in the criminal cases because they have to wait so long to be tried in the court. The Coast Guard at that time was trying very hard to handle these cases expeditiously so there wouldn't be those lags.

Q: Isn't it hard to be continually retrained? Every time I've talked to you, you've had a new type of training, a new school, a new type of duty.

Rhodes: You could look at it that way but on the other hand you're learning something new, and it's important or you wouldn't be going to that school. You've got to be very much interested in it. I felt that it was a great privilege to be able to learn something new which would not only be a satisfaction to me but would make me more valuable in any assignment that I might be assigned to. For example, if I ever was assigned to a higher spot where I would be in charge, the hearing and examining officers, as well as all disciplines throughout the area of the maritime services, as well as communications, engineering, and so forth, a little bit of training in all of those things would be very valuable. As long as you had training and experience in so many facets you're much more fitted for command later on. I found it very interesting.

Q: What happened when you finished your shooling? Did you go back to Seattle?

Rhodes: Yes, and got there just a short time before it was time to sail. There was a lieutenant commander of the Coast Guard that was going on one ship. He had been up in the Arctic with me also, Gradin was his last name. He was a gunner on the NORTHWIND when I was a navigator of the ship, so we were both out in Seattle assigned to this duty as ice pilots. We were both trained in this duty of examining officer so one could be acting as the hearing officer while the other would be acting examining officer.

Q: How many ships?

Rhodes: There were three ships. One ship was the schooner HOLMES, navigator, Johnny Backlund that went to the Arctic several years and traded with the Eskimos and villages, Lieutenant Commander Gradin was on a ship, and I was on another ship. There were two liberty ships and another cargo ship.

Q: Were they fitted out in any special way for an Arctic expedition?

Rhodes: No, they were not. They were strictly ordinary liberty ships and cargo ships. We figured as far as liberty ships were concerned, the main objective was to get the cargo up there and unloaded. If something happened to them on the way back or while we were there, it didn't make too much difference because this was toward the end of war anyhow and they were changing from liberty ships to faster vessels. Liberty ships were no longer of any great value because we were in the Pacific now. The Atlantic had been taken care of so the main objective was to get that cargo landed on the beach up there.

Q: Was that your idea or did somebody pass on word to you saying, "Don't worry about the ships, worry about the cargo."?

Rhodes: In talking it over, prior to sailing, I was given that impression. This was not my own impression but I certainly could agree with it because the idea was that this cargo was desperately needed up there and we should do everything possible to get it unloaded where it was needed. If some damage was done to the ship in the process, that wouldn't be nearly as important as having the ship damaged before the cargo was unloaded. Make sure that you played it safe until you got up there where you were unloading the cargo and then with ice closing in while you were unloading, and so forth, things can happen that would be beyond your control. The main thing was to get them into position and get unloading cargo so that they could have that cargo that they desperately needed up there.

Q: What exactly does an ice pilot do? What was your relationship to the commanding officer?

Rhodes: The ice pilot generally advises the commanding officer in approaching the ice, and in navigation. I helped in navigation all the way through because I had had many trips up in that area. He had never been there before. Whenever he encountered ice, he would transfer the conn of the ship to me and I would personally supervise it unless we were going along and his watch officer would actually conn the vessel and I would merely advise the watch officer. Of course, I would keep the captain advised at all times what the situation was. He was naturally quite leery of getting in the ice at all. In that area you've almost got to have ice around you all the time. I would say that without my presence there, he probably never would have gotten the vessel up there.

Q: Why wasn't there a Coast Guard ice breaker leading the expedition?

Rhodes: There weren't any available at that time and the Coast Guard had several ice breakers built during the war but they were practically all transferred to Russia. As fast as we would build them and try them out, they would be transferred to Russia. Our activities with ice breakers were up around Greenland and the Canadian Arctic at that time so that was the location of any ice breakers that we had. There was practically no activity around the Alaskan Arctic.

Q: How did the voyage go?

Rhodes: We managed to get up there all right and once the ice came in we had to go around to the east side of Point Barrow toward the Canadian border. There is a little place around there where you can go when the ice starts coming in that's fairly safe. The trouble is, while we were fully loaded we had to drag bottom to get around there --a shallow place we had to go over. We did that once and then got back. It was a very interesting method of unloading. We had a group of Seabees on board, an armed guard on board, and the ship's crew was also engaged in unloading. The ship's crew would unload one hatch, the armed guard would unload another hatch, and the Seabees would unload another. Of course, the Seabees also manned the beaches. We carried these great big barges on the sides of the ship on the way up there. We got them in the water and then they put what they called mules on the end of them which amounted to real large outboard motors that they clamped on the stern of the barges --these were big diesel engines that they ran but the principal was exactly the same as an outboard motor on a smaller vessel.

We got all the stuff unloaded on the beaches up there but I had a partial load for Wainwright, which is down on the Alaskan coast. I was ordered to, as soon as I unloaded the Point Barrow cargo, go down and unload at Wainwright, but just as I left the fog was closing in.

Q: Did you go over there, one ship?

Rhodes: One ship, yes. They were still unloading up at Barrow when I left. The fog was closing in and the ice was closing in and although they were still clear up at Point Barrow, I ran into ice coming down toward Wainwright. They had an intermediate place down there, Sea Horse Island which had a lot of shoals and so forth, and the ice closed in to such an extent that I couldn't get to Wainwright and I couldn't get back to Barrow. I remembered the circumstances down around the Sea Horse Islands so I went down and anchored in behind some large pieces of grounded ice. As the ice pressure came in, it surrounded the ship and even many of the pieces came up on the deck of the ship. We were so-called "beset." But we were anchored and those grounded ice packs protecting us broke up the heavy ice to such an extnent that I felt we were perfectly safe. When the fog cleared away and they flew down and took a look at us, they thought we were goners. However, I assured them that we would be all right. Pretty soon the wind shifted and the ice started loosening up and I made my way down to Wainwright and everything was just fine. The only thing is that the sides of the ship looked almost like a washboard because the ice had pressed it quite a little. If it had been an ice breaker, it wouldn't have had any marks on it at all except take the paint off. But you could see where every frame was along the side of the ship.

Q: You mentioned a plane came down and looked at you. Did you have planes with you?

Rhodes: Up at Point Barrow.

Q: How big was Point Barrow when you were there?

Rhodes: I would say that they probably had somewhere between seventy-five and a hundred people living up around Point Barrow when

I was there in the old days. Of course, during this expedition, if you counted all the Navy contract people it's grown to quite a size. But when I was there in the '30s they had a good sized settlement of about seventy-five or a hundred people. It was a very, very interesting place to go to. When we were unloading up there, they took us out on the plane, scouted the ice, and saw just what the situation was, so we also had a good look at the ice by plane.

Q: Were the people up there in the Navy researching the same oil field that's in the news today? *Prudhoe Bay?*

Rhodes: Yes, definitely. Even when I was up there in the '30s and long before that, there were places that you could go out in the tundra and cut the ground away. This was oil soaked grass.. The oil was oozing up out of the ground. This was done many, many years ago. The only thing is nobody knew what was down underneath. The Navy had taken out oil preserves up there and they wanted to see just what was underneath because with the second World War there was a great demand for oil and you never knew when the oil might be shut off. One of the big priorities at that time was to see whether they had a reserve under there that would stand us in good stead.

Q: How long had they been there?

Rhodes: I don't know exactly but I'm pretty sure it was just about at the beginning of the war when it looked like BLOCKADES and everything else might disrupt our fuel system, especially being at war with Japan and the Dutch Indies oil being lost to us at that time, it made the situation quite serious. I think they decided to go after that about the time they were talking about building the Alcan Highway up there.

Q: Do you know if they had in any way considered how they would get the oil out if they had to?

Rhodes: Actually, when you need oil there's always ways of getting it out. It's just a matter of spending the money. The main thing was at that time, to find out whether they had oil. They weren't worried so much how they were going to get it out because in time of war, if that was their only oil supply, they would find a way of getting it out. Right now they're considering the cost of getting it out commercially. That's an entirely different problem. Of course, you're interested in the cost in war, also, but if that's your only source of oil, they'll find a way of getting it out and getting it out in a hurry.

Q: Was it a secret activity?

Rhodes: Yes, it was at that time.

Q: So your family didn't know where you were going.

Rhodes: They knew that I was an ice pilot but that was about all. They didn't know why. They knew that I was an ice pilot because I was experienced in the ice and that's about the only thing they knew.

Q: You said during the war the Coast Guard was doing very little ice breaking and what it was doing was around Greenland and the Canadian Arctic. What happened to the settlements that the Coast Guard used to visit before the war, where you were the only contact to the outside world, bringing the mail, the nurses and teachers, and supplies, and so forth. What happened to them during the war?

Rhodes: The Bureau of Indian Affairs had a vessel up there which took care of supplying the school teachers up there. The hospital at Point Barrow had been transferred to the Public Health Service before the war started, so there was another contact. Also the Army and Navy were up in Alaska more. The Coast Guard was still up in the Alaskan waters --mostly in the Aleutians, and so forth. There was still activity but there wasn't as much activity of the type that we used to do in peace time because we were cruising up there trying to help the natives as much as possible. Also there was a lot of flying up there. The Army Air Force built a big air station at Nome, Alaska, for example. So there was a great deal of activity by the military in those areas but most of it was supported by air as far as the everyday supplies were concerned, and commercial ships could go up in the summer time and unload the large cargo.

Rhodes #7 - 275 -

Q: You were a Coast Guard officer on a civilian ship and *The Master* was a civilian. How did you get along with him?

Rhodes: Just fine. We were very friendly. These were selected crews, so therefore they were fine men all the way through. Apparently this was something that all of them would like to have the experience of doing. Very few of them could take a ship into the ice in the Arctic so the crews with the best record were generally assigned to that job. These were ships under contract to the Navy but there's ways of rewarding crews who really have a good record and have done a good job. There was no trouble at all, they worked fine with the armed guard, the Seabees and myself. Everyone seemed to outdo themselves to be helpful, so it was a very, very fine experience as far as all of us were concerned. I think we all enjoyed it.

Q: You hear a lot of stories about the conflicts that took place in the war between the merchant marine and the Navy.

Rhodes: There was a setup for this when you stop to think that several groups working together, there's always the possibility for friction. You have your little squabbles which is normal but nothing reached any proportions where it was thought necessary to notify me. Certain things came to my attention but they were not at all important and it was merely a long cruise with all these people kidding each other. Sometimes it comes close to getting into a fight but in this case everyone was very, very careful to see to it that the little friction didn't develop into something important.

Q: How long did the voyage take?

Rhodes: It seem to me we left in August and got back around the end of August or early September. We had the side trip to Wainwright and then we had to pick up cargo at Dutch Harbor, I believe. I've forgotten just what the situation was there. The main reasons for being there had been accomplished by the time we got back to Dutch Harbor. We stopped there, and I know we had to take on fuel at Dutch Harbor to get back.

Q: What did you do next when you got back to Seattle?

Rhodes: When I got back to Seattle, I reported to the Coast Guard district commander at that location as my orders required. I was detached from the vessel that I was on and ready for a new assignment. The district commander wanted me to request assignment there to SEattle. Of course, I would have enjoyed assignment in SEattle but I told him that I would request that unless they could assign me a command out in the Pacific -- I wanted to get out there. So we called up Coast Guard headquarters and told them what the situation was and they said that they were looking for someone like me for a command in the Pacific. So my assignment came through as commanding officer of the attack transport THEENIM, AHA-63.

Rhodes # 7 - 277 -

Q: What did the district commander want you for?

Rhodes: I believe he had in mind operations officer for the district.

Q: What was the THEENIM doing. Where was she when you were ordered?

Rhodes: This was about the time that the war ended in the Pacific. The atomic bomb had been exploded. When I arrived out there the war was over. They sent me all over the place to try to find the THEENIM, her whereabouts were secret, I remember one time they sent me to Okinawa and I found out when I got to Okinawa that she hadn't been there, so I went back to Guam and they checked it out and she was up at Omanata, Japan, with a load of cargo up there. So they sent me up to Yokohama and Tokyo to join the ship there because she was due down there from Omanata. I remember riding on the electric railway going from Yokosuka to Yokohama on the first day that they opened the Japanese railroads to American troops. Then when I got up to the command ship at Yokohama, they put me up to wait for her, and then I was called in by the admiral and told that the ship was going to have to by-pass Yokohama because of a typhoon that was coming up and going to strike the Japanese islands so she was being directed to go back to Manila. I had to arrange transport back there, but the surprising thing was that the typhoon took an odd course and on our way back to Guam we had to land at Iwo Jima because the typhoon was in Guam. I learned later that that typhoon coming up there had diverted the THEENIM into Yokohama. If I had just waited there I could have made it.

Q: Why this big rigmarole? Why didn't they just come right out and say, "This is where your ship is and you can pick her up there."?

Rhodes: Because ships don't stay in one place. Sometimes it's days before they know where she is. For example, the mistakes that they make by reading these messages --one message says "Omanata" and with the garble they think it must have been Okinawa; they've never heard of Omanata so they sent me to Okinawa. That was just a plain routing error on their part because they didn't know she was in Japan, they just knew the place where she was. Of course, this isn't the top admiral that routes you. These are the people strictly working in transportation that would route you that way. The senior admiral out there running things was the one that told me that I should go back to Guam and meet the ship in Manila because she was going to by-pass Yokohama, and that was his orders, because of the typhoon. So I felt that I was perfectly correct in getting sent back. On the other hand when the typhoon was coming up the coast and would have been out to sea and going to miss Japan, he ordered the ship into Yokohama for shelter until the typhoon got out of the way. That's the reason I had to go to Iwo Jima because the typhoon was coming right up there and Guam was battered down because of the typhoon.

Rhodes #7 - 278 - A

Q: Where did you finally find the ship?

Rhodes: I finally joined it in Manila but first, of course, I had to go back to Guam and get to the Philippines. Then I had to wait in the Philippines about two weeks before I ever joined the ship. She had to make her way down.

Quite often the people in the routing department, the travel department, didn't know the details of the operation because all the operations were kept very secret and so he knows about where the ship was but he didn't always know where the ship was going to be. That's what made it hard.

Q: You were in Japan at one time?

Rhodes: Yes, I went to Japan before I joined my ship.

Q: You were there after the surrender, as well. What was it like? What were the conditions like?

Rhodes: They were pretty terrible, as far as the Japanese were concerned. However, the Japanese people couldn't have treated us better. When I went up there from Yokosuka to Yokohama on the railroad, I was all alone in my uniform and many of the Japanese on the train could speak English and they were trying to be helpful and talking back and forth, perfectly friendly. I told them where I wanted to get off was Yokohama but none of them had ever heard of

Yokohama. Finally in hearing them talk in Japanese, I heard them say something like Yō'kəhä'mə and I told them I wanted to go to Yō'kəhä'mə, and they said yes they knew exactly where I wanted to go so they helped me off with my luggage even though they weren't planning on getting off there, and made sure that I got the right place. This was a real experience. I had several pleasant experiences out there. When I left Japan, the pilot had me go up in the cockpit when he took off and he took me over the bombed areas and then he took me over to circle the Imperial Palace, and we flew up an circled the peak of Mt. Fujiama. In those days, apparently the pilot did try to give you an idea of what things were like from the air if he only had one or two high ranking officers.

Q: What did the THEENIM do when you finally joined her?

Rhodes: The first duty I had was to be the commanding officer of a task FORCE of six ships similar to the THEENIM and lead them, loaded with cargo, from Manila to Yokohama. It was very simple as far as that was concerned, except we had to go through the mined channels. We had charts of ALL the mined channels but never-the-less I had to escort these six ships up through there, and having never been there by sea before, and conditions being as they were, you just hoped that you knew where you were the whole time so that you knew that you were in the proper channel instead of out in the mine fields.

Q: Why hadn't they swept the mines?

Rhodes: It was too early. It would take too much time. They wanted to get the supplies to the occupying forces up there. We made it all right and we broke up the task group there. They unloaded us one at a time. Generally we were assigned to the "magic carpet" which was the method of getting the boys home to the United States in a hurry. In other words, these ships out there were due for overhaul, so what they generally did was take these ships and them load a cargo either at Guam or the Philippines, bring it up to Japan, and load up with men and supplies going back to the United States. Even though you weren't equipped to haul men, you'd put them aboard some way. You'd generally be overloaded and you didn't have good accomodations for everyone but they were willing to put up with it because they were heading home. We were assigned to go back to Portland, Oregon for overhaul and we had a real full load of men who were anxious to get back.

Q: I hadn't heard of the "magic carpet."

Rhodes: That was the organization set up to get the boys home in a hurry. When they got so many points, they were eligible to go home. But they couldn't get home without this transportation for them. The transportation was the "magic carpet." Flying home on the "magic carpet," something unexpected. These ships come in and perhaps weren't scheduled to take back troops and didn't have the accomodations for it, and yet these men, in order to get home, would be willing to put up with it. So that's the way they got them back in a hurry.

Q: What did you do when you got to Portland?

Rhodes: We actually had our big ship's party. Although I had just joined the ship, many of the officers and crew had not been back in the United States for about two years, so in Portland we had the big ship's party and arranged for all the overhaul that was necessary. I guess we were there close to six weeks and then we were sent down to San Francisco-Oakland to load up for a supply cruise back to the Pacific.

Then I went back out to the Pacific and you just could not get unloaded out there because Guam and the Philippines didn't want any more. They had whole stacks of supplies at Guam and Manila. All these things we had on board had been ordered, they were in the supply line, and they didn't want us to take them back to the States. What would they do with them if they came back to the States? So Washington kept ordering them to unload it, and they kept delaying. They didn't have enough men or equipment to unload it, or space on the dock. We finally got unloaded in Guam and we went to Subic Bay. We just layed there trying to get to the dock. We kept asking them to let us have space at the dock so we could get unloaded, and nothing doing. Even then they said they didn't have manpower enough to unload us. Finally I told them that my own ship's crew would unload the ship if they could loan us the trucks, and so forth, to truck it away and tell us where to put it. So finally, to get me out of their hair I guess, they gave me space at the dock and my crew worked around the clock driving the trucks, unloading the cargo, and so forth. Finally we got unloaded. Then I got orders to fly back to Washington on a new assignment and turned the command over to my executive officer, who was quite capable.

Q: Was that the rule all over the Pacific that everything all of a sudden got jammed up after the war?

Rhodes: That's right because you've still got the supply lines going. These people in the forward area, although they ordered the stuff, they had no need for it.

Q: The material that you were bringing over was ordered before the war ended?

Rhodes: That's right. It took some time for them to get it together and as a result it didn't get out there until the war ended. Of course, the war ended suddenly --you've got to remember that. There was no one had any idea it would end suddenly like that. They all thought that they needed a lot of supplies to build up for the invasion. Also we were very anxious to bring the troops back and therefore those supply vessels were getting short on manpower, considering all the stuff that we were still shipping out there and they still had to ship the stuff up to Japan. Manpower was an item because they were continually losing their men, too.

Q: What was your new assignment when you left the THEENIM? Did you know what it was going to be or did they just say, "Go to Washington."?

Rhodes: I was pretty sure what it was going to be. It was to be in communications, I knew that, and it was to relieve Capt. L.T. Jones in the very highly classified communications.

Q: This was a different type of job from what you had before?

Rhodes: That's right. This was to take advantage of the training I had in the Signal Corps. Perhaps you might know, at that time they set up special combined agencies. It was a joint service agency and the Treasury Department was not included so therefore, the Coast Guard was out of that particular group. We had to close up our particular organization that had to do with that. It was very highly classified and they were trying to completely reorganize. Every service kind of had their own before that and they were putting it under a central head and only certain people would be invited to keep up with it. Although we still would keep our hand in a little, still we would not be into it nearly as deeply as we had before. So there I was sitting in Washington and had just about made the relief, when it was decided to close up the agency. Then they had to find another job for me.

The chief of communications wanted me to be his assistant chief, and they also offered me the job of chief of intelligence Division but the communications department used so much pressure that they decided to put me in as assistant chief of communications rather than to ~~put~~ *assign* me as chief of the division of intelligence.

Q: Which did you personally prefer?

Rhodes: I personally preferred assistant chief of communications, which I got because I didn't have too much interest in the intelligence picture. I'd been trained in communications, I was interested in communications, and I was interested in advancing in communications which is closely allied to operations, whereas intelligence is somewhat off to one side. No one knows what you're doing and no one knows what anyone else is doing in the way of operations. You know what they're trying to get away with, perhaps, sometimes, but that never interested me a great deal. I'd rather be in the swim where things are really happening.

Q: During this time the Coast Guard was going through a gigantic upheaval. I was talking with Capt. Capron who was really involved in that as he was in enlisted personnel. People were leaving the Coast Guard and the Coast Guard was having to get rid of people. Not only were there people that wanted to get out but there were people who had to get out. Q: Were you afraid of what was going to happen to you?

Rhodes: We were not only concerned, but we were directly involved.

Rhodes # 7 - 285 -

For example, Capron, myself and all our class and several other people were demoted. Here we were captains and they put us back to commander. We didn't know whether they were going to put us back any farther or not. A lot of people had that uncertainty. It was very difficult for a morale situation. You see you're losing a lot of your good officers and you don't know what you're going to get to replace them. You've got more men in one rank than you need and not enough in another, all your trained radiomen are leaving. You just don't know from day to day what you were going to have because you're in operations and it was personnel who were discharging your men. So it was awfully hard for you to keep advised as to what you're going to have tomorrow.

Q: You didn't have any say in it?

Rhodes: We did in the beginning. For example, we were making all of the assignments of communication personnel right up in communications. We were requesting personnel to make these assignments. Then during this mess, Capron was one and the rest of personnel had to get these things into their own hand because they were also resposible for personnel. So arrangements were made that they would assign personnel. They would be responsible for providing the proper rates that we said we needed. So they had a lot more resonsibility then. We used to train communicators, radiomen, communications officers, and so forth, and we still had an advisory capacity, but we were really doing a personnel job as well as a communications job. When Capron came in there, we got along fine, and it gradually shifted the personnel where it should be. We advised but we didn't actually have a direct authority to tell personnel we want this person assigned here. We never wrote orders for anyone to be assigned, we would merely write up requests to personnel to have them assigned and they were always assigned as we desired. During this upheaval, that's when the responsibility was put back in personnel's hands.

Q: This part of the war is the one that has always interested me the most because when the war began, the need was apparent and you said, "Okay, we need fifteen radiomen, let's go out and find fifteen radiomen. If you can't find them, train them." So it was sort of a forward looking effort. You knew what you had to do and you knew how to get the means to do it. At the end of the war, all of a sudden the Coast Guard is confronted with not doing as much as it was doing before, not having as much money, as many men, and so forth. How did you know where you were going to go the next day or the next day?

Rhodes: We continually had meetings and we were putting ships out of commission right and left in order to get the men that you had to release becasue you had a lot of men that you had to release. But that meant, then, that you were transferring men all the time -- transferring your men who were permanent Coast Guardsmen off these decommissioned ships to the regular Coast Guard ships which you expected to keep.

Q: How did you know what you were going to keep?

Rhodes: We were manning a lot of Navy vessels. The GENERAL MEIGS and the THEENIM were Navy vessels, so the Navy has got to release us from manning those because they've got to furnish the crews themselves. The Navy was laying up a lot of ships too in order to get the men to man a nucleus of a Navy rather than a wartime Navy. So they were having their troubles trying to release our men from these ships that were being laid up. First you had to get them to lay up yard, and so forth, and then you had to release your men and some Coast Guardsmen would have points, they'd be in the reserve and have points enough to get out and they wanted to get out. You had regular career men who wanted to stay in and they had to stay in anyhow because their enlistment hadn't expired. The regular officers, of course, they weren't going to let go anyhow. But you did have to let a lot of the reserve officers go and a lot of the reserve enlisted men. Many of the men in the Coast Guard had enlisted in the Coast Guard rather than be drafted into another service. Then they were required, when their enlistment expired, to extend their enlistment to the end of the war. So many of them had their enlistments expiring at the end of the war. Of course, legally the war hadn't ended. Congress carried it on so that these men's enlistments didn't expire because the war hadn't ended, but we arranged a system of points whereby a person with a certain number of points, we would let him go.

Q: In communications, you have to have people manning the radios. How did you know how many radios were going to have to be manned?

Rhodes: That's one reason why we had to turn all this over to personnel because they would just take rates, rather than names. They knew from the service records of these people whether they were going to get out or whether they were going to stay in, whether they had a hold on them. What they would do is transfer the people who they had a hold on to regular Coast Guard cutters, which were losing their reserve communication personnel. In peace time we wouldn't have nearly as many radiomen on our regular cutters. That's another way that we got by --we no longer had war time compliments on our ships. It had to go back in personnel because we no longer had control and we didn't know where the men were or where they were coming from. We couldn't keep track of it in communications. They had computers down in personnel, IBM machines and so forth, that they could keep track of the personnel.

Q: What kind of planning did you do? Were you in on the planning?

Rhodes: To a certain extent. We were working with the over-all planners but we couldn't say we'll keep this ship or not keep that one. That was the top planners, although we were advising. We were in the group. Of course, most of these extra ships that we were running were not Coast Guard vessels. But there again look at all we had to do. We had to fold up our shore patrol, our beach patrol, horses and dogs. To a certain extent we had to fold up our security organizations and these organizations were all over the world as well as the United States. It is a big problem.

Q: What exactly were your duties in communications division. I've read the organization manual and those things usually say one thing and what actually happens is another thing.

Rhodes: One of our major duties in communications was to arrange your communications in such a way that you serve operations, and that's basic. As a result of that, you've got to keep in touch with operations at all times, who is really the boss of communications to find out what the requirements are going to be. Then after that, operations, and communications advised personnel. This is what we need in the way of personnel. We've got to advise engineering what type of equipment we're going to need to accomplish the mission, and how many. So we've got to keep liason all the time with all these other groups. We've got to know what their plans are, what they're going to do so we can advise the equipment and the manpower necessary to accomplish this. At the same time, with the new developments in communications and electronics in the war, we had to look into new equipment and plan --you aren't going to get it right away. You've got to plan the development of it and aquisition of it and installation of it, and so forth. We were setting up groups right then to decide what equipment, and so forth, would serve our purposes best because we knew a lot more at the end of the war than we did at the beginning.

Q: Was Loran part of communications or was it an engineering function?

Rhodes: It was part of navigation and yet we were very closely involved in it. We had to supply communications to all these Loran stations and although we weren't directly involved in the Loran itself, we had to be aware of it because it was operating on communications frequencies, so we had to obtain their frequencies for them, and so forth. We were involved but still it was what we called aids to navigation division and the engineering division who were, you might say developed, and were directly in charge.

Q: What was your thinking at that time as to what the Coast Guard should do or should have ten years from then? What direction were you trying to go once you had your problems straightened out as to how many people you had and where you could put them, and so forth?

Rhodes: At first we in communications didn't have that particular type of duty. We engaged in all the meetings, and so forth, but our job mostly was to see to it once the decision was made we were going to get into something, that we provided the proper communications set-up for it. For example, search and rescue. We could see that that was going to be one of the most important jobs of the Coast Guard because we had been all over the world in search and rescue during the war. We learned a lot about it and the airplane and the helicopter were coming along. What we wanted to do was develop communications so that you could use the helicopter in all kinds of weather. At that time they still couldn't fly helicopters in bad weather. I remember one of the major developments was ~~to fly~~ light weight communication equipment that could be used effectively in a helicopter. Also we were looking for new life boats that we could use and patrol boats, small, and good reliable communication equipment that we could maintain communications on those. Then the Coast Guard was assigned a great responsibility, say in search and rescue, and that meant a terrific communications problem because you had to maintain communications with units of the Navy, units of the Air Force, units with commercial aviation, commercial ships, and keep complete knowledge of where all of those units were that you could call on for help in case of emergencies. We had to maintain at our large units such as Eastern Area and Western Area so we would know where all commercial ships were on the ocean and we'd have them plotted so in case a disaster came up, anywhere in the world, we would be able to get ahold of a ship, or land station, and notify them of the situation and ask them to assist. In the meantime we would be alerting others of the possibility that they might be able to assist. That is a great communication responsibility to try to maintain rapid communications with all those separate units. Also when you have all those different units, you might have a Navy ship, a Coast Guard plane, a Coast Guard ship, and a commercial ship out there working together. You've got to designate someone in command on the spot and have him be able to communicate with all these people who are trying to help. It's that kind of thing.

Then, of course, we had the ocean station vessels. We had to see to it that they were able to communicate with all planes of all nations, and all ships of all nations.

Q: Where did the FCC fit into this?

Rhodes: The Federal Communications Commission only fits into the picture as far as the commercial communications were concerned, and private communications. They were not into the government communications and that's where we had what we called IRAC, the Interdepartmental Radio Advisory Committee which advised the President on radio frequencies. Every time that we would agree as to radio frequencies, the President would have to assign these frequencies by executive order. So all the government agencies, such as the Army, Navy, civil aviation, Coast and Geodetic Survey, Coast Guard --actually I represented the Treasury Department and the Department of Health, Education and Welfare on IRAC. We were involved in frequency assignments to various government agencies. But the Federal Communications

Commission only assigns them to commercial and private U.S. government operations. IRAC assigned them to all U.S. government but they only do that through Executive Order of the President.

Q: You spent from 1946 until 1969 . . .

Rhodes: That's right. That was as assistant communications director. And then I went back to sea as commanding officer of the icebreaker, NORTHWIND.

Q: Was the NORTHWIND one of the cutters that had been given to the Russians and taken back again?

Rhodes: No, this was the second NORTHWIND. The first NORTHWIND had been given to the Russians so they had to build another one and this NORTHWIND that I was on made a big expedition up in the Arctic around Greenland. That must have been in the neighborhood of 1946, then in '47 I think she went down to the south polar expedition with Byrd and then in '48 I believe she made an Alaskan Arctic cruise. Then I was on her from April '49 until October, 1950.

Q: That was a fairly new ship.

Rhodes: Yes, she was completed at the end of the war and her first major task was up in the Greenland area.

Q: Why did the Coast Guard have ice breakers and the Navy have ice breakers up until now when the Coast Guard has all of the ice breakers?

Rhodes: The Coast Guard always had ice breakers because we had to take care of commercial shipping in the rivers, Great Lakes, Arctic. We were always in search and rescue work so far as commercial shipping was concerned. We went back even when the whalers were up in there in Alaskan waters and kind of acted as a mother hen up there. If anyone got in trouble they called on the Coast Guard. We needed ice breakers for that purpose. I think that the Navy got interested in ice breakers because of this supply requirement for the big oil fields that they expected to discover up in northern Alaska, and also the expeditions to the south polar regions. Admiral Byrd had gotten them interested and I think as a result of the second World War, the Navy got extremely interested in the northern Alaska region and also the south polar region. You've got to have ice breakers to operate in those waters.

Q: Did they use experienced men from the Coast Guard to start them off?

Rhodes: They actually assigned people to our ice breakers, but their first ice breakers were sister ships to the Coast Guard ice breakers, the NORTHWIND, and so forth. After they had experience with that type, then they saw the need for one even bigger than that and they built the GLACIER. All those ships now have been transferred back to the Coast Guard. But the Coast Guard is especially interested in getting a nuclear ice breaker which would have far greater capabilities than the present ice breakers up there.

Ques.: You can see yourself as a communications man, but you've spent almost as much time in breaking ice.

Rhodes: That's true. Remember too, that I had to be with the operations people all the time to look at things from the operations officer's view point in order to find out what the communicators should do to furnish the tools to carry out operations. Communications has no reason for being unless you can support it by the needs of operations, which is really the job. Communications, itself, could be a hobby but in order to get the job done and to get it done rapidly, you've got to know what the man responsible for a big operation is. He's got to keep in touch with all the people that he has command of so that he can act as a team. For example, a fleet has got to be completely in touch with everyone. In search and rescue operations, if you had been out there and couldn't get in touch with someone whom you desperately needed to get in touch with, you'd know that you'd want your communicator to find a way of keeping you in communications. My main interest was in operations. My curiosity interest was in developing a tool which would be useful to doing a good job. The Coast Guard always prided themselves in the fact that they could almost immediately get in touch with all the units and their units could intercommunicate with each other as well as communicate with other civilian and military units. It's probably one of the only outfits who really can do that in a big way. That is a real challenge in communications is finding ways of doing these things, and often you might have to do the things illegally --operate on other people's frequencies, which you're not supposed to do, just to alert them to a situation that's right on their doorstep but they don't know anything about it. You have no right to operate on their frequencies except in an emergency. We used this emergency thing many times in the Coast Guard to call for assistance. When people we know are right in the vicinity and we can't reach them any other way, so we go on their frequency and alert them. Of course, no one's ever called our hand on it because we had justification in doing it in an emergency. We wouldn't have had justification if it wasn't an emergency.

Q: I know that navigating in polar waters is difficult. Was communicating in polar waters difficult?

Rhodes: Yes, that's probably the most difficult there is because you're completely blanked out there every now and then. Sometimes you can communicate beautifully but other times there will be two or three days at a time that you can't raise anyone outside of the Arctic when you're up there in the ice. I think they've explained that with the Aurora Borealis up there, which is very, very effective and very beautiful at times. It is greatly responsible for cutting down the ability to get out on high frequencies in that area.

Rhodes #7 - 297 -

Q: So actually you were a good man to have up there.

Rhodes: It was a good experience for me, too, because here you are an outpost and you've got to find out how you're going to maintain contact with a lot of these places. For example, these Alaskan villages. Most of the school teachers had a little radio to get out but they wouldn't be listening all the time. You had to know when they would be listening, you had to know their habits and get aquainted with them so you could arrange your schedules and give them a call every now and then and see how they're making out. There again we were operating on their frequencies in order to do that because they couldn't operate on ours. In order to maintain communication with the Eskimo villages, we would operate through the school teachers with a little two way radio up there. Many of them might be somewhat of an amateur radio and have their own radios, but we had to know all of the little details of each village and each camp up along the beaches up in Alaskan waters. Also in each fishing group. There's a lot of fishing up there in Alaska so you had to know how to communicate with them, and they had to know how to communicate with you.

Q: What did you do on the NORTHWIND? Where did you go?

Rhodes: We contacted every settlement and village in Alaska, all the way to Point Barrow. My first cruise there was an especially interesting thing that came about. The Navy needed ice breakers to supply their stations up along the northern Alaskan SHELF — all the way to Barter Island which is just about the Canadian border. So their expedition up there with supply ships had the BURTON ISLAND ice breaker going along, escorting them through the ice. It was the northern part of Alaska and she got in heavy ice and broke her propeller. Knowing the Navy was up there, I had deliberatly gone up to that area without going all the way just so I wouldn't be too far away. When I heard about her breaking a propeller I started proceeding in that area and they asked for the NORTHWIND to escort these ships since the BURTON ISLAND could go no further. So I was assigned to report to the Navy commodore up there in charge of that expedition, Capt. Scruggs. After meeting with Capt. Scruggs, the commodore in charge of the operation, he explained to me that the BURTON ISLAND was half way to Barter Island laying the ice along with a couple of LSTs and asked me what I would need on the NORTHWIND to relieve the BURTON ISLAND and continue the escort. So I suggested that we could certainly use the helicopters, pilots and so forth, so he arranged that when we met up with the BURTON ISLAND we'd transfer the helicopters, pilots, the repair parts, all the gasoline from the BURTON ISLAND to the NORTHWIND. Also we only had enough men in the engine room to operate two engines around the clock so they transferred about thirty naval engine room personnel so that we could operate all six engines around the clock. There were other special equipment and personnel that was also transferred from the BURTON ISLAND to the NORTHWIND, so we proceeded as fast as possible and we docked right alongside the BURTON ISLAND, right in the ice, and proceeded to make the transfer which was completed in about three hours time. Then we proceeded to escort the LSTs to Barter Island. As it happened, we had good ice conditions, although the NORTHWIND had to remain out in deep water and break ice all the way through. The LSTs with their shallow draft were able to operate in shallow water where there was very little ice. They made the trip, unloaded and we came back without us having to help them once. We did use the helicopters to scout a bit and that was a great help. It was a potential use for the NORTHWIND to go there and they probably never would have tried to get the LSTs to Barter Island without the presence of an ice breaker because they could easily get fouled up and need an icebreaker to break them out.

Q: What other type of things did you do?

Rhodes: We supplied medical and dental treatment to all the Alaskan natives. Also on that cruise, they didn't have a method of fueling the light stations and Loran stations in the Aleutian group and they had me take on board a large, ten thousand gallon barge loaded on the flight deck, and we had to transfer fuel oil to light stations and Loran stations along the beach. One of the toughest places was at Scotch Cap, right out in the Pacific at the entrance to Bering Strait between the Pacific and the Bering Sea. There was a lot of outlying rock, and so forth, and at one time all of our boats and the barge itself was aground in there. We just had to operate between storms, and still there was always a big swell in there which could break the boats to pieces in there in a hurry. So it was a very difficult thing and I told them they should never try that again. These lighthouse tenders and buoy tenders are much better equipped to do that kind of work.

Q: They just weren't available at that time?

Rhodes: They didn't have enough of them and they needed them for other purposes. This was somewhat of a test to see whether we could do it or not. We did it but it was a test we never should try again because the NORTHWIND rolls a lot more than other vessels and you try to lower a big barge from your flight deck into the water with the ship rolling --you can kill a lot of people that way. We just didn't have the equipment to handle a big thing like that and still keep it from swinging around and hitting the side of the ship and sweeping the flight deck.

Q: You spent one season on the NORTHWIND?

Rhodes: Two seasons.

Q: What other things did you encounter?

Rhodes: One interesting job we had was burning the old light house at Schizmeref. They built a Loran station there and a new light so they wanted us to burn down the old one. We also had to carry a jeep up to St. Paul Island in the Pribiloffs to supply the fish and wildlife people up there and that was a very difficult job. As I say with the NORTHWIND out in the sea ways with the swells running and rolling deeply, to load a jeep into a LCVP boat with it bouncing along the side.

Q: You went all the way up there with a jeep?

Rhodes: They sent us a new jeep from Seattle to deliver it up there to them. We always went around the Pribiloffs, anyhow, and worked very closely with the fish and wildlife people up there.

Interview #8 with Capt. Earl Rhodes, U.S. Coast Guard (ret.)

At his home, Takoma Park, Maryland   September 20, 1970

Subject: Biography   by Peter Spectre

Spectre: Captain, the last time we talked, we covered your tour of duty on the NORTHWIND. Can you tell me about your next assignment?

Capt. Rhodes: When I returned from duty on the second cruise on the NORTHWIND, I was transferred to Washington, D.C. Coast Guard headquarters as chief of the communications division.

Q: Was this a normal assignment for you?

Rhodes: This was something I had been looking forward to because Capt. McKay, who was chief of communications when I was assistant chief, had indicated that he was going to recommned that I be assigned as his relief when he left for other duty. He had already departed Washington when I arrived. His assistant, Capt. Jocahce, had taken over until I arrived to assume the duties as chief. It was not a surprise that I received these orders although there was no certainty that I would receive them. We had discussed it previously.

Q: Was this something that you wanted?

Rhodes: Yes. Actually communications had been somewhat my hobby from the very beginning and I had had a great deal of duty and training in communications. Practically all my shore duty had been spent in communications AND related subjects and, of course, while I was at sea I took a great interest in mobile communications of all types.

Q: When you first got there, what did you want to achieve and how did it stack up with what you finally achieved at the end?

Rhodes: One of the big things facing me at that time was the forthcoming International Conference on Radio Frequencies. We always hoped in cases of that type, to maintain our position, at least, and better our position if possible. There had been many years since an International Conference had been held due to the war years, and the realignment of nations and governments had changed to such a degree that there was no certainty that we would come up with an agreement that would be satisfactory. Also the state of the *arc?* had greatly expanded during the war years and thereafter, so many more uses for the radio spectrum than there had been previously. Of course, the short wave and ultra short wave had been discovered and utilized to a great extent. For example, the very high frequency, ultra high frequency of your voice communications and your radar, and so forth. Your aids to navigation, such as Loran, were in the spectrum. There was a far greater need for more spectrum space and there was an essential need for an international agreement to the sharing of the frequencies.

Q: Had there been an agreement before this?

Rhodes: Oh yes, there had been, but this was back in the '30s. This was revising it and bringing it up to date because the state of the *art* and the change in the national need for frequencies had been greatly changed. For example, Russia was in great need of radio frequencies compared with her status in 1930. There was hope that we could reach an agreement with Russia at this stage, whereas it was difficult in the 1930s.

Q: How was it decided who was going to get how much space and what space they were going to get?

Rhodes: That is through need and negotiation, and also you can share frequencies provided you're far enough apart and friendly enough so you don't start a fight every time someone uses your frequency. Quite frequently if you study your use of the frequency, and another's use of the frequency, you can easily agree to share that frequency. Of course, in the United States, we often have to share frequencies on mutual agreement. We do that also with Canada and with the Central and South American countries, but it is very difficult to share a frequency with someone who wants to claim that frequency as their own.

Q: Say there's a frequency that's been assigned to Britain. The war comes along and if one international agreement is abrogated like a treaty, why couldn't something like a frequency agreement be abrogated, as well, so that if the Germans decided they needed an extra frequency, what's to stop them from using a British frequency? Did that type of thing happen during the war?

Rhodes: It would be very easy to go on someone else's frequency but it's also very easy for them to retaliate and come on your important frequencies, so it's a you stay out of my back yard and I'll stay out of your back yard type of an agreement. For example, after the war, you'll probably remember how the Russians tried to interfere, and did interfere with the broadcast made by Voice of America, and so forth. It's very easy to interfere with someone else's communications but generally if a country's communications are so important that they will give up quite a little in order to have reliable communications of their own, if you notify them that they are interfering with you, they will attempt to stop that interference. It is strictly a give and take proposition --if you don't agree to try to eliminate interfering with another country's communications, they will come back and interfere with yours, and it's far more important to you to communicate with your own units than it is to interupt the other country's communications with it's units.

Q: So during the second World War, there wasn't any problems with this?

Rhodes: During the war, there were many problems. On the other hand, a great deal of the communications during the war were silent. So many units practiced radio silence so the enemy would not be able to know where they were, that your radio communications, especially, were lessened. The German submarines, of course, would have to communicate with their bases but they would shift frequencies and condense their message to such an extent that it would just go out as a "mffft" and that was all it was. It was very rapid and they would have to have a special machine to decode it on the other end. If you listened on the radio spectrum, during the war, it was fairly quiet except for propaganda broadcasts, and so forth, but the communication frequencies themselves were not very active. Another reason for that was they were traveling in convoy a great deal and they communicated among themselves with very high frequencies which only traveled for the line of sight and therefore you didn't have to worry about anyone at any great distance hearing you. That caused much less interference because your signal is not traveling over a great distance.

Q: On the conference that you attended while you were chief of communications, were you attending as a Coast Guard representative or as a United States representative?

Rhodes: I was designated as an advisor to the State Department but I was actually representing the Treasury Department and especially the Coast Guard. We were especially interested in the frequencies to be used for search and rescue and that was international frequencies that would be used so that no matter what the nationality was, they would be able to call us, we would be able to talk to them, and we'd all be able to talk on the same frequencies in an emergency.

That is one of the major things that we want in the Coast Guard and of course, then we had to have very excellent frequencies for use by the Coast Guard themselves, so that you'd be able to keep in contact with your ships and airplanes at all times and in all circumstances.

Q: In other words, different interests in the United States have representatives who were ~~revising~~ ADVISING the State Department.

Rhodes: Exactly. Ambassador Butterworth was assigned as chairman of the delegation to the Radio Conference at Geneva, Switzerland, in 1951. You had the Navy, Air Force, Army, Coast Guard, the FCC had several representatives, and also representatives from our companies such as RCA, the Telephone Company, McKay Radio, and so forth.

Q: How did you prepare for this?

Rhodes: We used to have meetings for about a year in advance about every week or two preparing our own position trying to determine what we required in the United States and how we could coordinate our requirements with the requirements of other countries. Also we had meetings with Canada several times so that we would be sure that we coordinated Canadian needs with our needs here in the United States.

Q: Were the Canadians going to be at the conference?

Rhodes: Yes, they were at the conference, too. It was highly desirable that we be able to present a joint agreement between Canada and the United States because we were going to interfere with each other a lot more than we would interfere with the other countries on the other side of the ocean.

Q: Would this apply to Mexico as well?

Rhodes: It applied to Mexico except that Mexico actually was not using frequencies a great deal at that time. Therefore we were not able to get together with her. We had some dealings with Cuba but most of our dealings with Cuba were over at the conference itself, because over the years, the Cubans had gotten onto the Coast Guard frequencies. One reason was whenever they needed help they could always call us so they got to feel that that was their frequency and they were almost ruining our communications down in the Caribbean because they had equipped their radios with Coast Guard frequency and they were actually using it among themselves rather than just using it specifically to call the Coast Guard for help. We had to come to a very close agreement with them but that was made over there.

Q: When you decided what your position was going to be in the United States, and even with Canada, did you bargain in the way that you go to a used car dealer and bargain? In other words, did you ask for more than you really wanted so you could give concessions back to this point?

Rhodes: We did to a certain extent except that of course, there had been an agreement back in the '30s so we had to start from that. We were operating on these frequencies assigned in the '30s but we needed additional ones. The other countries had to come in and say these were the frequencies that they had several years back but they needed additional ones so we had to figure out ways of sharing frequencies and narrowing the band. You see the *state of the art* had changed a great deal and it was possible to share frequencies in different ways. You could narrow the band. You didn't need the wide band for the modern equipment. Also they could operate on a single side band --you could operate on one side of the frequency and another one operate on another side. So these modern developments had to be taken into consideration when they decided on how wide the band needed to be. For example, if you were going to use voice it had to be wider than if you were going to use CW. On the other hand there were many things you could put on a narrow band such as teletype and facsimile, and so forth. It's surprising how many more things we could put on the radio wave and get our information through much more rapidly than we could in the old days. You could send a whole map in just a few minutes by facsimile.

Q: Was that being done in 1950?

Rhodes: Yes, I had equipped the Coast Guard vessels with that so instead of sending them a lot of data so they could make up their own weather map, we would send the weather map by facsimile so all they had to do was hook up their facsimile attachment and their weather map would be cranked out. They could reproduce as many copies of that as they wanted to after they got it aboard ship. It was certainly a big advantage in having all this different equipment. You wouldn't stay on the air quite as long to send the message --you could say a great deal more. The state of the ART required this conference, and this gave many people an opportunity to get together with their counterparts of different countries and see if they could share. You could have time sharing --RCA would be on a frequency maybe at certain times of the day, and maybe Russia could share that at certain other times, or England could share it at certain other times. You could have time sharing where a great deal of information could be transmitted in a short period of time.

Q: When you were preparing your position, did you look totally at your own needs or, in other words, study what this country needed in various parts, organizations, and people in this country that were communicating, and say, "Okay, this is what we need and now we're going to go over there." or did you also study what other countries needed and say, "Look, this is what England needs and we're looking realistically at it. This is what they need and this is all we're going to give them." ?

Rhodes: That is a very good question. We definitely had to look at the needs of the other countries as well as our own. Our own, of course, were paramount. We knew more about our own needs than we did the needs of some of the other countries. We had been working with the other friendly countries right along and exchanging information so that we were pretty well advised as to what their actual needs were. Each country had to look for expansion. For example, India had very little need for radio frequencies, but she wanted to get frequencies assigned to her by population so that if her population was double ours, she thought she should have double the number of frequencies that we were getting. Now there is a point where perhaps in order to satisfy India so that she would agree, you could get different countries to share a frequency with India, knowing that India had nothing to transmit on this frequency, you figured you would get very little interference from her. It was that type of agreement in some cases that you had to arrive at. There was a lot of political requirements in this meeting which were definitely not supported by communication requirements.

Q: Where did you get your information about unfriendly countries and their communications?

Rhodes: It's surprising but, for example, the Russian technicians, and so forth, were quite reasonable. However, their head of the delegation would have to speak in accordance with his orders from back home. We could meet with the Russian technicians to see how we could share frequencies. They wanted to communicate and we wanted to communicate, and we didn't want to interfere with each other --not unless it was deliberate. So technically, we could very well see where we could get along just fine. In that way, we came up with a very practical recommended agreement for sharing frequencies. Now Russia was the only one who didn't sign the agreement after the Geneva conference had closed. However, we knew and they knew what frequencies they should go on. They did that and we got along very well. There was no interference except when it was deliberate such as trying to interfere with our, you might say, propaganda broadcasts, and their propaganda broadcasts. Outside of that, we generally got along very well. If they started interfering with us, there were ways of letting them know about it and the same way with them --they could let us know about it and we would try to accomodate them. That's something you can't afford to do, is get a real fight in a radio spectrum. No one can communicate if you start to do that.

Q: So really the conference was not really an antagonistic type of conference --from the beginning everybody realized that a compromise had to be worked out.

Rhodes: Exactly. We were trying to arrive at an agreement from technical points. It was quite possible to do that although very, very difficult, but it was a real challenge and most of the people that we were dealing with were practical people who knew what the requirements were, knew what they could live with, and knew that they had to come to an agreement of some kind. It would be impossible to operate unless they did come to a reasonable agreement.

Q: There must have been a lot of people there. If the United

Rhodes #8 - 313 -

States had representatives from all the organizations that you say they did, then all the other countries must have the same types of representatives. There must have been hundreds and hundreds of people.

Rhodes: That's very true. I think they United States had around fifty in its delegation, and England, France, all the other countries had a great many people in their delegation, so it was a real large conference. There were also many sub-conferences going on among different people. For example, I met several times with the Cubans because we were having a great deal of difficulty because the Cubans were coming on our frequency all the time, so we had to agree that they would have certain frequencies and we would have certain frequencies and they could not put out their boats with our frequencies. It was all right with us if they put their headquarters with our frequencies so that they could notify us if one of their vessels were in danger, but we didn't want them to equip all their vessels with the Coast Guard frequency. They finally saw the light.

Q: There must have been five hundred people involved in this, all meeting on the same subject. How did you organize? Were you broken up into smaller committees that touched on different parts of the problem, or did you all meet together?

Rhodes: We would have a so-called plenary session maybe two or three times a week when everyone would meet together, but of course, only chairmen of the delegations would speak and only a few delegations would have anything to say. We had simultaneous translation so that no matter who was speaking, you'd be listening to a translater if it was not in your language so that you could hear what was going on all the time. Each delegation, then, would submit papers and they would be distributed to all the delegations so that at this meeting all the delegations had received this paper and then the paper would be discussed. Most of the actual work that was done at the meeting was agreed to among small working groups. We had a great many small working groups going, and generally you would get agreement for an area of the sharing of the frequencies, then you would have to bring all these areas together and agree over all. But you had your position papers first that would be distributed among the delegation. Then your full meeting would be called to discuss these position papers and perhaps they could arrive at a solution there, but many times politics would be injected into the main meeting so it was very difficult to arrive at a true technical agreement.

Q: How do you mean politics?

Rhodes: For example, Russia would want more frequencies than we were getting, and we would want more frequencies than Russia was getting. From a technical point, we could justify the frequencies we wanted but perhaps they were asking for something just to have more than we were getting. India had nowhere near the transmitters that they were asking for frequencies for. We couldn't imagine their using these frequencies but they would insist on getting assigned so many frequencies because of their population. It was that type of thing that would be injected in the main session, whereas they would very seldom be brought up in the technical sessions where you were detailing the use of these various frequencies for the various countries.

Q: Had the Korean War begun when you were there?

Rhodes: Yes, the Korean war was already going on because that started when I was on the NORTHWIND, up in Alaska. I had to go within a half a mile of Russian shores and, of course, Russian planes were flying over all the time. I remember definitely that I was somewhat uneasy about it. I couldn't go anywhere but what I was shadowed by Russian planes, so therefore, definitely the Korean war had started at that time.

Q: Did that war affect your conference in any way?

Rhodes: I doubt it because remember there was a cold war already going on before the Korean war started, you might say a propaganda war between us and Russia. I don't believe that the Korean war, as such, had any affect on the conference, as a whole.

Q: During the conference, did the countries tend to align the way they align in the UN, or align politically? Did the Communists have a Communist voting block at this conference and did the free

Rhodes #8 - 316 -

world have a free world voting block, and did the non-aligned countries do the same thing?

Rhodes: Yes, strictly in the main conferences, first one would speak and then another would speak in the Communist country block, and they would say practically the same thing in different words. But that was the propaganda speech that was being made. That wasn't the way it worked in the technical sessions, where you're trying to get an agreement of sharing a proper assignment, and so forth. Generally speaking, that did not come up there because we were trying to find a way of operating together, and we were not trying to feed each other propaganda, we were trying from an engineering point of view to arrive at a gentleman's agreement as to the sharing of these frequencies. Then, of course, when it came to trying to get to an agreement on the floor, the head of that delegation was the one to make the propaganda statements. We were able to get a practical, suggested agreement and Russia and the other Communist nations didn't sign it and agree to it, but their technical people knew what it was, and we knew what it was, so we adhered to it and they adhered to it. That's the way it went. We were just hoping that this under the table maneuvering and technical work that we had done over there would be sufficient for them to follow that as far as their operations were concerned, and we certainly intended to follow it as far as our operations were concerned. We were very pleased to find that it worked so well. You always have difficulties, of course, where you haven't really come to solid agreement, but it was to their interest and to our interest to get along well with each other as far as operations were concerned.

Q: In your Coast Guard biography it says, "During 1951, Captain Rhodes was lauded by the State Department for helping solve a communications problem between the U.S. and Canada through his technical abilities and cooperation."

Rhodes: That was prior to the International Conference and when I returned from the International Conference, I also received commendation from the State Department for being a member of the delegation. Apparently that was not taken into consideration in that write-up.

Q: So the problem they speak of in there was working out the agreement with Canada before the --

Rhodes: That is true. We had several meetings with the Canadians before we went over to Geneva to work out the international agreement because we work so closely with Canada here, and they use frequencies a great deal because of a lack of land lines. They have a large area and they have to depend a great deal on radio. We also depend a great deal on radio and unless we had a very firm, workable agreement, we would be in each other's hair all the time. I would say that in many ways we had to spend a lot more time with Canada than we did with the other nations because the close-in frequencies, the line of sight frequencies in many cases, and the two megacycle frequencies especially, which are short distance frequencies but will carry several hundred miles under certain conditions. The spectrum just wasn't big enough to accomodate all of our needs, and that's where we had to hammer out agreements that certain cases we could share, certain cases we couldn't share. We wanted good reliable communications all the way through and Canada and the United States, after very rugged meetings, finally came to an agreement that we could take with us to the international meeting.

Q: The Coast Guard was physically handling the transmissions of Voice of America?

Rhodes: While I was chief of communications, we put into operation a ship with large transmitters and actually we had a balloon that they sent up to take the antenna up in the air. That was stationed on the island of Rhodes right near the Turkish coast.

Q: Was Rhodes selected because of your name?

Rhodes: No, it wasn't, but that gave me the opportunity that I had been looking forward very much to visit the island of Rhodes and see how our communication's ship was doing. Actually, while I was there the Turkish consul gave a dinner in my honor. I think part of it was because my name was Rhodes.

Q: Why was the Coast Guard doing this? Why wasn't, say, the

Navy, the Army, the State Department?

Rhodes: I think that this has been demonstrated many times, the usefulness of the Coast Guard for something like this. In the first place they needed someone who knew the sea and how to handle a ship. They had to have someone be able to handle rigging, and so forth, in order to get this balloon up and down all the time to take the antenna up and keep from fouling it. They also had to be able to send someone in to that area who would not disturb the equilibrium of the very sensitive areas. What could be better than a life saving group like the Coast Guard? No one could take offense at the Coast Guard in an area where there were very touchy political difficulties because we had no record of being spies, or were not pugilistic in any way, but were more like the Red Cross. We went in wherever somebody needed help.

Q: Weren't you afraid that broadcasting the Voice of America would give you a reputation?

Rhodes: That could to a certain extent. However, we were never actually doing it, we merely had the base of operations. However, it wasn't strictly the Coast Guard's desire to do this. Remember the Coast Guard didn't want the job, but it was national policy that the job be done.

Q: Were you there when this began?

Rhodes: Yes, it started when I was chief of communications. So due to that fact, when they decided it should be the Coast Guard, we were asked if we could do it, and of course we could do it, so we were told to do it, but it wasn't the Coast Guard asking for the job. Another example of how the Coast Guard gets involved in things like that was when they were having real trouble in Spain, they sent a Coast Guard cutter there and the American ambassador had his living quarters on a Coast Guard cutter. This was during the late '30s, during the Spanish Civil War. Finally, at one time, it was just unsafe for Americans to be there, so the ambassador made his headquarters on the Coast Guard ship. A Coast Guard ship could go in there but it might be a little bit ticklish for a Navy ship to go in. It would look like the Navy was going to occupy the place. The same down in the Caribbean --quite often they've sent Coast Guard ships down there when it would be very undiplomatic to send a whole Navy squadron down there. You might upset certain people who were in charge down there whom you didn't want to upset. The Coast Guard can go down with the idea that they're going down to help out because that's generally what the Coast Guard is doing, especially in peace time. When you have a world-wide reputation, the Coast Guard can go into many places where you wouldn't want the Army and Navy. There is a real different implication when the Army or Navy goes in than when the Coast Guard goes in

Q: If the Coast Guard didn't want to do this, did you actually oppose it or did you say, "We don't want to do it but we'll do it if you say we have to do it."?

Rhodes: I don't think we opposed it. This was in the executive branch --it was not, you might say, taken through Congress. It was decided very high up in the executive branch that this would be done, and, of course, the decision there was the State Department and the Voice of America, and then probably at the Cabinet meeting it was decided who could better furnish the means of doing it. Probably the Secretary of the Treasury was asked if the Coast Guard could do it, and he said he'd check. Apparently the agreement was made high up that if the Coast Guard could do it, they were the ones to do it. So when they asked us, could you do it? we'd say we could, we don't want to, but we could. They said, "Go ahead and do it then." Of course, the money came from the Voice of America so our costs of equipping the ship and the cost of manning it, and so forth, even though it was manned by Coast Guardsmen, the salaries would be paid for by the Voice of America. But that put a transmitter right down exactly where they wanted it --very effective from all reports.

Q; What else were you involved in during that time?

Rhodes: I think probably one of the big things was we were manning the ocean station vessels at that time. We had to maintain communications with aircraft of all nationalities. I was very much involved in what they called ICAO, the International Civil Aviation Organization. One of my last conferences, by the way, was to Paris in 1954 on communications and ocean station vessel conference for ICAO in Paris.

Q: So communications were involved in civil aviation?

Rhodes: Definitely. Our ships had to communicate with all of the foreign planes regardless of the languages, therefore we had to have an international voice language, which we would be able to handle and the planes would be able to handle because we had ships both in the Atlantic and the Pacific and we had to communicate with them. Every time they passed over we had to give them the local weather and their position. We would know our position, generally, better than they would know theirs, then they would fly over the ship and we would give them our position. We'd also give them the surface weather and a more detailed report than they would be able to get on their own frequency.

Q: What do you mean by an international voice language? Do you pick a language, like English, and say this is what we're going to speak?

Rhodes: We had to have a phonetic language. For example, in the old days "a" was affirm, but we had to change affirm to alpha so they would all recognize that. All of the letters of the alphabet had to be changed. Then once you could pronounce these letters so that everyone would recognize the letters, then you could send coded messages. In other words, you could say SOS is a call for assistance or in very great danger. Mayday is the spoken language for SOS. SOS is on your CW international signal, and mayday is your international spoken distress signal. Of course, mayday means in French, "assist me."

We had to have international agreement there as to how we would handle these and we had to have international code messages so that they could send a few letters and right away you'd know what they meant. The three letters might mean a great deal to these people.

Q: During this same period of time, port security became an important thing again for the Coast Guard. It was during the second World War and then all of a sudden during the Korean war, port security became a big question. Were you involved in any of this in any way?

Rhodes: Yes, I was involved but you might say in a very minor way because we just had to see to it that they had proper communications. Having gone to all these conferences, and so forth, it was very easy for us to see to it that they did have proper communications. We were in on all the conferences when these ships were built and also just what the operations would be, but there was no great difficulty there. I would say that port security operated mostly on district frequencies and the districts then would have communications with all their units so it was just another unit as far as we were concerned.

Q: On a theoretical plane, or philosophical plane, I've seen a lot of the training movies on port security during that period of time and there seemed to be a very shrill, harsh attitude about it, very much more so than what we have now. Do you think that McCarthyism had anything to do with the fact that port security was pushed so hard during that period of time?

Rhodes: No, I don't think so. Of course, that's my own thought. I think that the period that we went through had a lot more to do with it. I think McCarthyism was a result of people being upset over what was happening. For example, you probably remember Churchill's speech with the Iron Curtain coming up. Also there were a lot of trials being brought up and we were told by our newspapers that our atomic secrets had been let out by spies in our midst to the enemy. I think McCarthyism was a result of that and not these activities that we took as a result of McCarthy. I think McCarthy saw an opportunity just like a lot of people see an opportunity in these days for being against the war. That's a popular thing and they're riding it for all it's worth. I think McCarthy did that. What he was doing was popular and it makes no difference whether he believed what he said. He was trying to make political hay on a popular subject. I think port security was very necessary because regardless of McCarthy, or no McCarthy, there were a few people in this country who, if they were allowed to get in where they could do a lot of damage, would certainly do that damage. Just like we find right now. We have people in this country, native people, who will go out and blow up universities, and burn this, and burn that, and unless we can control that type of thing, we're in very bad shape. I think we were in a similar situation at that time although these times are much worse because we've allowed it to get worse. For example, there was a great deal of propaganda against McCarthyism and that somewhat soothed the people so that it was a bad name if they said you were trying to be another McCarthy. Now were paying for that type of propaganda. We have a lot more people in our midst now who will go out and burn and destroy, and give us a reason for having port security, whereas, if we had maintained a *balance* and not gone overboard like McCarthy did but just be sensible all the way through. The pendulum swung the other way after we condemned McCarthy and we were too soft on those people. We should have kept watching all the time.

Q: Was the Coast Guard affected during that period of time? McCarthy said he found people in the State Department. Did the same thing happen in the Coast Guard?

Rhodes: So far as I know there was no one closely connected with the Coast Guard itself but the assistant Secretary of the Treasury, who had been the assistant Treasury and went over to the World Bank (I had personal relationships with him when he was with the World Bank) was accused by McCarthy, White was his name, of being associated with the Communists. I remember when I was chief of communications, he asked me to come over and visit him. He wanted to set up some kind of communication for the World Bank. I was certainly surprised to hear shortly after that, McCarthy accused him of that kind of operation. It is very difficult in a case like that because probably within a year after that, White died under mysterious conditions.

So it was never settled one way or the other but he admitted certain things that looked very odd for a person in that position to be doing. As I say, there were a lot of false accusations made at that time and that is what hurts. If he had been sure of his facts --a lot of the things he said were factual-- but a lot of them were propaganda. The exaggerations, and so forth, were very, very bad. I think that's one thing that hurt him more than anything else was to accuse innocent people because at least you shouldn't accuse people unless you can prove them guilty. To the public, they appear innocent until proven guilty, therefore when you start naming people you should be pretty careful.

Q: How was the Coast Guard, itself, doing during this period of time? This is toward the end of your career.

Rhodes: The Coast Guard was expanding and getting more jobs assigned to it at this time, right along. We also could see great future for the Coast Guard and its activities because as the United States stretched out through its international air lines, and so forth, the need for the Coast Guard was great --also for aids to navigation, assistance to commerce, both shipping and air. The Coast Guard always was involved in anti-pollution, especially around the waters, so it looked like we were going to expand there. Of course, the yachting, private boat ownership, expanded, and there were cries for more Coast Guard, more Coast Guard, all the time. We were being supported by local requirements. We didn't have to ask for expansion except to point out that these people were insisting that we put someone there to help them out so if Congress wants us to do that, we'll just need more money. The Coast Guard never had to go in and pound the table and say we need this, and we need that. Generally, the people who wanted the Coast Guard to be in their neighborhood to protect them, the boating public, the fishing fleets, the merchant marine requirements, the aeronautical requirements, they were all asking for our help.

Q: That's a nice position to be in. In the services it's scratching all the time.

Rhodes: That's right. We don't generally have a time when we are up against it, unless the whole nation is up against it. The Coast Guard was hurt during depression probably as much as any one else but the main reason for being hurt was the money wasn't available for that type of purpose. But the need was there, and as soon as money became plentiful, the Coast Guard was built back up again.

Q: In 1954, you then went to Honolulu. That must have been a great change in assignment.

Rhodes: Yes. I was looking forward to that very much and I certainly enjoyed it while I was there.

Q: What did you do?

Rhodes: I was in charge of operations for the whole Pacific area and we had stations on almost every island. We had ~~four~~ six stationson Japan. I believe we had six in the Philippines, one on Korea, as well as Guam and many other islands in the Pacific. We had to have construction battalions to construct these places and maintain them, also stationed on Okinawaw, Iwo Jima. One of my first jobs was to go out and inspect all these stations. It takes you a month to fly under all kinds of conditions to see every one of them. Then when you get back, it's lucky you took pictures, and so forth, because it helps to bring back memories of just how the station is. One of our stations on Bataan Island, up toward Okinawa from the Philippines, had lost a station twice through typhoons. The typhoons are terrific over there. That is one difficulty we had in constructing stations that would stand up out in those locations. You had a situation in the tropics and also, for example, Iwo Jima, where the sulphur just bubbled up from the fountains out of the ground, and the sulphur fumes would --you'd paint a station white one day and it would turn black the next day. It smelled terrible. I never realized what the boys went through on Iwo Jima, but when you see all that sulphur around there --war might be Hell, but war on Iwo Jima was two Hells, as far as I could see.

Q: What else did you do in the Fourteenth District there? Was there anything new that you instituted when you were there?

Rhodes: No. The volcano erupted while I was there on the island of Hawaii. We had to evacuate some of the people there and our lighthouses right there had to be evacuated. I had to fly over several times and I never saw anything like it, to see those actual rivers of lava flowing down the mountain side and into the sea. It would send up steam for very great heights. Flying over this hot lava made it very rough. The air currents would be heated up over a stream of lava. The air currents would be going up there and down in other places. It was really a terrific sight and if you flew over there at night it was even more of an unusual sight. There was lava also spouting up into the air a few hundred feet and big rocks coming up. It looked for a time like we might have to evacuate Hilo, but we didn't.

Q: You retired in November, 1955?

Rhodes: Yes. My heart attack was in May of '55, therefore I only had duty in Hawaii from September of '54 to May of '55. There wasn't much that I could do except become familiar with what was going on. We were holding practical ditching operations with the commercial planes out there. About once a month we would have crews of certain airlines come out. They would get in their rafts and simulate getting from the planes into the rafts and the Coast Guard picking them up under various situations so they were used to our procedure and we were used to theirs. We got acquainted with them and they got acquainted with us and our procedure so they would know exactly what we would expect them to do if they had to ditch.

With that type of procedure held every month, and the preparations to be made, it kept us awfully busy. We not only had to maintain all those stations out there but we had air detachments at Hawaii, Guam, the Philippines, we had planes flying out from San Fransisco, supplying us, and getting out to all the stations. If you need something in a hurry or need to evacuate somebody, air is the only way to do it in a hurry. We also had our aids to navigation out there to take care of all the lights and the buoys throughout the whole area. We had to operate ocean station vessels out there so there was plenty of operation just to try to get familiar with and carry out the operations, and take care of the emergencies that came up.

Q: When you had your heart attack in May, were you able to work from May to November?

Rhodes: No, it took me some time to recover. I stayed in the hospital probably six weeks, Tripler Hospital out there, because about two weeks after I had the first heart attack, I had another one right at the hospital. I was planning on going back to work after I recovered from the first one, but to have a second one right on top of it, it left me in much poorer condition and the doctors advised me strongly not to attempt to go back because apparently there was a reason that they couldn't discover for having one attack on another. It did my heart a great deal of damage so when I was able to travel, they sent me to a hospital in Baltimore and they checked me over very carefully at the Public Health Hospital in Baltimore. While I was still there, my retirement board was held and they retired me for physical disability. The reason there was ~~so~~ *THAT* much difference was it took me quite a while to recover from that, and actually you never do recover, you just learn to live with it. You do get some of your strength back.

Q: We've come to the end of your Coast Guard career. I'd like to ask what you consider your single most important accomplishment?

Rhodes: That is a very, very difficult thing to answer but I would probably say my decision to go into communications was most gratifying of everything that I have ever had because I have felt that I was able to help the Coast Guard more by improving communications than I could have in any other way. I don't care how much equipment you have, how good men you have, you can not have an efficient operation without good communications.

INDEX FOR

INTERVIEWS WITH

Captain Earl K. Rhodes
Captain, U. S. Coast Guard (Ret.)

Aleutians, 136

ALEXANDER HAMILTON, sailing vessel, 23-25

AMMEN, DD, 49

Anzio Beach-head, 249-250

APACHE, Cutter, 61

Arctic navigation, 150-54

Aurora Borealis, 296

BEAR, cutter, 128-130; 139, 147

Bering Sea Patrol, 136, 162

BREMEN, ocean liner, 75

Burton Island, Icebreaker, 298

Caliendo, Capt. Anthony J., 183

Capron, Capt. Walter C., 25, 164

Coast Guard: state of enlisted men prior to WW II, 46-48; DD duty, 51-52; nomenclature, 65; painting of ships, 66; administrative decisions in field, 95-96; effects of Great Depression on, 105; efforts at union with Navy, 106-108; East Coast oriented, 118-119, 120-122; administrative matters, 166-168; organization prior to 1930, 182-183; bad weather warnings, 188-189; headquarters in WW II, 238; policy on wartime assignments, 240-242; decade of the 1950s., 326; navy control in WW II, 218-219; status, post WW II, 285-288

Coast Guard Academy: life there, course of study, physical description, seamanship, 11-27, 34-35; law enforcement courses, 27; cruises, 30-31, 36, 37; assignment from Academy, 43; confidence of an Academy graduate, 44-45

Coast Guard Auxiliary, 183, 185-186

Coast Guard Aviation: flight training, 109-111; state of, 112-114

Coast Guard Communications, 16-17, 63-64; 79-82; navy relationships, 83-84; 170-172, 197, 206-210; Communications Security, 211a-213; wartime measures (WW II), 214-218; wartime lessons, 220-226; 283-4; post WW II changes, 285-6, 288; communications division duties, 289-290; Loran and communications, 290; search and rescue, 291-292; communications vs. operations, 295-296; communications in polar waters, 296; Chief of Communications, 302-303; use of facsimile in post war period, 309-310

Coast Guard, Public Relations, 62-63; bad publicity, 93-94

Code Breaking: early attempts, 52-58; codes vs. ciphers, 226-227; substitution code, 229-230; breaking our codes, 230-231; enemy code breaking, 231-234; diversionary moves, 235-236

Commercial Salvage - C. G. relationships, 125-127

Customs Bureau, cooperation with, 100-101

Demock, Professor Chester, 19

Dutch Harbor, 136

Escanaba, ice breaker, 174

Fourteenth District C.G. operations, 327-328

Friedman, Col. and Mrs. Wm. F., 194

General Greene, oceanographic cutter, 70-71

GENERAL MEIGS, troop transport, 244-247; first assignments, 249-50; 251-255; description of ship, 256-259

GLACIER, Navy icebreaker, 294

Godfrey, Arthur, 83

Gradin, Lt. Comdr., 267

Great Lakes district, 168ff, 186-187

Guam, 277-278a

gyro compass, difficulties with in arctic areas, 150-51

Hearing and Examining Officer, U. S. Coast Guard, 261-262, 263, 265

Helicopters, 291

HOLMES, schooner, 160, 267

Hoover, President Herbert, inauguration of, 66

ICAO, International Civil Aviation Organization, 321; discussions of problems in civil aviation and communications, 322

Ice Breaking in Arctic Waters, 133-134; 146, 294

Ice Pilot, description of duties, 268

International Ice Patrol, 67-70, 72-74; cost of maintaining, 75; suggested use of planes, 76-77

IRAC, Interdepartmental Radio Advisory Committee, 292

Japan, conditions at time of surrender (1945), 278a-279

KRASSEN, Russian ice breaker, 130-131; intelligence on Russian vessels, 132

Life Saving Service, Revenue Cutter Service, discussion of and amalgamation, 32-33

Life Saving Stations, 180-182, 216-217

Lighthouse Service, 149, 179-81

Lighthouse Tenders, use of, 176-177, 181

Life Saving Stations, communications, 79, 169; Great Lakes, 174-175

Magic Carpet, 280

Manistee C.G. Station, 8

MANN, troop transport, 253

McCarthyism, 323-325

McDOUGALL, DD, 49

McKean, Capt. George, 245

Midnight sun, 149

MODOC, C. G. Cutter, 69

MOJAVE, C. G. Cutter, 24, 56, 66-69, 71-72, 78; general duties, 84-85

Nome, Alaska, 136, 148

NORTHLAND, Icebreaker, 127-129, 133, 136-138, 140-146, 150, 155

NORTH STAR, Indian affairs ship, 161

NORTHWIND, ice breaker, 147; NORTHWIND II, 293-294; duties of in Alaskan waters, 297-299, 300

Nurses, Public Health Service, 138-140

Omanata, (Japan), 277

O'Neill, Admiral Merlin, 183, 248

Paulding, DD, 49

PERSEUS (Patrol Boat), 41; characteristics of, 114-115, 125, 193

Pilot Service, 264-265

Point Barrow, 136-137, 149

Pollution in Great Lakes, 189-192

PORTER, DD, 43, 48-50, 52, 56, 60, 63, 193

Post, Wiley, aviator, 136

Pribiloff Islands, 136

Prohibition, 28-29; discussion of repeal, 99

Prudhoe Bay, oil reserves, 273-3, ff

Radar, 219

Radio Frequencies, International Conference, 303, 307-308; discussion of need, 304-307; technical and political problems, 311-316; pre-conference agreement with Canadians, 317-318

Rescue work, question of negligence in, 91-92

Rhodes, Capt. Earl K.: early life, 1-8; first contacts with C.G., 8; C.G. exams, 8-9; family reactions, 42-43; personal life in wartime Washington, 236-240; heart attack and retirement, 329-331

Rogers, Will, 136

Rosetta Stone, 227

ROWE, DD, 49

Rum runners, methods of avoiding intercept, 58-59; underway replenishment, 58; harrassment of, 60; C.G. boarding of fishing vessels, 60-61; forfeiting of their (rum runners) speed boats, 63; distribution of C.G. vessels, 97-98; sea-going experience gained from trailing, 54

Sarratt, Comdr., 144

Scammel, Comdr. Wm. K., 142, 153

Schizmeref Light, 300

Scientific Teams for Arctic, 155-156

Search and Rescue Operations, 158

Siberia, visits to various villages, 163-164; Russian authorities' attitude, 163-164

Signal Corps School of Cryptanalysis, 192-207, 211

Spring Floods, 178-9

Steamboat Inspection Service, 264

Tampa, C. G. Cutter, 69

Teachers in Eskimo Service, 138

Tenth Mountain Division, U.S. Army, 254-255

THEENIM (AHA-63), attack transport, 276-281

Traverse City Air Station, 187

Voice of America, transmissions from Rhodes, 318-321

Waesche, Admiral Russell, 183

Wainwright, Alaska, 270-271

WAINWRIGHT, DD, 96-97; special searchlights, 102-104; target practice, 102-103, Henry Coyle, skipper of, 102-103.

Washington, D. C., in wartime (WW II), 239-240, 242-243

Webster, Commodore, precursor of Coast Guard communications, 80-81

Whaling Fleet, 134-136

White, Harry Dexter, 325

Yachting regattas, C. G. patrol during, 85-87; Chicago incident, 88-90

Yardell, Capt. Steve, 60-61

Zeusler, Comdr., 143-144